CORPORATE NONUNION COMPLAINT PROCEDURES AND SYSTEMS

CORPORATE

NONUNION

COMPLAINT

PROCEDURES

AND

SYSTEMS

A Strategic Human Resources
Management Analysis

DOUGLAS M. McCABE

Funded by a grant from CUE—An Organization for Positive Employee
Relations—an educational subsidiary of the National Association
of Manufacturers.

New York
Westport, Connecticut
London

Copyright Acknowledgments

I would like to thank the National Association of Manufacturers for permitting quotations of prose from the following single copyrighted works: Harvey S. Caras, *Peer Grievance Review— A Proven Approach to Employee-Problem Resolution* (Washington, D.C.: CUE—An Organization for Positive Employee Relations, National Association of Manufacturers, Number 41— Studies in Employee Relations, 1986); Robert E. Bales, *Appeal Systems—A Different Approach to Resolving Employee Problems* (Washington, D.C.: CUE—An Organization for Positive and Progressive Employee Relations, 1981); and Brian W. Gill and Daniel B. Loftus, *Union-Free Complaint Procedures—25 Samples* (Washington, D.C.: CUE—An Organization for Positive Employee Relations—An Educational Subsidiary of the National Association of Manufacturers, 1984).

Library of Congress Cataloging-in-Publication Data

McCabe, Douglas M.
   Corporate nonunion complaint procedures and systems : a strategic
human resources management analysis / Douglas M. McCabe.
     p. cm.
   Bibliography: p.
   Includes index.
   ISBN 0-275-93059-9 (alk. paper)
    1. Grievance procedures—United States. 2. Grievance arbitration—
United States. I. Title.
HF5549.5.G7M33   1988
658.3'155—dc 19   88-11758

Praeger Publishers, One Madison Avenue, New York, NY 10010
A division of Greenwood Press, Inc.

Printed in the United States of America

The paper used in this book complies with the
Permanent Paper Standard issued by the National
Information Standards Organization (Z39.48-1984).

10 9 8 7 6 5 4 3 2

This book is dedicated to my parents, Mrs. Helen McCabe and Mr. Douglas McCabe, who made it all possible.

Contents

Foreword

History demonstrates, time after time, that conflict is a basic and vital element of the human nature. The human relationships that occur within the associations we create increase the complexity of conflict. This book is concerned with the conflict that manifests itself as grievances or complaints in the workplace. Left unattended, they are disruptive, costly, and ultimately destructive. There can be no doubt then that employees and employers want and need a known and workable system that will answer complaints swiftly and justly. In the case of employee complaints and grievances in nonunion firms, the scope of this research, management has much latitude of action in designing due process procedures and systems and in amending them promptly when deficiencies are revealed.

The research for and the writing of this landmark book was conducted by Douglas M. McCabe, Ph.D. associate professor of human resources management at Georgetown University's School of Business Administration, Washington, D.C. It was funded as part of the academic research program of CUE—An Organization for Positive Employee Relations—an educational subsidiary of the National Association of Manufacturers. Dr. McCabe served as principal investigator of this research project entitled "Improving Employee-Oriented Management: Complaint Procedures and Systems in Non-Union Environments" from September 1986 to October 1987.

This comprehensive study focuses on the many forms of complaint procedures (including arbitration, internal tribunals and peer review systems, open-door policies and formal appeal systems to higher management) currently in operation in nonunion companies. Despite the number and variety of the systems presented, the goal is simple and singularly important—to achieve harmonious and cooperative employer-employee relations in the handling of employee complaints. It is highly recommended reading for both practitioners and academicians alike in the field of strategic human resources management.

Bernard H. Trimble
Executive Director
CUE—An Educational Subsidiary of the
National Association of Manufacturers
Washington, D.C.

Acknowledgments

Many have helped directly and indirectly in the writing of this book. Thanks are especially due to Bernard H. Trimble, Executive Director, CUE—An Organization for Positive Employee Relations—An Educational Subsidiary of the National Association of Manufacturers, Washington, D.C.; Jill Henderson, Publications and Research, CUE; Quentin Riegel, Deputy General Counsel and Assistant Vice President, National Association of Manufacturers, Washington, D.C.; James R. Dunton, Senior Editor, Business and Economics, Praeger, New York City, New York; Karen O'Brien, Senior Project Editor, Praeger, New York City, New York; and Lisa MacLeman, Copyeditor, Praeger, New York City, New York, for providing valuable guidance and direction.

In addition, special commendation is due to my manuscript secretary, Peggy Sorbera, Quick Turnaround, Inc., complete Word Processing Service, Herndon, Virginia, for her meticulous work on my behalf. Her yeoman work efforts will always be most appreciated.

Additional thanks are also due to the 78 vice presidents of human resources management of some of the leading nonunion companies within the umbrella of the National Association of Manufacturers who supplied the excellent primary source documentation and accompanying, explanatory archival material, which is synthesized and analyzed by this author in Chapters 3, 4, and 5. For their individual time and effort in the area of their concern for the improvement of the management of human resources and for their concern for building linkages between practitioners and scholars, I am grateful.

No field study is possible without the wholehearted cooperation of people in a position to provide access to needed information and to provide other resources to help complete a book. Thus I would like to thank the following individuals for their help: Jan S. Amundson, vice president and general counsel, National Association of Manufacturers, Washington, D.C.; Cynthia J. Anderson, manager, Peat Marwick Main and Co., Washington, D.C.; Elizabeth W. Barton, director of administration, School of Business Administration, Georgetown University, Washington, D.C.; William E. Blasier, senior vice president, Finance/Administration Division and treasurer, National Association of Manufacturers, Washington, D.C.; Patricia DiGiannantonio, financial management officer, Office of Sponsored Programs, Georgetown University, Washington, D.C.; Sherry L. Dott, senior assistant to the Provost, Georgetown University, Washington, D.C.; Virginia N. Flavin, director of faculty services, School of Business Administration, Georgetown University, Washington, D.C.; Nancy L. Fullerton, member services, CUE—An Organization for Positive Employee Relations—An Educational Subsidiary of the National Association of Manufacturers, Washington, D.C.; Brian W. Gill, president, Master Printers of America, Inc., and senior vice president, Printing Industries of America, Arlington, Virginia; Lenola M. Greene-El, administrative assistant, School of Business Administration, Georgetown University, Washington, D.C.; Randolph M. Hale, Vice President, Industrial Relations Department, National Association of Manufacturers, Washington, D.C.; John E. Hill, Senior Military Analyst, National Security Analysis, The Orkand Corporation, Silver Spring, Maryland; James G. Hogue, Vice President, Employee Relations, Florida Steel Corporation, Tampa, Florida; Edward K. Kimmell, International Trade Specialist, U.S. Department of Commerce, Washington, D.C.; Kathleen M. Kozar, Associate Director, Office of Sponsored Programs, Georgetown University, Washington, D.C.; Doris J. Lyons, Director, Office of Sponsored Programs, Georgetown University, Washington, D.C.; G. Brent Stanley, Vice President, Employee Relations, Marriott Corporation, Washington, D. C.; Karen M. Sullivan, M.B.A. Research Fellow, School of Business Administration, Georgetown University, Washington, D.C.; Alexander B. Trowbridge, President, National Association of Manufacturers, Washington, D.C.; and James T. Wilson, Administrative Assistant, School of Business Administration, Washington, D.C. To these and many others who have given their time and assistance, I extend my sincerest thanks.

The material in this book was prepared under a Grant from CUE—An Organization for Positive Employee Relations—An educational Subsidiary of the National Association of Maufacturers, through the Office of Sponsored Programs, Georgetown University, Washington, D.C. Georgetown University Business School faculty members undertaking such projects under a grant through Georgetown University's Office of sponsored Progarms are encouraged to express freely their professional judgment. Therefore, points of view or opinions stated in this book do not necessarily represent the official position or policy of the National Association of Manufacturers, its educational subsidiary, CUE, or Georgetown University.

Thus, grant-sponsored research undertaken by the Georgetown University Business School is always independent and impartial, and dedicated to the improvement of management practices. Information and data that are generated by Georgetown faculty members who are sponsored by outside grant support are made available to a wider audience at the discretion of the faculty member. While a sponsor's inputs about factual accuracy and equitable presentations are always solicited, CUE did not have approval rights on any product of this research project.

Finally, I wish to express my deepest love for my parents, without whose unending encouragement and total support in my pursuit of an education this project would not have been possible.

PART I
INTRODUCTION AND
OVERVIEW

Part I sets the stage for this study. Beginning with a strategic overview of the subject matter in Chapter 1, the objectives of the study are then indicated, together with the issues to be investigated. The order of presentation of material is also delineated.

In Chapter 2 the literature regarding nonunion grievance procedures is examined. Provided in Chapter 2 is an analysis of the strategic issues regarding nonunion grievance arbitration systems, internal tribunals and peer review systems, and open-door policies and formal appeals to higher management. Furthermore, the following emerging issues are studied; due process for non-unionized employees; the relationship between the doctrine of employment-at-will and nonunion grievance procedures; the corporate ombudsman in relationship to the nonunion grievance procedures; and employer-employee relations in the nonunion setting: the role of the nonunion complaint procedure. General principles emanating out of a study of the literature are also delineated.

1
Design and Scope of the Book

INTRODUCTION

The scope of this study encompasses an analysis of corporate nonunion complaint procedures and systems in 78 of the leading nonunion companies under the umbrella of the National Association of Manufacturers (NAM), with particular attention to the most significant issue in that area at the operating level of individual companies and firms: the *procedural* requirements with respect to the processing of employees' complaints and grievances.[1]

STRATEGIC OVERVIEW

The intention of this overview is to stimulate awareness in management, and particularly among the employee relations and human resources management personnel who write companies' employee-relations manuals, of the inherent complexity of the process of resolving employees' grievances. The preparation of the Grievance section of a manual is not a task which the person who is assigned to it may deem to be secondary to his or her other duties, and similarly top management, when it approves the prepared draft, may not deem it a project meriting only perfunctory attention. All concerned must be acutely conscious that what is at issue is ethical employer-employee relations, worker satisfaction, and, from management's self-interest viewpoint, the paramount factor of the morale of that group of men and women whom all companies in theory, and some in practice, define as "our most important asset." And underlying all of this is a concept that is very simple to define yet very difficult to administer: justice.

If justice is easy to administer, why is it that, among the 78 employee-relations manuals and accompanying primary archival source documentation studied, all of them prescribe a complicated procedure for the appeal of an employee's grievance from an unsatisfactory decision of the immediate supervisor through sequentially higher levels of management? Why is it that one-third of them include, as an appeal "step" at a relatively high level, what this writer calls an "internal tribunal," that is, a jurylike committee consisting generally of two or three management personnel, one of whom invariably is drawn from the human resources management department, and in many companies two or three of the complaining employee's "peer" fellow employees, who provide the tribunal with a desirable "democratic" environment? And why is it, if justice is easy to administer, that 6 of the 78 companies, despite the disinclination of management to place its destiny in the hands of outsiders, authorize a complaining employee not only to process a grievance through successive levels of higher management but also, finally, to invoke the decision of a professional arbitrator? Why is it, to pursue this line of questioning further for the sake of emphasis, that at least one of the companies surveyed by this writer deems it a matter of "fair play" to authorize an employee, in a search for a satisfactory solution of a grievance, to obtain a total of six management decisions, one by the immediate supervisor and five appeals through ascending levels of management? Is "justice" as elusive as it is here being pictured? The evidence in this research is that the top management of the 78 surveyed companies obviously thinks so, and is appropriately conscientious in the matter.

It should also be noted that this study is limited to companies, or to divisions or plants of companies, which do not have unions. The grievance resolution procedure in a unionized company is established at the collective bargaining table, and the question being investigated by this writer is what formal provision is made by nonunion companies for management's fair treatment of employees' complaints.

It is evident that top management recognizes the inevitability of employees' grievances against management. The size of a company is apparently irrelevant, inasmuch as companies varying from 30 employees to over 60,000 submitted formal grievance procedures for this research. The inevitability of grievances is due to a number of causes, some the fault of the employees concerned and some the fault of their supervisors and managers. Both groups are subject to "human frailty," which is undoubtedly the basic problem in all phases of employee-management relations. Specifically, as a few companies state in their employee-relations manuals, grievances may be generated either by employees or by their supervisors as a result of ambiguity in a company's published rules or by misinterpretation of rules which are not obviously ambiguous. Another probable frequent cause of grievances is "personality conflict" between employees and their supervisors, with the fault being on either side or both sides. No company surveyed discussed this matter directly in its employee-relations manual, undoubtedly for reasons of diplomacy, but quite a few companies recognized the subject indirectly by providing that an employee may, for a "personal" reason or otherwise to avoid "embarrassment," bypass the immediate supervisor when initiating a grievance. The point here is that employees' grievances, whether they are the fault of the employees or of management personnel, are so inevitable that good business practice dictates that companies make provision in their employee-relations manuals for a *formal* procedure for resolving grievances. Peculiarly, some companies appear to be allergic to the word "grievance" and refer in their manuals only to employees' "problems and questions."

Why does a company have a formal procedure for resolving employees' grievances? What is desired here is not an ostensible answer to this question but a deeper, more fundamental one, an answer that reflects pertinent elements of economic and business philosophy. Is the providing of a formal procedure merely an incidental feature in the operation of a company, or is it the implementation of an ethical obligation which top management feels toward the employees, or toward the company itself, or perhaps both? And even if ethical obligation is fundamental in this matter, are grievances, which are complaints against the ways management treats employees, sufficiently numerous to justify the elaborate systems established by many companies for resolving them?

It is reasonable to conjecture in some instances that a grievance resolution procedure is primarily not a system established for the benefit of employees but rather a means for management to correct its own mistakes, even though in some instances the problem is a misunderstanding of company policy or rules on the part of employees. Credence is furnished for such a conjecture by the plausibility of observers who assert that business executives do not generally submit their proposed actions to an ethical test. What is being proposed here is that what inspires some, but not all, companies to install grievance resolution procedures is not a sense of ethical obligation to employees but rather management's self-interest in maintaining a body of employees whose morale is high as a consequence of being well treated by management. It is a truism that it is mandatory for the success of a business enterprise, as it is for the success of a military enterprise, that the morale of the organization's members be at a high level.

The question raised by this discussion is whether the effectiveness of a grievance resolution procedure is independent of the motive which established it, either the motive of a felt ethical obligation toward employees or the motive of management's self-interest. The importance of this question is in the fact that the motive for doing something is the inspiration that generates energy in accomplishing it, especially in the fact that—in the case in which the motive of felt ethical obligation toward employees' conflicts with the motive of management's self-interest—the stronger motive will prevail. This discussion is more than merely academic. Its practical aspect is indicated by the following instance of conflict of motives. In the late 1940s, in a division of one of the country's largest corporations, middle management decided to expand one of its operations and hired five or six new "exempt" employees. A week later higher division management cancelled the expansion program, caused the new employees to be discharged, and ignored their claim that the company, at the very least, had an ethical obligation to refund to them the fees they had paid to the employment agencies with which the personnel department had dealt.

That division of that company at that time did not have a formal procedure for the resolving of the grievances of "exempt" employees, leaving them at the mercy of arbitrary management decisions. Even if the middle management that had hired the new employees felt an ethical obligation toward them, it is doubtful if it had the courage to lecture higher management on the propriety of considering ethical precepts when making business decisions. And as for higher management, its decision was obviously one of its own self-interest, namely, the holding down of operating costs. Higher management's worst mistake in pursuing its own self-interest was its failure to consider the detrimental effect of its decision on the morale of the division's "exempt" work force, which could not help feeling that "If management can treat those poor fellows that way, it may do the same to the rest of us."

The concept being developed here is not that management should abandon self-interest as a basic operating motive. Self-interest is too instinctive in human nature to be abandoned. The concept being developed here is that *it is actually in management's own best self-interest to recognize that it has ethical obligations toward employees which, when properly implemented, advantageously rebound to management's own benefit by assuring that employees' morale, which is indispensable for a company's success, is maintained at a high level.*

Examine the case of England's King Richard III (reigned 1483–85). Political leaders instinctively pursue their own personal self-interest as their primary objective, and Richard III acted accordingly. He established a grievance resolution procedure in civic affairs for the people in the county of Kent but, despite the magnanimity which can be read into the words of his proclamation, his motive was not a sense of an ethical obligation to the people but his intensely felt need to obtain their local support in his struggle against his political enemies. The proclamation was designed to raise the people's morale under his rule. It stated his determination

to see due administration of justice throughout this his realm . . . and to reform, punish, and subdue all extortions and oppressions in the same. And for that cause . . . that every person dwelling within the same . . . do make a bill of his complaint and put it to his highness, and he shall be heard and without delay have such convenient remedy as shall accord with his laws . . . for his grace is utterly determined that all his true subjects shall live in rest and quiet.[2]

What is the relationship between Richard's proclamation and companies' formal procedures for resolving employees' grievances? First of all, in both instances the emphasis in on cure, not prevention. It is true that punishment for government officials is mentioned, but, if the emphasis were on prevention, a detailed procedure for effecting prevention would have been provided rather than only a procedure for submitting citizens' grievances. And second, the objective in both instances, stated in Richard's words as "that all his true subjects shall live in rest and quiet," is thwarted by the existence of circumstances that render persons so unhappy that they must resort to the unpleasant act of filing grievances.

The point being developed here is the conclusion that companies' obvious need for formal procedures for resolving employees' grievances is a consequence of companies' failure to avoid the situations that generate the grievances. In all the employee-relations manuals studied, the emphasis is solely one of cure, not of prevention, of the two recognized types of causes of employees' grievances, namely, misunderstanding by employees of companies' policies and rules, and improper treatment of employees by managerial personnel. What does the phrase "employee relations" signify? In the documents which, for the sake of simplicity, are called "employee-relations manuals," although companies have various titles, the subject matter is invariably employees' relations with management, and not management's relations with employees, other than management's willingness to listen to employees' grievances. What is absent, in other words, is the giving of attention to companies' policies and practices, if any, designed to minimize employees' grievances.

This discussion would be incomplete if it did not stress the importance of the prevention of employees' grievances. If management could have prevented a certain grievance, then it is unethical for it to claim that its conscience is clear because it decided the grievance in the employees' favor. It is questionable whether management's decisions regarding legitimate grievances are generally fully compensatory of the damage done to the employees. If a rendered decision is not appealed by the employee to higher management, this fact does not certify that full compensation has been accomplished. It may be that the employee thinks it is the best decision he or she can obtain, or the employee may be dissuaded from appealing by some felt disinclination to intensify the battle for his or her perceived rights.

Furthermore, the emotional aspect of a grievance must be considered. In civil courts, plaintiffs are awarded remuneration not only because of physical damage incurred but also because of associated emotional pain. Considerable emotional pain may be expected to ensue not only as a result of the cause of an employee's grievance but also, additionally, due to the stress inherent in a struggle for personal vindication. And a further consideration is the traumatic rupture of the friendly association of managerial personnel with employees when the former reprimands, either justly or unjustly, the latter, leaving scars in the emotions of the latter which may take years to erase. Every indication is that a grievance is an evil, even when justified by the circumstances, of such a proportion that "an ounce of prevention is worth a pound of cure."

The prevention of grievances has an ethical factor which may not be ignored in the case of justified grievances caused by the treatment of employees by supervisory or managerial personnel. Ethical considerations will be ignored if top management's ethics, or, more correctly stated, lack of morality, is exhibited by an inordinate preoccupation with the color of the ink on the annual profit-and-loss statement, with top management instilling that preoccupation in all its subordinate management levels.

This overview may be summarized as follows: It is necessary for a company to have a formal grievance resolution procedure, but the greater necessity is to have a grievance-prevention procedure.

This overview closes on a very positive note by means of the following "true story," which is an excellent example of the proper attitude of management personnel toward their subordinates. It was told to a friend of mine by Joseph Houdek, who had been a foreman in defense production in a Chicago plant of the General Electric Company during World War II. The "Pat" whom Houdek mentions was Patrick Ryan, the plant's general manager, who later became one of the founders of the Burger King restaurant chain. Houdek speaking:

One day I goofed. It was a disaster, because it shut down the entire plant. I shivered in anticipation of my phone ringing and my having to endure Pat's bawling me out.

Sure enough, Pat called, and I was flabbergasted by his first words, which were: "Joe, I'm in trouble!" Gosh, I had thought that it was *me* who was in trouble!

Pat continued: "You've got to help me, Joe! You've got to get your department back to normal as soon as possible." That's all he said! How can you help loving a guy like that!

A few comments are appropriate regarding that story. It is obvious that the general manager could not correct the error and had to rely on his foreman to do it. Furthermore, the general manager obviously understood human nature, and reasoned that, although the foreman fully deserved a tongue-lashing, nevertheless the latter was already in an emotional collapse and needed to feel above all other considerations that the general manager was a real and abiding friend.

That general manager spectacularly earned his salary that day in the area of ethical employer-employee relations and sound human resources management.

OBJECTIVES OF THE STUDY

The first objective of this study is to analyze the nonunion complaint procedures stipulated in the employee-relations manuals of 78 nonunion companies within the umbrella of the National Association of Manufacturers. Six grievance arbitration systems will be studied; 23 internal tribunals and peer review systems will be studied; and 49 open-door policies and formal appeals to higher management will be studied. These three major types of procedures account for the vast majority of nonunion complaint systems in existence today.

The second objective of this study is to appraise the current practices that employers and employees have evolved for resolving issues generated by complaints and grievances.

The third objective of this study is to attempt to perceive future trends in nonunion complaint procedures and systems, with findings of this study utilized as a basis for recommendations.

Statistical data, summations, and integrative analyses will be presented to clarify various situations and particularly trends.

SOME ISSUES TO BE INVESTIGATED

In nonunion companies, particularly with respect to the procedural composition of complaint procedures and systems at the operating level of individual firms, participative management and sound employer-employee relations can be looked upon as both an effect and a cause of the establishment of complaint procedures; that is, complaint procedures bring employers and employees together around a conference table, which is an effect, and contrariwise participative management and sound employer-employee relations has a very real causative influence upon the nature and composition of procedural complaint systems. Two issues therefore arise: the impact of participative management and ethical employer-employee relations on complaint procedures, and the impact of complaint procedures on employer-employee relations and nonunion participative management techniques. It does not suffice to call these two impacts the two sides of a coin; they are two separate, even though mutually interacting, realities. Those two impacts need to be considered both separately and jointly in a study that examines the issues of nonunion complaint procedures in a number of individual companies in depth, and in the industry generally, within the milieu of contemporary employer-employee relations and the changing face of current industrial relations and human resources management.

Nonunion Grievance Arbitration Issues

Should nonunion grievance arbitration be nurtured? Where is it going in the future? Why has the use of this new employee relations tool become adopted by some companies? What are some potential problems connected with the remuneration of impartial and neutral third party arbitrators under this system? How active should the American Arbitration Association and the

National Academy of Arbitrators be in this process? If the concept of employment-at-will in the nonunion employment sector continues to erode, will employees seek and managers turn more to the process of nonunion grievance arbitration? Can the Expedited Labor Arbitration Rules of the American Arbitration Association be utilized to obtain an equitable and impartial review of employees' complaints and grievances? Does the sheer popularity of the most experienced arbitrators make them practically unavailable for the nonunion process? Should companies select less well-known arbitrators? What are the cost considerations in nounion grievance arbitration? Who pays for the arbitrator—the company, the employee, or both in nonunion systems? Should and how have companies limited the scope of nonunion arbitrable issues? Under such a system, does the employee tend to push every case up the procedural steps to arbitration?

Internal Tribunals and Peer Review Issues

What should be the composition of internal tribunals? Should most consist of three of the complainant's peers and two management representatives or should the opposite composition be the norm? Should the decisions of these tribunals be advisory or binding? Does the institutionalization of a peer review tribunal broaden employee rights? Do peer review tribunals build an atmosphere of mutual trust between employees and employers? Do internal tribunals impinge upon traditional managerial rights and prerogatives? Should boards determine policy or merely review contested applications of company policy? Do internal tribunals force supervisors and middle managers to follow company policy more closely? In deciding cases, who are tougher on the complainants—their peers or their supervisors? Are internal tribunals too costly and time-consuming? What are the benefits of peer review to both employees and managers? What are the limitations of internal tribunals? How has their scope been restricted in companies? Will peer review tribunals continue to grow? For purpose of membership on tribunals, how are "peers" defined? Does a peer review process provide for an increased sense of industrial fairness and security against arbitrary and capricious decisions? Can the involvement of a worker's peers in a company's problem-solving process pay real dividends to the firm or organization? Can a peer provide salient background information for helping management correct improper managerial practices or job-related working conditions? What are the key outcomes of peer grievance review systems? Can internal tribunals of a peer review composition be a win-win program for both employees and employers? How does top management preserve its right to run its business? What kind of training should there be for employees who serve as potential panelists on peer review internal tribunals?

Open-Door Policy Issues

How do we explain the preponderance of open-door policies in organizations? Why are there truly significant gaps in our understanding and comprehension of the concept of open-door policies and their implementation in firms? What are the procedural patterns followed by companies in this area? Do employers, executives, and managers recognize and accept the thesis that other procedural means besides the formal chain of command should be made available to workers for the expression of their grievances? Why do open-door policies, combined with formal appeals to management, seem to be more ubiquitous than peer review and arbitration systems? Do employees fear reprisal from their supervisors under these policies more so than the other types of procedures? Why do open-door procedures range widely from informal statements that workers can talk to any member of management at any time on any subject to highly specific and structured steps through the regular scalar chain of command? Are delays in investigating facts and taking corrective action more of a problem in informal open-door systems? Why is the open-door policy so often and badly-maligned? What is and should be the role of the human resources department under open door systems? Should an employee with a complaint go to his supervisor or take his grievance directly and immediately to someone higher above or even outside of the chain of command? Do scholars and practitioners have doubts about the equity of this type of system? Do employees see little chance of getting adverse supervisory decisions modified? Must the employee put the complaint in writing at any step? What are the limitations of this system? What are the various variations of the open-door policy? What aspects of open-door policies are good, and what are bad? How should open-door systems evolve in periods of rapid and evolutionary company growth? How does a firm increase employee awareness of the procedure? What are the advantages and disadvantages of formalized appeal mechanisms versus informal mechanisms? How does a company achieve a credible and expedient open-door process? How do these systems actually work? Are they truly effective in resolving organizational conflict?

Due Process Issues for Nonunionized Employees

Why are expectations about due process in organizations increasing? How are these expectations being exhibited? What is the nature of organizational justice and organizational due process in relation to nonunion grievance and complaint procedures? What human resources management devices can be utilized to enhance equity in companies? What is the nature of fair treatment of employees in relation to nonunion grievance procedures? What are the idiosyncrasies of institutionalized due process? In what various organizational ways can the concept of due process be assured?

Employment-at-Will Issues in the Nonunion Setting

What is the unique relationship between the currently debated issue of the employment-at-will doctrine and the issue of nonunion grievance procedures? Should an employer be aware that the existence of a complaint procedure may legally restrict the employer's right to fire an employee? Has the introduction of nonunion complaint and grievance procedures been construed by some state courts as giving employees certain employment contractual rights? Are state and federal courts attaching legal import to employee-relations policy handbooks and manuals? Can failure by management to follow nonunion grievance procedures to the letter lead to a lawsuit on the part of a disgruntled employee? What can management do to protect itself? If an employee submits a nonunion complaint to a decision by management, can management then forestall the employee from appealing that decision to the local civil courts?

Corporate Ombudsman Issues in Relation to the Nonunion Grievance Procedure

What are the most commonly asked questions by executives and human resource managers exploring the potential implementation of this idea? What is the working and operational definition of an ombudsman? What are the functions and purpose of an ombudsman? What can or should be his or her relationship with the complaint/grievance resolution process, procedure, or system? How can we use this technique to improve organizational employer-employee relations? How would a corporate ombudsman operate in a firm or organizational context? What are the major objections and concerns to a corporate ombudsman system?

Employer-Employee Relations Issues in the Nonunion Setting: The Role of the Nonunion Complaint Procedure

Can a nonunion complaint procedure delimit some of the conditions that may lead to unionization? How does the existence of a nonunion complaint system fit into an employer's overall organizational strategy for remaining nonunion within the framework of public policy? Is the existence of a nonunion compliant procedure directly or indirectly related to the process of remaining nonunion?

METHODOLOGY

The need for field research in the area of corporate nonunion complaint procedures is substantial. The reason is that previous studies have been principally at a very broad level of discussion.[3] This study fills a major gap in the literature by addressing the key *procedural* issues and questions at the level of individual companies and firms, specifically those within the umbrella of NAM.

The research involved in this study was divided into two areas: library research and field research.

The library research was conducted in the following libraries: the Library of Congress, Washington, D.C.; Lauginer Library, Georgetown University, Washington, D.C.; Georgetown University Law Center Library, Washington, D.C.; Martin P. Catherwood Library, New York State School of Industrial and Labor Relations, Cornell University, Ithaca, New York; and the Eastman Arbitration Library, American Arbitration Association, New York City.

Bibliographies, books, manuscripts, theses, dissertations, periodicals, magazines, newspapers, and government documents were examined. The work done in the library research provided the informational background required for directing the field research into meaningful and constructive channels.

The field research consisted of three elements. First, examination of relevant documentation, including employee-relations manuals and other accompanying primary sources of written archival information relating directly to the procedural requirements of nonunion complaint systems, provided by 78 of the leading nonunion companies under the general umbrella of NAM; second, interviews with managers and human resource executives where needed in order to clarify, explain, and supplement the primary sources of information; and third, interviews with informed neutral parties.

Although the interviews with the knowledgeable parties provided a clarifying supplement to the written record, some of them, being confidential, were not used directly in this study but served to enhance this writer's understanding of various facets of the study.

ORDER OF PRESENTATION

The scope, purpose, strategic overview and objectives for this study having been outlined in this chapter, it is now desirable to indicate the groupings under which the subsequent text material is presented.

In Chapter 2 the literature regarding nonunion complaint procedures is examined. Provided in Chapter 2 is an analysis of the strategic issues regarding nonunion grievance arbitration systems, internal tribunals and peer review systems, and open-door policies and formal appeals to higher management. Furthermore, the following emerging issues are studied: due process for non-unionized employees; the relationship between the doctrine of employment-at-will and nonunion grievance procedures; the corporate ombudsman in relationship to the nonunion grievance procedure; and employer-employee relations in the nonunion setting: the role of the nonunion complaint procedure. General principles emanating out of a careful study of the literature are also delineated here.

Part II of the study comprises an analysis of the nonunion grievance procedures stipulated in the employee-relations policy manuals of some leading nonunion companies who are within the aegis of NAM. More specifically, Chapter 3 studies the procedures of six nonunion grievance arbitration systems. Chapter 4 studies the procedures of 23 nonunion internal tribunals and peer review systems; and Chapter 5 studies the procedures of 49 open-door policies and formal appeals to higher management. Each one of these three chapters contains a requisite and comprehensive Integrative Analysis.

Part III states the findings of this study. Chapter 6 outlines the executive summary of general principles (that is, the human resources management lessons to be learned); delineates policy recommendations for human resource managers; and offers recommendations for future research.

Lastly, what is probably the most comprehensive bibliography on the subject of nonunion complaint/grievance procedures and systems has been compiled for use by both scholars and practitioners.

CONCLUSION

This writer has endeavored to present all pertinent evidence from the primary sources of documentation available to him without regard to whether that evidence appears to favor or to be critical of the companies being researched and critiqued. If he is to be criticized, it probably will be regarding his frequent personal interpretations of the evidence, which are clearly identified as such.

Nonunion complaint procedures are a very serious matter. Hopefully, this study will shed substantial light on what the procedures and systems are really all about; that question involves considerations on both sides of nonunion employee relations which go much deeper than the matter of the procedural requirements per se of the grievance systems themselves. The determination and comprehension of those deeper considerations, which concern the aspirations of both employers and employees, are the purpose of this study.

NOTES

1. For purposes of this study, the term "complaint" and "grievance" will be used interchangeably because at this time there is still no universally agreed upon definition of the two in the *nonunion* setting. In the literature, for example, scholars often use the two words interchangeably. Likewise, practitioners do the same in the nonunion environment when discussing their own procedural systems. It should be noted, however, that the leading practitioners on the cutting edge of the implementation of procedures in the nonunion setting prefer the term "complaints" in order to distinguish these from the concept of "grievances" in unionized firms in the traditional labor relations nomenclature.

For purposes of clarification and further study, this writer will now list a few of the more common definitions of "complaints" and "grievances" found in the literature.

"A *grievance* is an expression of dissatisfaction by an employee for which formal procedures for handling it have been established. A *complaint* is an expression of dissatisfaction by an employee that is handled by some means other than the formal grievance procedure." See Thomas W. Comstock, Ph.D., "Dealing with Complaints and Grievances," in *Modern Supervision* (Albany, NY: Delmar, 1987), 374.

"A *complaint* usually consists of any individual or group problem or dissatisfaction which employees in nonunionized companies can channel upward to management personnel." See Theo Haimann and Raymond L. Hilgert, "Handling Employee Complaints and Grievances," in *Supervision: Concepts and Practices of Management*, 3rd ed. (Cincinnati, OH: South-Western, 1982), 396.

"At one time or another, each of us had complained or expressed dissatisfaction with some turn of events. These are not grievances; they are merely expressions of dissatisfaction. Grievances are complaints that have been formally registered with the employee's supervisor or some other management official in accordance with the recognized grievance procedures. Grievances usually arise when an employee thinks he has been done an injustice. Maybe nothing wrong has been done, but if an employee thinks he has been treated wrongly, he can file a grievance." See Claude S. George, Jr., "What is a Grievance," in *Supervision in Action: The Art of Managing Others*, 3rd ed. (Reston, VA: Reston, 1982), 91.

" 'Grievance procedure' is the term most commonly employed to describe the fourth channel as a result of its use in the union contract process. But many organizations wish to avoid the use of union terminology and any overtone such terminology might have. Among other terms employed in the nonunion context are 'complaint procedure,' 'employee communications procedure,' 'solving dissatisfactions,' 'bitch belt,' 'gripe system,' 'settling problems,' 'I Want to Know,' and 'fairplay program.' However, most employees still settle on the term 'grievance procedure.' " See Wiley I. Beavers, "Employee Relations Without a Union," in *ASPA Handbook of Personnel and Industrial Relations, Volume III, Employee and Labor Relations*, ed. Dale Yoder and Herbert G. Heneman, Jr. (Washington, D.C.: The Bureau of National Affairs, 1979), 7–53.

"The term 'grievance' seems to have a rather unpleasant connotation to some nonunion employers. As a result, some companies have attempted to use substitute language and have established their written procedures under a number of different titles. It may be difficult to get away from the term 'grievance' and still retain the sense of the word, but the following alternative titles, which have been used, may suggest a less provocative term: Complaint Procedure; Gotta Grievance? Adjustment Procedure; Adjustment of Complaints; 'Beef' Control; Problem Solving Procedure; Guarantee of Fair Treatment, Settling Disputes. But regardless of what an individual employer chooses to call his particular procedure, chances are that the employees in the plant—and even first-line supervisors—are quite likely to refer to the situation it involves as a 'grievance.' " See Industrial Relations Department, National Association of Manufacturers, *Settling Complaints in the Union-Free Operation* (Washington, D.C.: National Association of Manufacturers, June 1982), 4.

2. See Paul Murray Kendall, *Richard the Third* (NY: W. W. Norton, 1955), 337.

3. The following are the major nationwide and regional studies in research monographs and journal articles: William G. Scott, *The Management of Conflict: Appeal Systems in Organizations* (Homewood, IL: Richard D. Irwin, and The Dorsey Press, 1965); Ronald Berenbeim, *Nonunion Complaint Systems: A Corporate Appraisal* (NY: The Conference Board, Report No. 770, 1980); Mary Green Miner, *Policies for*

Unorganized Employees (Washington, D.C.: The Bureau of National Affairs, Personnel Policies Forum, PPF Survey No. 125, April 1979); James J. Bambrick, Jr., and John J. Speed, *Grievance Procedures in Nonunionized Companies* (NY: National Industrial Conference Board, Studies in Personnel Policy, No. 109); William G. Scott, "An Issue in Administrative Justice: Managerial Appeal Systems," *Management International* 1 (1966): 37–53; Alan Balfour, "Five Types of Non-Union Grievance Systems," *Personnel* 61 (March-April 1984): 67–76; Richard L. Epstein, "The Grievance Procedure in the Non-Union Setting: Caveat Employer," *Employee Relations Law Journal* 1 (Summer 1975): 120–27; Stephen R. Michael, "Due Process in Nonunion Grievance Systems," *Employee Relations Law Journal* 3 (Spring 1978): 516–27; Donald A. Drost and Fabious P. O'Brien, "Are There Grievances Against Your Non-Union Grievance Procedure?" *Personnel Administrator* 28 (January 1983): 36–42; James P. Swann, Jr., "Formal Grievance Procedures in Non-Union Plants," *Personnel Administrator* 26 (August 1981) 66–68; 70; Maryellen Lo Bosco, "Nonunion Grievance Procedures," *Personnel* 61 (January 1985): 61–64; Ronald L. Miller, "Grievance Procedures for Nonunion Employees," *Public Personnel Management* 7 (September-October 1978): 302–11; James K. McCollum and Dwight R. Norris, "Nonunion Grievance Machinery in Southern Industry," *Personnel Administrator* 29 (November 1984): 106–9, 131; Thomas J. Condon, "Use Union Methods in Handling Grievances," *Personnel Journal* 64 (January 1985): 72–75; Sharon L. Yenney, "In Defense of the Grievance Procedure in a Non-Union Setting," *Employee Relations Law Journal* 2 (Spring 1977): 434–43; Walter V. Ronner, "Handling Grievances of Nonunionized Employees," *Personnel* 39 (March-April 1962): 56–62; Maurice S. Trotta and Harry R. Gudenberg, "Resolving Personnel Problems in Nonunion Plants," *Personnel* 53 (May-June 1976): 55–63; Fabius P. O'Brien and Donald A. Drost, "Non-Union Grievance Procedures: Not Just an Anti-Union Strategy," *Personnel* 61 (September-October 1984): 61–69; Brian P. Heshizer and Harry Graham, "Discipline in the Nonunion Company: Protecting Employer and Employee Rights," *Personnel* 39 (March-April 1982): 71–78; Kenneth McCulloch, "Alternative Dispute Resolution Techniques: Pros and Cons," *Employment Relations Today* 11 (Autumn 1984): 311–19; Thomasine Rendero, "Grievance Procedures for Nonunionized Employees," *Personnel* 57 (January-February 1980): 4–10; and Reid L. Shaw, "A Grievance Procedure for Non-Unionized Employees," *Personnel* 36 (July-August, 1959): 66–70.

2

Nonunion Grievance Procedures and Systems: A Review of the Literature

INTRODUCTION

The purpose of this chapter is to integrate the findings of previous studies dealing both directly and tangentially with the subject of nonunion grievance procedures and systems. One of the processes in a chemical laboratory is distillation, the act of separating out and isolating the essence of a particular substance from the mass of material in which it is found. It is the task of this chapter's analysis to perform that function with respect to the bibliographic material garnered on this important human resources management topic.

In this distillation of research findings, significant minority views will not be neglected. Not only do minorities have a right to be heard, but they can influence employee-relations policy thinking and therefore employer-employee policy action.

Thus the scope of this chapter encompasses an examination and assessment of the major literature which deals with the strategic issue of the development of nonunion grievance procedures. There will be an analysis of the composite views of researchers on specific topics for the purpose of extracting whatever general principles appear to be valid deductions from the existing literature. The greatest weight will be given in areas where there is uniformity of thinking in the research, while, in areas which are controversial, conflicting viewpoints will be juxtaposed so that their relative merits can be analyzed.

In summary, all pertinent evidence from the literature will be presented without regard to whether that evidence appears to favor one type of nonunion grievance procedure or another in the many detailed aspects of the interrelationship between nonunion grievance systems and human resources management. Hopefully, this chapter will shed substantial light on what non-union grievance procedures and systems are really all about.

STRATEGIC ISSUES

Three major strategic issues emerge out of a careful study of the literature pertaining to the resolution of nonunion grievances: the nature of grievance arbitration systems; the nature of internal tribunals and peer review systems; and the nature of open-door policies and philosophies, especially with formal appeals to higher level management. Each one of these three major issues of import will be examined here.

Nounion Grievance Arbitration Systems

According to one author, it is somewhat significant to note the increased use of grievance and complaint arbitration in nonunion employer-employee relationships. The utilization of this new human resources management technique has become so widespread that the National Academy of Arbitrators recently placed it on the program of one of its recent regional meetings.[1]

One practicing arbitrator describes the process as follows:

In the nonunion setting, arbitration takes many forms. Protesting employees may represent themselves or may bring friends, fellow workers, or attorneys.

Some companies assign a person from the personnel department as the grievant's representative, or the enterprise may even employ a full-time ombudsman whose sole function consists of the processing of employee grievances. The arbitrator may be selected by the company, or management may ask an agency such as the American Arbitration Association to appoint an arbitrator. Occasionally, the case is heard by three arbitrators: The employee and employer each designate one person to act as arbitrator, and the two select the impartial panel member.

The extent to which management will allow the grieving person access to its records and to other employees varies. So far, I have not had the feeling that employees were handicapped in the handling of their cases.[2]

This same arbitrator also poses a number of interesting problem areas in this arena. For example, "what happens in the cases of a nonunion employer in the absence of a just cause standard who has traditionally enforced a rule that strikes an outsider as unreasonable? Is the impartial arbitrator in such a situation relegated to inquiring only whether established *procedures* were followed properly?"[3] Furthermore, cases not involving discipline can sometimes even present worse difficulties. "In the nonunion situation we have to deal with a vaguely worded policy manual or employee handbook or, even worse, with just a carelessly tossed out promise. . . ."[4]

Also very problematical are questions connected with a arbitrator's re-muneration and fee structure. It may be questioned whether an arbitrator, when considering an employee's grievance, is influenced by the fact that his fee is being paid by management, or differently influenced if the employee pays a portion of the fee. Another question is whether an arbitrator is inclined, when reinstating a discharged employee, to grant him full back pay to help him pay the bills that accumulated while he was unemployed.[5] One professional arbitrator, as if he were replying to such hypothetical questions, has summed up his views of the nonunion grievance process by reminding his readers that professional arbitrators' careers depend on their reputation for impartiality and that, beyond that requirement, they have an obligation not only to their profession in general but also, in particular, to an agency which appoints them and therefore has its own reputation at stake.[6]

The president of the American Arbitration Association (AAA), Robert Coulson, also concurs with the efficacy of the nonunion arbitration process. Interestingly, "an informal arbitration system is now available through a simple reference to the American Arbitration Association's Expedited Rules."[7] Under a typical plan, "employees may submit grievances under the Expedited Labor Arbitration Rules of the American Arbitration Association thereby obtaining a fair and impartial review of their complaint."[8] According to Coulson, the operation of a plan is quite simple.

First, an employee must discuss the grievance with the immediate supervisor. The supervisor must respond within two working days. If the answer is not satisfactory, the employee may present the grievance in writing. The supervisor will answer in writing within two days.

If the supervisor's answer does not settle the affair, the employee may file the written grievance with the personnel manager. After consultation with the department head, the personnel manager must provide the employee with the final management position in writing within three days.

At this point, an employee can appeal to management or may submit the case to impartial arbitration. A request for arbitration must be filed within two weeks and must be in writing, delivered to the personnel office.[9]

What is interesting about this process and procedure is that hearings are held in the building, employees and workers do not lose pay for participating or testifying in an arbitration hearing, no transcripts or recordings are made, and the arbitrator must issue a decision within five working days after the hearing. Last, among the problems that may be arbitrated are failure to promote an individual employee, disciplinary actions, seniority rights, and other provisions covered in the employee-relations manual.[10]

Another observer, commenting on the utilization of third party arbitrators in the nonunion setting, states that "nonunion managements, in posing an alternative to unionization, need to show their workers that they are willing to restrict their use of power in arbitrary or opportunistic ways. One possible way to do this is to buy into a third-party arbitration mode for dispute resolution. Workers in certain kinds of cases would be able to appeal to such neutral bodies for relief rather than appeal to the courts."[11]

One lawyer states, however, that "substantial problems arise when administering internal, nonunion arbitration systems. For example, who is to represent the employee as the grievant presses his or her complaint through the system: an employee representative, management personnel, outside counsel? Moreover, what is the role of the personnel department once a grievance is filed?"[12] Additionally, he wishes to know how one can identify "legitimate" systems from illegitimate systems written by the company's public relations department.[13]

The most famous nonunion grievance procedure culminating in arbitration has been that of the Northrup Corporation. Northrup was the first union-free manufacturing firm to adopt formal grievance machinery and a concomitant process for both hourly workers and salaried employees which terminates in third party arbitration;[14] this was done in 1946 according to Littrell.[15]

A number of primary prerequisites were viewed as essential if this arbitration approach was to be a success. First, there was the establishment of a formal procedure through which facts are discovered. Second, there were lucidly formulated and widely distributed human resources management policies and employee standards of conduct, providing for a system of positive and progressive discipline. Third, there was the establishment of an organization of individuals with the responsibility of aiding workers in the complete resolution of their complaints.[16] The complaint procedure formally adopted in 1946 is essentially the same as that which exists today.[17] Discipline and discharge, according to Littrell's analysis of Northrup's experience, were the most frequent subjects grieved in that nonunion environment, with other grievances involving seniority in a layoff situation, the distribution of overtime among employees, time of reporting for work, pay, the classification of jobs, and promotion.[18] It is interesting to note that, while "discipline and discharge" are listed by Littrell as Northrup's principle subjects involving grievances, discharge is actually merely one of the penalties imposed on violations of discipline, in which sense it would appear proper for Littrell to have classified employees' dissatisfaction with the way they were disciplined as the principle cause of grievances at Northrup, thereby flagging the attention of top management to that human relations problem.

The fourth and final step of the Northrup procedure is interesting. The primary method of selecting an arbitrator is by mutual agreement between the grievant and the company, which is respresented by the employee-relations manager. If that agreement cannot be reached, which is seldom, a list of five arbitrators is obtained from a suitable agency, whereupon each party strikes out one name in an alternate manner until one name is left and becomes the arbitrator chosen.[19]

The corporate director of industrial relations for Northrup sums up the company's experience with their particular procedure as follows:

I have come to believe that without final and binding arbitration, a system of internal grievance handling, whether it be a simple "open door" policy or a more formal system, runs great risk of losing credibility in the eyes of the employees.

A further and very practical benefit flows from a system that uses arbitration; it forces the establishment of written personnel policies, rules, and regulations which add certainty and consistency to the treatment of personnel.

Perhaps the most beneficial effect of such a grievance system is that it makes people think before they take actions which may result in a grievance. No system will ever substitute for good supervisory judgment, but it may help some supervisors to exercise it, knowing that sometime in the future an independent arbitrator may be asked to judge the propriety of the action taken.[20]

One classic research study on nonunion grievance procedures found that arbitration is the system resorted to most infrequently.[21] According to this study, while many firms have considered arbitration, their most vociferous objections arise from two kinds of strategic and tactical considerations: cost and the invasion of management rights on issues that the organization does not wish to be arbitrable.[22]

In relation to the cost factor, first and foremost is remuneration for the arbitrator, an expense customarily assumed by management. Another key element in the cost variable is whether or not the organization also assumes the cost for a worker representative. Another potentially expensive item in nonunion arbitration costs is the expense of moving witnesses to the arbitration hearing.[23]

A second element in the establishment of nonunion arbitration systems is the potential invasion of managerial rights. According to that study, organizational experience with arbitration does not support this assertion. All firms have effectively delimited the scope of arbitrable issues.[24]

Finally, the study notes that in the few instances in which arbitration has been tried, "it does not produce the problems anticipated. Employees do not abuse the system and, in any event, management can limit the arbitrable issues. Among the companies interviewed, terminations were the most frequent, almost exclusive subject of arbitration. These particular arbitrations did not pose a threat to company policy, as all arbitrations were limited to review of contested applications of company policy—not of the policy itself."[25]

In another study of grievance procedures in nonunionized companies, it was stated by executives that the absence of a step culminating in final and binding arbitration did not tend to weaken their nonunion complaint procedures.[26] The primary rationale listed for not including arbitration was a sheer reluctance to place the ultimate power for final decision authority outside of the firm. These organizations felt that it was not desirable to bring in a third party totally unfamiliar with endemic firm practices to solve an internal dispute.[27]

Nonunion arbitration costs and concerns of "who will pay the bill" were other pragmatic objections of managers in many firms. Additionally, the meticulous prepartion of an employee's case for presentation before an arbitrator was not thought to be an easy job. The employee would have to do it on his or her own volition, or the firm would have to perform the task for him or her. Either method would raise serious problems according to these firms.[28]

Furthermore, the absence of a truly complete written statement of corporate or organizational policy was another key rationale cited by some executives for not having a terminal arbitration stage in their structured nonunion grievance procedures.[29] Finally, several managers expressed the concern that a final and binding arbitration stage might tend to weaken the effectiveness of the nonunion complaint procedure in that the firm and the worker might tend to push every single case to the arbitrator's hands.[30]

In closing this section on nonunion grievance arbitration systems, it should be noted that one professor states that the arbitration process has tremendous meaning for workers because, generally speaking, the arbitrator is equally obligated to both managers and employees.[31] He further states that in union-free companies there is no organization to pay for the worker's portion of the cost of the arbitration. He maintains that since the sharing of the cost of arbitration may be prohibitive for employees, this drawback may not make the system totally viable.[32]

The last word on the subject will be had by Professor Daniel Quinn Mills of the Graduate School of Business Administration at Harvard University. He states:

Some companies permit nonunion employees to take an unresolved grievance to a neutral arbitrator. The company ordinarily pays the costs of the arbitration and agrees to be bound by the arbitrator's decision. Although this is an infrequent procedure because most companies do not wish to grant a right of neutral arbitration of complaints to nonunionized employees, the American Arbitration Association, a professional service organization for neutral arbitrators, has recently established rules for the conduct of arbitration hearings involving nonunion employees.[33]

Internal Tribunals and Peer Review Systems

An increasingly large number of firms and organizations, often totally disenchanted with seemingly underutilized open-door complaint and grievance procedures, are establishing internal tribunals and peer review panels to resolve conflicts over promotions, disciplinary actions, and discharges. Some consist of three peers of the aggrieved and two management representatives and their decisions are final and binding on both employer and employee.[34] "The trend represents an effort by companies to broaden employees' rights in disciplinary matters. Companies also say the peer boards build an open, trusting atmosphere, help deter union organizing and, perhaps most importantly, stem the rising number of costly lawsuits claiming wrongful discharge and discrimination."[35]

According to *The Wall Street Journal*, about 100 companies now utilize internal peer review panels and tribunals, including Federal Express Corporation, General Electric, and Citicorp. "Such panels can be time-consuming and costly to run."[36] "Federal Express, for instance, says it has spent up to

$10,000 on a single case—transporting workers and managers to an off-site hotel, compiling documents and reviewing the testimony."[37]

A key issue, as in nonunion arbitration procedures, is that "managers often consider the boards an intrusion on their prerogative and say the panels are incapable of deciding subtle personnel issues."[38] However, most firms do not allow peer review boards to establish corporate policy, although some peer review panels recommend substantive and procedural policy changes that are sometimes adopted by upper level executives.[39] What is very interesting is that "the peer boards' very existence often prompts managers to adhere more carefully to company disciplinary policy and give subordinates more feedback."[40]

Two final interesting empirical research observations are made by *The Wall Street Journal*. First of all, peer review panels have generally sided with upper management's decisions about 60 percent to 70 percent of the time, and the "workers seem to be rougher on their peers than their supervisors."[41]

One author describes peer review as a participative management technique. He states: "As a system that falls within the participatory management umbrella, peer review allows for employee grievances to be appealed to a committee including one's peers rather than leaving final decision-making authority with management."[42] Furthermore, his research concludes with the following observation:

Peer review, when institutionalized in an employer's grievance procedure, has many sociological as well as legal implications. The goal of a particular employer may be to retain nonunion status, to facilitate better communication between employees and management, to provide an orderly and efficient resolution system, to avoid lawsuits and agency investigations, or to increase productivity by enhancing employee motivation.[43]

According to *Business Week*, a handful of major firms have adopted peer review boards as a means of remaining nonunion.[44] They describe the process as follows:

Typically, peer review is simply added to a company's existing grievance process. At most nonunion companies with a complaint procedure, an employee tries to solve disputes first with his or her direct supervisor. If no agreement is reached, the employee can appeal to higher levels of management, including, in some companies, the chief executive officer. Peer review usually takes over after that process is exhausted.[45]

Business Week's research also discovered the following findings: both workers and executives are tangible benefits in the peer review process; some chief executives find that any form of peer review increases supervisors' awareness; supervisors tend to perform better because they don't want their subordinates to utilize an internal tribunal; the process of peer review is meaningless unless it is promulgated with top management's wholehearted support; critics of the system argue that the process creates discord among employees and yet the use of peer review boards will increase in the future.[46]

Four major companies with peer review systems have been discussed in the literature: Control Data Corporation; Trans World Airlines; the General Electric Plant in Columbia, Maryland; and Coors Container Company. The major research findings from the literature regarding these four companies will now be discussed here.

Over a quarter century ago, the Control Data Corporation was one of the first nonunion firms in this country to institutionalize a complaint procedure.[47] In 1983 the firm added to their employee grievance process a peer review system.[48] Its primary characteristic is a panel consisting of two peers randomly chosen by the employee, and one panel member consisting of a "disinterested" executive. This panel serves as an arbiter of major disputes arising out of the workplace. A decision is by a majority vote of the panel. Since two out of three members of the board are employees, complaint settlement power can be said to lie in the hands of the workers.[49]

As of 1984, the outcome of the peer review process at Control Data was as follows:

Eleven cases have reached the peer review board stage, with four decided in favor of the grievant. The three most recent cases have gone in favor of management. In two cases, the peer members out-voted the executive in favor of the grievant, while in a third, one employee sided with the executive in supporting management's position. Eight of the cases received unanimous decisions; of these, two went in favor of the employee and six were unanimous for management.

Nine of the eleven cases involved grievances over terminations.[50]

Once the employee asks for a peer review board, the company ombudsman helps the worker "complete his or her written presentation, convenes the board, and guides it through its deliberations as a nonvoting chairperson. The board, seeing only the written record of the case, acts as an arbiter rather than a mediator."[51]

" 'Peers' are defined as fellow workers in the same job family at a grade level equal to or higher than that of the grievant."[52] The company ombudsman's office "chooses two at random from a computer-generated list of employees nationwide. An executive is similarly chosen from a list of persons at the general manager level and above, excluding the very top tier."[53]

The three persons who are selected sign a statement promising confidentiality and receive casebooks containing statements by the employee and management, a separate statement by the personnel department, and pertinent policies and procedures, but with the names of affected persons and organizations deleted.[54] After the members of the peer review board have fully examined the record, the panel issues its recommendations to the personnel vice president.[55] As of 1984, no board decisions had yet been rejected.[56]

The ombudsman at Control Data Corporation summarizes their experience with peer review as follows:

Peer review is now a fact of life at Control Data. . . . As a result, we're seeing much more aggressive problem solving by local managers. From the rank-and-file we hear comments indicating an increased sense of fairness and security against arbitrary decisions. And at the corporate level, our legal counselors say that peer review almost certainly heads off litigation.[57]

We now turn our attention to the internal tribunal system at Trans World Airlines. What is unique in this company's nonunion grievance procedure is that it contains provisions for elements of peer review along with provisions for a professional arbitrator from the ranks of the National Academy of Arbitrators.[58]

Today, the nonunion grievance procedure at TWA is a three-step procedure. The first step is one in which the employee's complaint is listened to and answered to in writing by the complainant's immediate boss. The second step in the procedure is one in which the employee's complaint is listened to by a middle manager who is outside the complainant's immediate scalar chain of command. Complaints appealed to the third step of the process are then reviewed by a panel of three individuals—called at TWA the System Board of Adjustment—whose internal composition depends on whether the complaint involves a dismissal.[59] If the case does not involve a termination, the board's chairperson is a personnel department executive, the other members being a vice president selected from a rotating list of vice presidents, and a nonunion employee selected by the grievant.[60] If a termination is involved, a member of the National Academy of Arbitrators is chosen as chairperson of the Board, with the personnel executive and the grievant's selected peer being the other members.[61]

In a termination case an attorney may represent the grievant, but only in the last step, and in that situation an attorney represents the company, but otherwise the company is represented by the employee's supervisor.[62]

The former staff vice president of personnel of Trans World Airlines states the following:

One interesting feature of TWA's procedure is the ability of a grievant to involve coworkers in the processing of a dispute. This was initiated by the company in the early 1970s to help eliminate the perception that the procedure was biased in favor of management. In establishing the members of the System Board of Adjustment— the third step of a procedure—provision is made for the grievant to name a coworker as a member. The coworker can be any other noncontract employee, management or nonmanagement, from the employee's location. The peer involvement feature has been extremely successful, and has generally enjoyed very responsible support from the employee board members and representatives.[63]

Furthermore, this former TWA vice president makes the following observation:

The involvement of employees' peers has paid real dividends to the company since the coworker often has insights on an issue that would not be available otherwise. And while there may be a tendency on the part of the coworker to support the grievant in spite of the evidence, there have been many instances where the coworker has supported the denial of a grievance based on the facts brought out during the hearing, some of which may not have been obvious or available earlier.[64]

Finally, the company's policy is to pay the travel expenses of grievants and persons participating with them, and grievants may receive pay for attending hearings on company time.[65]

Another fascinating internal tribunal peer review system that has received considerable attention in the literature was the one operational in the General Electric Plant in Columbia, Maryland.

In 1982, peer grievance review (PGR) was implemented in the GE Columbia plant.[66] The PGR panel consisted of five members.[67] "In Columbia, the plant manager and employee relations manager were permanent members of the panel. The remaining panel members were selected at random from the trained employees participating in the program."[68] According to the founder of the peer grievance process for resolving employee grievances at the Columbia facility, "other locations have chosen to use various combinations of management representatives. In every instance, only two management people are involved in the panel decision. The three additional panel members have been peers of the grievant."[69] He further notes: "The one common thread that runs through all organizations using this review system *is that the number of peers on the panel is greater than the number of managers* (emphasis added). Each panel member has an equal vote in determining the outcome of the grievance."[70]

An important consideration in PGR is the jurisdiction of the panel. "The PGR panel cannot change company policy, set the rates of pay or benefits, or change the work rules."[71] "Essentially, PGR works like a 'jury.' In this country the legislature makes the rules, not the jury. The jury only decides whether the rules have been followed or else the proper remedies instituted when they have not been followed. The Peer Grievance Review panel has the same authority—not to make the rules but to see they are followed."[72]

The founder of PGR states the following regarding employee perception of the system:

Employee response has been overwhelmingly positive, due mainly to key differences in employee perception of the normal traditional grievance procedure and Peer Grievance Review. Employees often think of the traditional, one-over-one grievance procedure as being nothing more than a rubber stamp. They feel that no manager will overturn a decision made by a subordinate because if managers do not back up their people, they might lose them. The new Peer Grievance Review is seen as a factual review of the problem.[73]

The key outcomes of PGR can be summarized as follows: It builds commitment and trust; it breaks down the we/they barriers; it assures a very factual review of problems; it adds defensibility in third party reviews; it reduces conflict between employees and management; it eliminates a key union organizing issue; it requires supervisors to do their job correctly; and it maintains managerial prerogatives and rights.[74] Also, under PGR, management does not lose control of the business; employees do not lack responsibility to make good decisions; the process is not administratively cumbersome; the confidentiality of the employee is not violated; and employees will not always support each other.[75]

Finally, "peer grievance review has provided to be a win/win program in Columbia. It has also been a win/win program in the 12 other General Electric plants that have implemented it, including Louisville, Kentucky, with its 5,000 salaried employees."[76]

The remaining company that has been cited in the literature for its peer review system is Coors Container Company.[77] Under the Coors system, "company policy is not appealable, but the application of that policy is."[78] Furthermore, all terminations are appealable, as well as any form of discipline.;[79] "In addition, any employees who feel that they are treated unjustly under existing company policies may request an appeal board hearing."[80]

The Coors's appeals system is as follows:

When an employee wants to appeal, the first step is always through the immediate supervisor. The exception is when the problem itself is the immediate supervisor. In that case, the employee proceeds to the next step.

The employee discusses the problem with the department manager or, in manufacturing, the general supervisor. If the employee receives no satisfaction at this step, the appeal process proceeds to the third step.

The employee talks to the "function head," the superintendent in a manufacturing area or the manager just below the officer level in any other area. If, again, the problem is not resolved to the employee's satisfaction, an appeal board is requested. . . . The employee requests an appeal board if the problem is not resolved to his or her satisfaction. Once the appeal board has been formed, it hears the appeal within 10 days. Sometimes it may take longer because of vacations, work schedules, shifts, etc. In all instances, however, the employee is told why the problem has not been heard within the 10 days.

The board itself is composed of five members. Two of them represent management. They are the personnel officer and the appropriate division head, either an officer or a director from the same division as the employee with the complaint. Two other members of the board are chosen by the employee, without regard to position shift or schedule. These individuals are usually friends of the employee, but they cannot have family ties. One-half hour before the appeal is heard, the individuals selected by the employee and the management representative meet to select a fifth member.

Only one rule governs selection of the fifth member: the person cannot be a relative of the employee. . . .

After they have settled on two or three candidates, the four members take a 15-minute break and the potential fifth members are contacted in priority order. More than one person is selected, because an employee has the right to refuse participation on an appeal board. Rather than reconvene the four members, a multiple listing enables the system to continue quickly and efficiently. Once a fifth member is chosen and agrees to serve on the appeal board, it's usually only a matter of minutes before the appeal itself can begin.[81]

What is very interesting at Coors is that "results of an appeal, however, are never made public. A statement outlining the statistical makeup of appeals, that is, how many, percentage of modified decisions, etc., is included in the annual report to the board of directors. No other publicity about appeals is made to either management or to the employees in general."[82]

The peer evaluation system at Coors has seemed to produce the following results: the breakdown of the age-old barrier between employees and management has occurred; employees now realize that a decision to discipline or terminate an individual is not an easy one, and that the supervisor goes through a large amount of frustration in his or her decision-making process; supervisors are more skilled at relating to employees; managers realize their decisions are open to scrutiny; supervisors and managers give appreciably more and better thought to their decisions; and the peer review system is a simple yet very effective tool for resolving employer-employee problems with particular emphasis on discipline, discharge, and other supervisory and managerial actions.[83]

Finally, in relation to peer review, one auther notes that the chief benefit of this type of system is its perceived justice.[84] He also states that an individual who is not familiar with the process of review by peers might anticipate that worker representatives will tend to side with the subordinate and that representatives of management with the supervisor or executive.[85] However, in his experience, members of peer review tribunals have very often acted in a very impartial manner.[86]

In closing, he issues a minority viewpoint that the process is not perfect. He perceives that the endemic nature of the peer review process also means that a decision will not be handed down by employees with excellent knowledge of the intricacies of human resources management. Therefore, the final decision may be totally unsuitable.[87]

In summary, firms that tend to favor peer participation in the complaint review process put forward the following key arguments: workers truly feel that a decision in which their fellow employees have fully and truly participated guarantees a maximum amount of just and equitable treatment; workers are given extra courage to put forward their complaints; peer panel members often make excellent recommendations which provide a highly workable means to solve the complaint; and providing employees with a real and truly legitimate voice in the management of firm organizational justice meets a fundamental and a basic employee desire for participative management.[88] In a similar vein, "peer review committees tend to be conservative in their interpretation and application of established policies. Moreover, the peer committees have been reluctant to use the procedure as a 'back door' for sanctioning a practice where policy does not exist or is incomplete."[89]

Open-Door Policies and Philosophies

Our attention will now turn to the third type of nonunion grievance procedure: the corporate nonunion open-door policy. Unlike its predecessors—binding, outside arbitration, and juries by peers—open-door policies have received very mixed reviews in the literature.[90]

According to one study, "virtually all managers profess to have an 'open door.' That is, if the manager has done something that irks an employee, the employee is free to come to him or her and complain about it."[91] This study states the following concerning open-door systems:

It's difficult to gauge the extent to which open-door policies succeed as an appeal system. They seem to be more popular with professional and white-collar employees who are accustomed to dealing directly with management than with blue-collar employees who prefer more formalized procedures. For employees who lack individual bargaining power, whether they are blue-collar or white-collar, the open-door system offers no protection at all. The *system* does nothing to protect their interest, although individual managers may administer the procedures involved justly.

A final, potentially dangerous problem exists when no complaints are presented despite the availability of an open door. One interpretation of this situation is that few problems exist; the other is that employees do not believe the appeal system will work, so they bypass it for alternative ways of showing their displeasure. The employer who assumes that a lack of complaints reflects a lack of problems can be wrong—and the consequences can be quite expensive.[92]

A contributing editor to *Employment Relations Today* makes the research observation that "many companies practice a rather loosely defined 'open-door' policy, whereby aggrieved employees at all levels can address superiors informally, often without a written record." What is interesting, however, is that "some of those companies are tightening up their policy. Stricter application of an open-door policy allows a company to post its grievance resolution resources and expertise with the company managers, who spend the most time handling such problems and are best prepared to do the work."[93]

For example, when MCI Communications had about 3,000 employees in 1982, the chairman of the firm "was able to know many employees by name, and the open-door policy admitted anyone to his office who wished to register a complaint. It proved a practical and effective method."[94] However, after faster than projected growth, neither the chairman, nor any single executive today, could possibly be expected to hear all grievances and run the company productively.[95] MCI has thus "introduced a practice to deal with expanded numbers and yet be responsive to employee concerns. This provides for more structure and results in quicker responses."[96] The total system still occasionally deposits a problem at the doorstep of the vice president for human resources, "but more often troubles are resolved at lower levels. When open-door complaints are registered, complete files are kept to formalize and ensure expected resolution. However, file contents are usually reviewed at lower levels."[97] Hence, some commentators feel that the "open door" must evolve in a period of managing growth.[98]

Two senior human resources management scholars state the following:

A case can be made for the open door procedure. But we are convinced that inherent disadvantages—both short-term and long—more than outweigh short-term advantages.

Where there are several levels of management, it is organizationally unsound to invite employees to bypass a lower-level supervisor and take complaints directly to a member of higher management or Personnel. Undesirable consequences include the following:

It prevents the supervisor from getting prompt, firsthand information that is stated or implied in a complaint. But first-level supervisors need this kind of information—whether it concerns allegedly unsatisfactory work conditions or merely the feelings of some disgruntled employee.

When the complainant does not go directly to the first-level supervisor, members of higher management and personnel officers lose a valuable opportunity to assess the skill of supervisors in the leadership aspects of their job.

The open-door policy inevitably weakens the authority of management representatives who are bypassed. First-level supervisors lose face with their immediate organizational supervisors, and with their subordinates as well, when dissatisfied employees can go straight to the top or to Personnel.[99]

Berenbeim's classic study on corporate nonunion complaint systems delineates the basic characteristics of the open door. First of all, there is a company commitment to an open door as a matter of basic company policy, with the policy being stated in employee handbooks. Another characteristic feature is that the handbooks assert that employees using the open-door systems need not fear reprisal.[100] Furthermore, the doors of executives at all levels are open to employees, although the latter are encouraged to go first to their immediate supervisors if the employees' situations do not make that inappropriate.[101] Finally, most open-door systems provide employees with appeal steps more or less similar with those in more formal grievance resolution procedures, but with the emphasis on resolving a grievance at the initial stage.[102]

A recent article in the *Harvard Business Review* states that "managers in some companies claim that an 'open door' policy exists, which suggests that it is possible to go over the boss' head or that the personnel department offers an alternative route. But most companies don't have the clear policies and supporting procedures necessary to make these additional routes a credible resource for a broad range of employees and problems."[103] Furthermore, "most employees—support staff and managers alike—definitely do not want to take a complaint 'up the chain' past their supervisor. They understand all too well the taboo against going over a boss' head and they actually fear reprisal for doing so."[104] It is noted that "for professionals, the fear may not be of immediate reprisal but rather of a deferred reckoning that would upset their careers years down the line."[105]

One senior manager describes his experience with the open-door policy as follows:

I have never questioned the value to my company of an open-door policy. And without doubt, trust, as with so many issues, is the key. When employees don't know where else to turn, they have to be confident that they can go to you without the slightest fear of being labeled a whistle-blower, being ostracized, or worst of all, being fired. At the first sign that the policy can backfire on an employee, it will lose its usefulness. Your managers, if they are to be effective in their work, have to be confident that you will not undermine them and that they will be given a fair hearing, whatever the charge against them. All in all, an open-door policy is definitely a challenge, but one in which the payoffs can be immeasurable.[106]

It has also been noted that the "door is always open" method of adjusting grievances has several weaknesses and can break down in practice.[107] First of all, "few employees possess the courage to confront middle and top managers in their offices."[108] Second, "these executives are frequently inaccessible at the time a problem arises. Listening to employee complaints is but one of their many responsibilities. The complaint that seems urgent to an employee often seems of little consequence to an executive who, at the very moment an employee is seeking an appointment, is feeling pressured by a major planning, policy, or strategy problem involving productivity and profits."[109] Last, "when top management encourages employees to bypass their immediate supervisor, the status of that supervisor suffers. He or she finds it increasingly difficult to command the respect of subordinates. Furthermore, supervisors ordinarily look with disfavor upon anyone who bypasses them. Subordinates usually understand this; and fearing reprisal, they hesitate to make use of the "open door."[110]

Nevertheless, "the most popular procedure for responding to employee complaints is the open-door policy."[111] It seems from the literature that "although an open-door policy provides an avenue for employees to express their complaints, it does not always function very effectively. The social distance between production workers and the company president is usually exaggerated when viewed from the bottom of the hierarchy, and it can destroy an employee's willingness to share a problem."[112] "On the other hand, a true open-door attitude toward subordinates on the part of the immediate supervisor is very helpful in improving communication. If the supervisor is receptive to relatively free talk from subordinates, there is opportunity to promote good organization morale."[113]

In summary, this literature review regarding open-door systems reveals a very mixed reaction among practitioners and scholars concerning its efficacy. This certainly was not the case for nonunion grievance arbitration systems and peer review procedures. It can be concluded, however, that all organizations need some form of appeals procedure. "The traditional standby for companies without set procedures is the open-door policy."[114] And since "the courts seem to be moving toward requiring nonunionized organizations to show just cause and due process in disciplining or discharging employees... many organizations have established appeal procedures for disciplinary actions taken by management. The most common type of nonunion appeal procedures are open-door policies and step systems that allow employees to bring appeals to successively higher levels of management."[115]

Furthermore, "part of an open-door procedure is assurance that reprisals will not be taken against workers for using it."[116] "However, employees are often skeptical of this approach, feeling that their complaint would probably be viewed as an unnecessary 'rocking of the boat.' "[117]

It can also be said that "in an open-door problem, employees can go to any manager with a complaint. In this case justice may not be served because the manager who handles the grievance is frequently a party to it. If so, he or she lacks credibility and is unlikely to act fairly."[118] But "for an open-door policy to be effective, managers must be sincere in acting on and correcting the problems that employees present."[119]

EMERGING ISSUES

Four major emerging issues emanate out of a careful study of the literature: the nature of due process for nonunionized employees; the nature of the relationship between the doctrine of employment-at-will and nonunion grievance procedures; the nature of the corporate ombudsman as a complement to the nonunion grievance procedure; and the nature of employer-employee relations in the nonunion setting—the role of the nonunion complaint procedure. Each one of these four major emerging issues of import will be examined here.

Due Process for Nonunionized Employees

One scholar has emphasized that nonunion "grievance procedures not only should be established to ensure due process for employees but also should be administered consistently and fairly. For example, evidence should be available to employee and employer, and both parties should have the right to call witnesses and refuse to testify against themselves. Furthermore, these grievance procedures should be clearly stated as company policy and communicated to the employees."[120]

One of the reasons, therefore, cited for the rise in nonunion grievance procedures is that the concept of "due process" is becoming more important at the workplace, the emphasis being on "fair and orderly" procedures in matters affecting employees' lives, and with their airing of their concerns and complaints without fear of reprisal.[121] A result of this development is the increasing acceptance of "progressive discipline," defined as reliance on responsive, corrective action rather than on severe disciplinary actions, together with increasing use of grievance procedures.[122]

Wendell French, a senior scholar of human resources management at the Graduate School of Business Administration at the University of Washington, defines the issue as follows:

In addition to being concerned with the substance of the decisions on human resources, people in organizations also tend to be concerned with the procedures used for determining what is equitable or fair. Further, they are concerned with the kind and quality of the avenues of appeal open to them. Thus both the quality of treatment and the procedures used in this treatment are important, and any discussion of organizational justice must include some emphasis on substantive and procedural matters pertaining to discipline, layoffs, transfers, promotions, privileges, work schedules, and wages.[123]

He further clarifies the issue:

A broader term organizational due process might be used for enterprises in general. This concept can be defined, tentatively, as follows: organizational due process consists of established procedures for handling complaints and grievances, protection against punitive action for using such established procedures, and careful, systematic, and thorough review of the substance of the complaints and grievances by unbiased or neutral parties.[124]

Thus, "the trends for the future indicate that grievance procedures will maintain their great importance as a means of ensuring employee justice."[125] For example, Professor Keith Davis in a classic exposition states that "the basic objective of grievance settlement should be *justice* which is defined as fairness according to established rules and relationships. Justice is a fundamental requirement in employee human relations because it gives substance and meaning to human dignity."[126]

One prolific writer on the subject, David W. Ewing of the Harvard University Graduate School of Business Administration, lists the following requirements for due process in any organization: "It must be a procedure, it must follow rules, and it must not be arbitrary; it must be visible and well-known enough so that potential violators of rights and victims of abuse know of it; it must be predictably effective and employees must have confidence that previous decisions in favor of rights will be repeated; it must be institutionalized; it must be perceived as equitable; it must be easy to use; and it must apply to all employees.[127]

Ewing also postulates that "fair hearing procedures, which are the corporate equivalent of due process,"[128] have a number of practical values. First of all, "they correct many injustices. The employee unfairly fired can get reinstated; the supervisor who harasses a subordinate is required to mend his or her ways."[129] Second, "they are the means of protecting such rights as freedom of inquiry, conscientious objections, and privacy."[130] Last, "they are helpful to management—despite the monetary sting they may produce."[131]

Ewing also states the following:

An effective form of due process has various advantages for a company. It helps to clear the air so that rumors of an abusive discharge or unfair handling of an objector do not circulate and build up and sometimes, in the end, create a worse situation than the original event. It is valuable for morale. Reportedly it has a salubrious effect on supervisory behavior; just knowing that a conflict may be aired in front of an impartial investigator may be incentive enough for a supervisor to attack it more constructively. . . .

The only *real* costs of a corporate response to dissidence is the wounded pride of managers and supervisors whose judgments can be questioned. If a managear feels that he or she can't manage without total power to compel obedience, then due process is indeed an ominous threat, and if top executives don't want managers to have to worry about such a threat, they shouldn't toy with "open doors," employee assistance offices, ombudspeople, or fair hearing committees. But if managers are confident of their ability to manage nonautocratically, then due process makes good sense.[132]

Last, Ewing notes that there seems to be a growing support among executives for means and methods to assure due process for all employees.[133]

In terms of a careful reading of the literature, a number of points can be made. First of all, "the political concept of due process has been evolving for over seven hundred years, but its application is still imperfect and its scope is still limited. We are probably witnessing a small segment of a long period in the evolution of industrial due process."[134] Furthermore, "we can expect that its use will spread in all kinds of organizations and that its form will become more complicated and sophisticated as well as more successful in resolving superior-subordinate conflicts."[135] Second, a major right or entitlement commonly demanded by workers today is "the right to due process procedure for grievances against the employer."[136] Third, an organizational justice system of complaint machinery "also offers the employee security in knowing that the organization is less likely to make arbitrary decisions."[137]

Fourth, there is "a positive advantage to management in providing a meaningful internal appeals system."[138] Fifth, "for many people, the most critical right of employees is the right to due process."[139] Sixth, "because due process involves a system of checks and balances, it increases the objectivity of decisions."[140] Seventh, "organizational due process is a fair and less costly means of resolving disputes than litigation."[141] Eighth, "the topic of due process in work organizations calls for much greater conceptual development, practical experimentation, and systematic research."[142] Last, "efforts to institutionalize fairness must concentrate on defining an open and participative process for making human resource flow decisions and resolving disputes that will surround them. Ignoring or suppressing different views or disputes will have a negative impact, leading inevitably to dissatisfaction, turnover, low commitment, a poor public image, and lawsuits."[143] "This calls for an industrial jurisprudence."[144]

Manual C. Velasquez, Professor of Business Ethics at the University of Santa Clara, states the following:

An ideal system of due process would be one in which individuals were given clear antecedent notice of the rules they were to follow, which gave a fair and impartial hearing to those who are believed to have violated the rules, which administered all rules consistently and without favoritism or discrimination, which was designed to ascertain the truth as objectively as possible, and which did not hold people responsible for matter over which they had no control.

It is obvious why the right to due process is seen by many people as the most critical for employees. If this right is not respected, employees stand little chance of seeing their other rights respected. Due process ensures that individuals are not treated arbitrarily, capriciously, or maliciously by their superiors in the administration of the firm's rules, and sets a moral limit on the exercise of the superior's power....

The most important area in which due process must play a role is in the hearing of grievances. By carefully spelling out a fair procedure for hearing and processing employee grievances, a firm can ensure that due process becomes an institutionalized reality.[145]

According to Patricia H. Werhane, Professor of Business Ethics at Loyola University of Chicago, due process—procedurally—should state that "every employee has a right to public hearing, peer evaluation, outside arbitration or some other open and mutually agreed upon grievance procedure before being demoted, unwillingly transferred, or fired."[146]

Finally, Thomas A. Kochan, Professor of Industrial Relations at the Sloan School of Management of the Massachusetts Institute of Technology, observes that "various scholars . . . have argued that *all* employees should have access to due process or dispute resolution procedures on a broad array of issues including unfair discharge."[147] And Mary P. Rowe, Adjunct Professor in the Sloan School of Management at M.I.T. states: "Most corporations I know eschew the term 'due' process (of uncertain meaning and widely misunderstood) in favor of 'fair process' or something like it, in the non-union arena."[148]

The Relationship Between the Doctrine of Employment-at-Will and Nonunion Grievance Procedures

Richard T. De George, Professor of Business Ethics at the University of Kansas, defines this issue very well:

In the United States, the traditional legal view of the employer-employee relationship has been known as the doctrine of "employment-at-will." According to this doctrine, individuals are free to work for whomever they choose, and employers are free to hire whomever they choose. Because the agreement is a mutual one, and both are free to enter an agreement, the employment agreement can be terminated at will, unless there is a contract that precludes it. If a worker wishes to move to another job, the worker may do so. If an employer wishes to fire an employee, the employer may do so. Both parties therefore work "at will."[149]

For purposes of this study, what is the relationship between the currently debated issue of the employment-at-will doctrine and the issue of nonunion grievance procedures? "It should be noted that, notwithstanding the benefits from establishing a complaint procedure, an employer should be aware that, unless precautions are taken, the complaint procedure may legally restrict the employer's right to discharge an employee."[150] To put it another way, "the introduction of a complaint procedure that gives employees a 'right' to air their differences or complaints could be and indeed has been construed by some state courts as giving employees certain employment contract rights."[151]

"Courts are increasingly attaching legal significance to employee handbooks and their contents. The same is true with respect to other personnel policies such as employee complaint procedures.... Consequently, before undertaking any such complaint procedure, an employer should realize that failure to follow these procedures in all cases could lead to a lawsuit."[152] Furthermore, "many courts have recognized that by undertaking affirmative obligations such as those spelled out in complaint procedures, an employer will be expected to follow those procedures to the letter and that failure to do so could give rise to a lawsuit on the part of an employee who was denied due process under such complaint procedure."[153] Thus, "complaint procedures should not be undertaken and adopted lightly and once they are put into practice, all levels of management must be prepared to honor the commitment."[154]

"Employers with successful complaint procedures place great emphasis on consistency and uniformity in its application. Therefore, employers should make certain that their complaint procedure machinery is working and that there is no deviation from it. In other words, once a complaint procedure program has been implemented, the employer should follow and abide by the format consistently."[155]

Without a doubt, the "right to discharge is generally looked upon as being total and even today the courts far more often than not sustain this doctrine when ex-employees contest it judicially. But for the first time such workers are winning some such cases."[156] Hence, "many employers have become increasingly uneasy about the real extent of their ability to discharge unsatisfactory employees."[157]

Concomitantly, "the increasing litigiousness on the part of workers is sending a message to the courts."[158] As a result, "nonunion companies, in particular, are instituting formal systems, similar to union grievance procedures, that enable workers to resolve job-related problems."[159]

Fred Luthans, Professor of Management at the Graduate School of Business Administration at the University of Nebraska, saliently points out the following:

Beyond the individual employee satisfaction that results from the adoption of a formal grievance procedure, the organization also receives a means to protect itself from litigation. The organization is protected from litigation because court decisions have specified that an employee must first exercise the grievance procedure before seeking redress in the courts. Thus, the process would help to resolve problems before they become costly legal battles. Additionally, the grievance procedure can act as a means to relieve pressure and inform management when problems are occurring, before they grow into major issues.[160]

As can be seen so far, "courts are finding that oral agreements, personnel policy manuals, and employee handbooks are implied contracts between employers and employees and that employers are not free to discharge employees in violation of these implied contracts."[161] As a result, "some attorneys are recommending the elimination of anything in policy manuals or employee handbooks that could be construed as a commitment to job security that the employer does not intend."[162] Concomitantly, "it is recommended that employers carefully document employee misconduct or inadequate job performance and provide the employee with notice of poor job performance. The affirmative strategy is to develop and implement clearly formalized personnel evaluation and review procedures, grievance procedures, and human resource development plans."[163]

Labor Law Journal has aptly discussed the issue in these terms: Problems can easily arise in the area of grievances. For example, a personnel director or director of human resources may attempt to foster positive worker relations and provide a mechanism for corporate due process by including a grievance procedure in employee manuals or handbooks. While this has traditionally been accepted as a valid personnel practice, it could spell trouble later if the company decides to fire an employee unless the company has strictly adhered to the described grievance procedures. Deviation to a significant degree by a company from a grievance procedure described in its literature may greatly weaken its case against a terminated employee.[164]

Thus, as in noted above, "courts have begun to enforce the substantive restrictions on discharge announced by an employer."[165]

In summary, what can managers, executives, and employers do to protect themselves? The Wall Street Journal forcefully states that "first and foremost, ensure compliance with company policies and procedures set forth in employee handbooks and manuals. The cirtical question: Are supervisors really following these policies when they take action against an employee?"[166] Also, personnel managers must ensure that supervisors are sensitive to the potential for wrongful-discharge actions. They must insist that supervisors know the policies and procedures in the manual, and that no one makes promises that cannot be kept."[167]

Another view is that "one of the first things a company can do is review employee handbooks, personnel manuals, employment applications, company brochures, advertisements, and any other written documents to be sure they do not contain any reference that might give support to a lawsuit."[168] Furthermore, it has been noted that in-house nonunion grievance procedures "give an employee the opportunity to have his or her 'day in court' with the company rather than with a judge. When there is a legitimate problem, the facts and steps taken by the company before termination will be documented. The written record can become an important asset to the company in court. Similarly, it can be to the employer's advantage if an employee has not taken advantage of an available grievance system."[169]

Harvard Business Review has suggested measures to take "that will give the employer a margin of security that helps the company win its case."[170] They suggest that a company look out for any sentence or phrase in its employee-relations literature that might be possibly interpreted to mean that a worker will be fired only for "just cause." Furthermore, they urge that if a company's employee-relations manual mentions a disciplinary process, such as a progressive discipline program, make sure that the firm follows the procedural steps exactly. Last, they exhault companies to be on the lookout for any language in their personal literature that might be obtuse.[171]

In closing this section on the relationship between the doctrine of employment-at-will and nonunion complaint procedures, it should be highlighted that "enlightened personnel management typically embraces a formal grievance procedure as a means to ensure fair and consistent treatment of all employees. Sometimes, however, management becomes entrapped by their own creation through failing to adhere to the mutually agreed-upon procedure."[172] It should also be highlighted that "when a multistep grievance procedure specifies time limits for filing and responding to a grievance, both parties have an obligation to observe such time limits. If the second step of the procedure requires the charge to be put in writing, management has the obligation to deal only with the offense specified in the first step, not another offense, when writing up its arguments."[173] Finally, "penalties should not be changed after the fact, especially to increase the penalty."[174]

The Corporate Ombudsman in Relationship to the Nonunion Grievance Procedure

Although "there is no universally accepted definition of an intra-corporate ombudsman,"[175] one preeminent authority in this field states the term ombudsman means a "neutral or impartial manager within a corporation, who may provide confidential and informal assistance to managers and employees in resolving work-related concerns, who may serve as a counsellor, go-between, mediator, fact-finder or upward-feedback mechanism, and whose office is located outside ordinary line management structures."[176]

Mary P. Rowe, President of the Corporate Ombudsman Association, points out the following:

One purpose of an ombudsman is clearly to foster and support fair and proper communications and processes. But, typically, the major purpose is to help with a very wide variety of problems and inquiries and concerns at work, in whatever ways are perceived as helpful by the employer and by the managers and employees of the company.[177]

For example, one of the functions of an ombudsman is the investigation of a complaint or a problem which can be formal or informal, with or without recommendations to an adjudicator—such as to a grievance committee or to a line or senior manager.[178] "These investigatory options are reported by ombuds practitioners, and are more or less common depending on the company and the ombudsman."[179] Furthermore, some common topics that they deal with are issues dealing with promotion and demotion, performance appraisals, salary and fringe benefits, job security, company policies, discipline, termination, personality conflict, and management practices.[180]

According to Rowe, "there is almost no general rule about ombuds offices that holds true for all such offices. But the overall ideas of listening to people as individuals, and of trying to deal with problems at an early stage, are clearly ideas of current interest to a wide variety of employers."[181]

Personnel Journal states that an ombudsman is needed for many reasons, especially when appeals procedures, when present, are perhaps rather cumbersome and difficult to pursue.[182] Hence, "employees need someone (in whom they have confidence and trust as being independent) to turn to who has the power to investigate complaints."[183] Therefore, the ombudsman (acting as an internal but independent authority) "can investigate each case and decide on the fairness of the decision that was made. This is of special importance to organizations in which the employees are not unionized."[184] Last, *Personnel Journal* notes that "there is little doubt that employee relations ombudsmen are needed in today's legislated, regulated, and complex industrial organizations to assist employees who—through no fault of their own, and, usually, no intentional fault on the part of the administration—have become helplessly entangled in rules and policies."[185]

A classic study on the subject has affirmed the idea that full-time and neutral ombudsmen could make many complaint procedures work much better.[186] The success of the idea depends on the personal stature of the ombudsman and the adequacy of the authority granted him.[187] Furthermore, according to this study, the function of an ombudsman is to assist "little guys" in a large organization to cut through the inevitable "red tape" and, in the case of a grievance, to serve as an expediter.[188] It was pointed out that the primary offender is neither the employer or the individual—it is the sheer size of the firm.[189] The large size of organizations commonly causes two key problems: a diminished voice for employees and greater pressure on the formal system, thereby resulting sometimes in much less expeditious service.[190] Thus, as firms have grown, the ombudsman can be a counterforce to make employees' voices more audible "as well as speeding service by reducing system pressure."[191]

The classic study also affirms the following tenets:

Finally, the newly-appointed ombudsman must have enough power to be heard effectively anywhere in the organization. There must be no doubt that he has the backing of top-most management. And the support must be overt and publicized, not merely implied.

In addition, pressure on the formal system would be reduced. The more serious and involved cases could still go the usual route. With these, complexity warrants taking sufficient time; seeming delay is merely prudent handling. For the bulk of relatively minor matters, however, where delay results from a system bogging down more than from the nature of the issues, faster service would be assured.

One possible misinterpretation should be clarified here. Major resistance to the idea is likely if the proposed ombudsman is seen as a substitute for the regular grievance procedure. This is not intended; the traditional system of industrial jurisprudence has worked reasonably well over the years, all things considered. But with changes in the labor force, and with growing organizations, it needs help.[192]

Without a doubt, more firms have institutionalized this concept. According to Professor Deborah M. Kolb, "in a small, but highly visible number of firms, the position of corporate ombudsman is intended to serve as a voice-giving mechanism in the absence of unions."[193] *Fortune* states that "making sure that bad news gets passed up the chain of command is a topic receiving a lot of attention in executive suites these days. Many companies have long had 'open door' policies. IBM, for example, guarantees the right of any employee to appeal a supervisor's decision without fear of retaliation."[194] But, *Fortune* has noted that "in the past few years, dozens of other major companies have set up formal 'ombudsman' systems, in which a senior executive operating outside the normal chain of command is permanently available at the end of a hot line to deal with employee grievances and alarms on a confidential basis."[195] But one of the reasons why the concept has caught on with a small number of firms is that "incorporating an ombudsman into the corporate structure has turned out to be a very tricky business."[196]

Harvard Business Review makes a strong case for the establishment of a corporate ombudsman office:

It is clearly in the long-range interest of the corporation to seek mechanisms to effect employee justice. If justice is a dominant value of American life, there can be no question that corporate employees bring this value into the office in the morning and leave it at night. Employees expect justice in their lives and cannot arbitrarily divorce their existence into "work" and "leisure" components. People do not create such simple categories, in either their conscious or their psychological lives. An employee who feels that his legitimate grievances are being justly dealt with cannot help but be a better employee.[197]

Harvard Business Review also plays the devil's advocate on the subject. It poses the following:

Possibly, the very existence of an ombudsman would encourage filing of numerous frivolous complaints; managers would spend all of their time answering baseless accusations, and corporate efficiency would be impaired. In law, this is called the 'flood of litigation" argument. However, such fears usually prove to be unfounded. Rarely does the trickle of complaints become a flood.[198]

In summary, "an ombudsman is a person who is assigned a special responsibility to hear complaints and mediate disputes between parties in an organization. The ombudsman must be a respected person with problem-solving and conflict resolution skills. Ombudsman have been used increasingly in some industrial settings."[199]

In effect, therefore, an ombudsman "operates a complaint office to which individuals may go when they feel that they have exhausted the more usual means of receiving an acceptable hearing."[200] Without a doubt, "the ombudsman's role in American companies has typically been to listen to employee complaints and select the appropriate organizational procedures in formulating a remedy."[201] Last, "ombudsmen are found in greater numbers in government and other nonprofit organizations than in private industry."[202]

Employer-Employee Relations in the Nonunion Setting: The Role of the Nonunion Complaint Procedure

According to *Personnel*, a nonunion complaint procedure in a union-free setting may help to eradicate many of the conditions that might typically lead to employees feeling that they need a union.[203] On the other hand, according to *Personnel*, "developing a union-avoidance strategy for its own sake usually results in a dysfunctional adversarial relationship between management and the workers. Management could better apply the same amount of effort and resources to creating a climate of trust and commitment by setting up a grievance procedure.''[204] Last,

in and of itself a grievance procedure does not provide a guarantee that employees will not perceive unions as necessary, but it does provide a medium through which a working philosophy can be established to bring the organization members' goals closer together. Benefits are widespread throughout the firm, and management is able to maintain control while gaining a productive, creative partner in the development of organizational policy.[205]

Personnel also addresses the question of how a nonunion complaint procedure deals with conditions that lead to unionization. First of all, "the grievance procedure makes possible the prompt, just, and consistent resolution of employee complaints. The first-line supervisor is forced to spend more time on employee relations. The very processing of grievances may make it apparent that restructuring is needed to give supervisors adequate time for subordinates.''[206] Frequently, a nonunion complaint system results in much higher job satisfaction for employees and greatly improved employer-employee relations.[207] Thus, this journal suggests "that modern organizations can use grievance procedures as a vehicle to etablish an 'employee-centered' philosophy without the attendant costs of unionization.''[208]

Many of these themes are reinforced throughout the pertinent literature. For example, Professors Elmer H. Burack and Robert D. Smith state the following forcefully:

Maintaining a nonunion work force is that part of industrial relations known as preventive labor relations and must be initiated long before there are any signs of union organizing activity. This consists of establishing and maintaining an aggressive employee relations program designed to build employee morale, loyalty, and commitment to the goals of the organization.

To maintain nonunion status it is usually recommended that the organization *create a procedure for addressing employee complaints* (emphasis added), maintain working conditions, pay, and benefits that are at least as good as those of unionized companies, and eliminate practices such as inequalities in the wage structure, arbitrary supervision, and threats to employees' job security. It is also recommended that the company establish a meaningful system of two-way communication between management and the workforce, adopt some form of participatory management style, and make the employees feel that they are part of the family.[209]

Business Week, in an excellent analysis, affirms that of all the tools that companies are utilizing to create a nonunion environment, probably the most important tool was created by trade unions. "It is the establishment of a system of adjudicating a worker's complaints about his job or his boss. Increasingly, companies are installing grievance procedures, often patterned after union systems, and sometimes even including arbitration as the final determinant, for non-union employees.''[210]

According to *Business Week*, the institutionalization of complaint systems in nonunion environments is partly attributable to management cognizance that today's employees are much better educated than ever before and partly to a very determined effort to keep trade unions out.[211] John G. Wayman, a senior partner of the Pittsburgh law firm of Reed Smith Shaw & McClay, was quoted as saying that a workable nonunion complaint procedure is "probably the single most important way to keep a union out of a plant."[212] Wayman concludes with the following: "It's essential that an employee has some way to present his complaint, to have someone pay attention to that complaint and give him what he will consider to be a fair answer."[213] *Business Week* concurs with Wayman by stating: "The ability of unions to protect employees from arbitrary actions by managers has probably been a more powerful attraction for workers than organized labor's wage bargaining power."[214]

Most of the pertinent literature affirms the basic proposition that the existence of a good and legitimate nonunion grievance procedure is a proper strategy or tactic for maintaining union-free status. For example, it is felt by some scholars that a nonunion grievance procedure is a means of keeping employee problems from becoming serious.[215] Furthermore, total commitment to such a company policy needs to start with upper management and be instilled in every manager and supervisor.[216] Last, "employees who believe that management is concerned with attempting to resolve their problems lack a major reason for needing a union."[217]

Daniel Quinn Mills, Professor of Industrial Relations at the Graduate School of Business Administration of Harvard University, notes the following: "In the absence of a union, grievances create a special problem for nonunionized companies. It is a basic characteristic of better-standards nonunionized firms that they establish formal methods of dealing with grievances since few nonunionized firms do so."[218] Mills also states that one of the major standards that help an ethical nonunionized employer avoid unionization is in those cases where the employee has readily available a practical grievance mechanism.[219]

A number of scholars concur with Professor Mills. For example, Professors William Holley and Kenneth Jennings state the following: "The fact that less than one-fourth of the nonagricultural labor force are union members is in part due to the nonunion employers' environmental characteristics and personnel practices."[220] Additionally, they maintain that nonunion policies must be carefully implemented in the following areas: instituting grievance procedures and "ensuring upward communication by use of group meetings, complaint boxes, ombudsman programs, attitude surveys, open-door policies, and counseling."[221]

Professors Louis Boone and David L. Kurtz hit the nail right on the head in terms of this analysis. They assert the following very strongly:

In many instances, management has chosen to offer a compensation and benefit structure comparable to those of unionized firms in the area. Provision of comparable wages and working conditions coupled with effective communications, emphasis on promotions from within, and employee participating in goal-setting and *grievance handling* (emphasis added) may be effective in avoiding unionization if the workers feel that they would receive few additional benefits from the union dues they would have to pay.[222]

Professor Kochan of M.I.T. terms the preceding the "indirect union-substitution approach,"[223] which he expands as follows:

While many firms that utilize advanced personnel policies do not do so solely, or even primarily, to avoid unions, but rather because these policies are effective in motivating, supervising, and satisfying employees, the fact is that the effect is to reduce the incentive to unionize. For example, a representative profile of contemporary strategies used to reduce the incentives to unionize would include most or all of the following components: (1) wages and fringe benefits equal to, or greater than, those paid comparable unionized workers in the industry and/or labor market, (2) high rate of investment per worker in human support programs such as training and career development, (3) advanced systems of organizational communications and information sharing, (4) informal mechanisms for, or encouragement of, participation in decision making about the way work is to be performed, (5) development of a psychological climate that fosters and rewards organizational loyalty and commitment, (6) rational wages and salary administration, performance appraisal, and promotion systems that reward merit, but also recognize the relevance of seniority, (7) *nonunion grievance procedure* (emphasis added).[224]

The classic research on this topic has been conducted by Fred K. Foulkes, Professor of Management Policy at Boston University's Graduate School of Management. His research indicated that "the most important single factor in keeping a company non-union was effective communications."[225] The nonunion companies that he studied had communication programs that "gave employees the opportunity to voice complaints, offer opinions, and make suggestions, while allowing management to uncover problems and respond constructively."[226] In addition to the wide variety of programs that encourage communications, the nonunion companies that Foulkes studied also had formal grievance procedures.[227] According to his research, "analysis of the formal complaint procedures in use suggests that their main value is the encouragement they give to managers and supervisors to resolve employee problems before they become formal complaints. The formal procedures stimulate and enhance the effectiveness of informal problem-solving behavior, for their existence helps keep managers and supervisors 'on their toes' with respect to the employee relations aspects of their jobs."[228]

Professor Foulkes is going to have the last word on this subject of employer-employee relations in the nonunion setting, with particular emphasis on the role of the nonunion complaint procedure. In his truly classic *Harvard Business Review* article entitled "How Top Nonunion Companies Manage Employees," he states unequivocally this thesis:

In my view, a nonunion company today should not be without some kind of formal complaint procedure.

This is especially so in today's environment because employees who feel discriminated against because of race, sex, or age or who think their work area is unsafe can take complaints to an outside agency for investigation. Wise executives prefer to respond to complaints through their own mechanisms rather than deal with requirements set by a government agency.[229]

GENERAL PRINCIPLES

A number of major generalizable principles relating to the establishment, implementation, and operation of nonunion complaint procedures emerge out of a review of the germane literature. These principles will now be summarized here.

According to CUE—An Organization for Positive Employee Relations—an educational subsidiary of the National Association of Manufacturers (NAM), a well-designed and managed nonunion complaint procedure will yield benefits from the employer's standpoint.[230] For example, it allows managers and supervisors to identify and solve legitimate causes of dissatisfaction; it enables managers and supervisors to handle and correct these complaints, thus preventing minor problems from mushrooming into egregious problems; it eliminates a potential major union organizing weapon; it provides a process for resolving complaints within a company, thus eliminating the costly resolution by an outside third party; and it provides a peaceful and nonacrimonious way of settling and handling complaints.[231] Furthermore, "by addressing the employee's need to be heard through a complaint procedure program and by communicating the employer's whole-hearted support, a positive environment is created which enhances a company's union-free status."[232]

This educational subsidiary of NAM also postulates that there are some very important prerequisites to consider before management jumps in with both feet. These prerequisites are that management must recognize that the interests and rights of individuals are involved; management and superiors must fully support the complaint procedure idea from the outset; management must realize that fair, well-defined human resource management policies that are effectively communicated to employees will create good employer-employee relations; management should also recognize that a complaint procedure is not a panacea, that is, it cannot eliminate all discontents or conflicts; and management should establish such a complaint procedure before minor problems become major ones—in other words, start a complaint procedure when employer-employee relations are calm, not in a period of crisis.[233]

Furthermore, CUE notes that "whichever complaint procedure is used, employers should emphasize that no reprisals or retaliations of any kind will result from an employee's use of the complaint procedure program."[234] It is also important that "all complaints be handled quickly. Otherwise, the effectiveness and viability of the procedure are harmed. So when a complaint is presented, quick attention and fast action in getting the right answer are necessary; likewise, prompt communication to the employee in question is also a must."[235] Last, and simply put, a "complaint procedure makes an important contribution to harmonious employee relations and can boost the morale and efficiency of the entire organization."[236]

CUE concludes by enunciating this very important principle:

Notwithstanding the benefits from establishing a complaint procedure, an employer should be aware that, unless precautions are taken, the complaint procedure may legally restrict the employer's right to discharge an employee. The introduction of a complaint procedure that gives employees a "right" to air their differences or complaints could be and indeed, has been construed by some state courts as giving employees certain employment contract rights.

More and more frequently, courts are attaching legal significance to employee handbooks and their contents. The same is true with respect to other personnel policies such as employee complaint procedures as discussed. Many courts have recognized that by undertaking affirmative obligations such as those spelled out in complaint procedures, an employer will be expected to follow these procedures to the letter and that *failure to do so could give rise to a lawsuit on the part of an employee who was denied due process under such complaint procedures.* Accordingly, complaint procedures should not be adopted lightly and, once they are put into practice, all levels of management must be prepared to honor the commitment.

Employers with successful complaint procedures place great emphasis on consistency and uniformity in their application. So employers should make certain that their complaint procedure machinery is working and that procedures are being implemented consistently.[237]

The Industrial Relations Department of the National Association of Manufacturers echoes CUE's principles by stating that "a clear and open channel for the expression of employee complaints is a fundamental principle of sound employee relations."[238] A successful complaint procedure can be a safety valve for an organization's temper; can make it possible for an employee to express problems and complaints with no fear of retribution; can help executives, managers, and supervisors identify and eliminate legitimate causes of dissatisfaction; can enable management to deal with these complaints, thus preventing minor problems from mushrooming into major and significant grievances; can provide a peaceful way of handling disputes and providing for conflict resolution within the firm; and can make a very important contribution to harmonious employer-employee relations and can favorably affect the efficiency and productivity of the entire organization.[239]

According to NAM, there are a number of prerequisites to grievance handling. If a nonunion complaint procedure is to work effectively, the following conditions must exist:

Top management must support the idea, fully recognizing the importance of resolving employee problems. All levels of management must be willing and able to take necessary actions. Management must understand that definite and fair personnel policies, known to all employees, are basic to good employee relations. A grievance procedure is not a panacea. It cannot in itself eliminate discontent or employer-employee conflicts.

The employer must realize that the procedure is best established in a period of normalcy. The wise employer will not wait until things are ready to "blow up" before launching a method for settling complaints of salaried as well as hourly employees.[240]

In a classic writing on the subject, Professor Keith Davis says that the "principal benefit of any grievance system is that it encourages human problems to be brought into the open so that management can learn about them and try corrective action."[241] Furthermore, according to Davis, the following are also benefits of complaint systems: they help to catch and nip problems early on before they become too serious; they are a means of giving employees emotional catharsis for their dissatisfactions; and their existence makes it a check-and-balance upon capricious employer and supervisory action.[242] Davis also maintains that there are four principal elements in satisfactory complaint handling: policies and organizational rules which are workable and acceptable to both the employer and employees; attitudes of mutual interest and integrative problem solving; complaint systems which are both workable and equitable, including absolute protection against retribution as well as the right of appeal; and communication in order to comprehend each other's problems and to convey to each other feelings of equity.[243] Last, Davis notes that the basic objective of complaint settlement "should be *justice*, which is defined as fairness according to established rules and relationships."[244] This writer could not agree more!

Professors Sterling Schoen and Douglas Durand concur with the preceding. They postulate that a complaint procedure in a nonunion situation must possess various endemic characteristics in order to be truly effective. First, it must be relatively simple, so that it can be easily comprehended and fully understood by both supervisors and employees. Second, it should give expeditious and courteous action in every case, for if the procedure is prolonged or dragged out over a long period of time, the employee is likely to feel very frustrated and stonewalled. Third, the procedure should be definite. That is, employees should know that the initiation of a complaint or grievance will result in certain actions on the part of management. Fourth, the whole procedure should be committed to writing, for a written statement makes the procedures more definite and less subject to misinterpretation. Fifth, employees must be assured that filing a grievance will not bring retaliation by executives, managers, or supervisors. Last, a staff specialist from the human resources management department should be available to assist supervisors and managers at all levels in their attempts to adjudicate the grievance.[245]

John S. Schauer, a member of the employment law firm of Seyfarth, Shaw,

Fairweather & Geraldson believes that there are many sound reasons why an employer should implement a nonunion appeal procedure, particularly as it would relate to discharge cases.[246] He hypothesizes:

It is my view that the only benefit a union contract offers to unorganized employees is the right to file a grievance and ultimately have it heard by an impartial arbitrator whose decision will be final and binding on the employee and his employer. If then an unorganized employer voluntarily offers an appeal procedure culminating in binding arbitration and otherwise provides its employees with competitive wages, benefits and working conditions, what incentive will employees have to reorganize?[247]

As the reader is now being made aware, a number of very important principles are emerging from a careful summary of the pertinent literature.

Professor Ronald L. Miller adds a number of other important general principles to the discussion. He asserts that a company must be prepared to invest in management development and employee training if a formal complaint system is to function effectively for both managers and employees.[248] He also asserts that any nonunion complaint procedure should have the following features in writing. First of all, "any limitations or restrictions related to the use of the procedure should, of course, be clearly stated."[249] Second, "employees who have access to the grievance procedure should be clearly identified in the written policy by their appropriate categories."[250] Third, "a precise statement of what categories of issues may be grieved is another key component of any grievance procedure."[251] Fourth, "the grievance procedure should identify whatever provisions, if any, are available for grievant representation."[252] Last, "the procedure should indicate management's intent to assist the grievant to identify and obtain relevant information."[253]

Professor Miller concludes his research by enunciating these opinions:

The future of employer controlled grievance procedures seems to be bright—if employer perceptions are correct. While the individual aspects of nonunion grievance procedures vary widely, most employers see them as successfully meeting a number of objectives: providing a forum for employee concerns, facilitating the redress of inequities, and acting as a "safety valve" for employee frustrations. Also, many employers consider the grievance procedures an important element in an overall strategy to reduce the potential for union organizing.[254]

Charles A. Myers and Paul Pigors, Professors Emeriti at the Sloan School of Management at the Massachusetts Institute of Technology, assert that the following series of questions can be used to judge (or be used as a criteria for) the effectiveness of a nonunion complaint procedure: Were the parties to the case able to reach rapprochement on the issues? Were the grievances concluded to the satisfaction of all parties? Did the manner of resolution of each complaint lead to greater organizational productivity and to a lowering of firm costs? Last, was there an understanding of the broad issues involved with individuals who were not directly linked to the initial grievance?[255]

Professor John M. Ivancevich believes that the lack of a complaint procedure in a nonunion firm can cause antagonism, frustration, and anxiety among employees.[256] Furthermore, "these feelings and attitudes are not healthy for good employee-management relations. They also can spark an interest to organize a formal bargaining representative."[257]

Professor Claude S. George, Jr., asserts that every manager and supervisor will get some complaints and gripes, no matter how good a job he or she does.[258] He hypothesizes that "when employees don't express complaints, many take this to be a sign of suppression, indicating that the employees are afraid to speak out. In the best-managed companies, therefore, you can expect a number of employee complaints."[259] George maintains that the following principles should be used in complaint adjustment by managers and supervisors:

1. Never ignore or take lightly a gripe, complaint, or grievance;
2. Know your grievance and complaint procedures and systems and follow them impartially and to the letter;
3. Be tactful;
4. Never hesitate to admit error;
5. Don't try to laugh off a complaint or downplay it;
6. Treat the employee and his complaint as being serious and important;
7. Don't withhold any concessions if in the wrong;
8. Listen attentively and carefully;
9. If an apology is called for, do it immediately and without hesitation;
10. Don't lose your temper—that is, don't let emotions get the better of you;
11. Don't make a decision until you have all the facts;
12. Address the problem;
13. Always explain why you made the decision you did as well as give the reasons;
14. Be fair, just, honest, and equitable;
15. Always be available to your employees and workers;
16. Don't hesitate to inform your employee how he or she can appeal your decision.[260]

Professor Gary Dressler follows in the footsteps of George. He maintains that there are three principles that can enhance the effectiveness of a nonunion complaint procedure. "First, the system should be formalized through scheduled meetings, suggestion plans, yearly surveys, and so on. Second, there must be a climate of trust in the organization, because subordinates are unlikely to speak freely (even anonymously) if they mistrust management's motives or have learned that they are simply blamed for mistakes."[261] Third and last, "supervisors must react to the opinions and problems expressed in upward communications, even if just to acknowledge that they have been received. If the problem cannot be solved it should be made clear why; if the problem can be eliminated it should be."[262]

Thus, "the sole purpose of any non-union grievance plan is to promote and encourage communications between management and employees and to project management's intention to give fair treatment to employees."[263] Such plans provide opportunities for two-way communication, give employees a structured opportunity "to let off steam" and provide nonunion employees with an alternative to join unions.[264]

In closing this section, a number of strategic summary points can be garnered from the literature. First of all, firms need to tailor their nonunion complaint systems to their own needs in order to obtain the benefits and reduce the drawbacks.[265] Second, a company that adopts a system tailored to its endemic and idiosyncratic needs is bound to improve its relations with employees and will in all likelihood reduce substantially the risk of lawsuits by aggrieved employees.[266] Third, the main purpose of these procedures and systems are to assure fairness in employee relations and to improve employee attitudes, rather than to interpret human resources management policies and practices.[267] Fourth, nonunion firms have much more flexibility in designing complaint procedures and systems that satisfy both management and employee needs.[268] Fifth, the procedure must be viewed by all employees as being both comprehensive and impartial.[269] Sixth, a well-designed system ensures that the employee has ample opportunity to make complaints without fear of supervisory or managerial reprisal.[270] Seventh, if the procedure is to function, the employees must be very well informed of the system and be totally convinced that management wants them to use it.[271] Eighth, the fact that a supervisor has received no complaints does not indicate that grievances do not exist, for in a closed and mechanistic organizational climate, workers may be afraid to voice their dissatisfactions to management.[272] Ninth, firms that fail to truly communicate with their employees and who seem disinterested in their employees' problems are those firms that can easily fall prey to unionization action.[273] Tenth, most complaint procedures of nonunion firms are usually delineated in an employee-relations handbook or a personnel/human resources policies and procedures manual.[274] Eleventh, nonunion complaint procedures serve as a positive motivator for lower level managers to take the initiative with employee problems.[275] Twelfth, a nonunion firm should not be without some kind of formal complaint procedure or system.[276] Thirteenth, a firm will have high turnover, higher labor costs, and lower efficiency if employees believe their human resource problems are consistently handled capriciously, with no right to an impartial review of decisions believed to be unjust and unfair.[277] Fifteenth, an employee procedure must have a time limit for each step of the appeal so that the employee has some sort of idea of when to expect an answer from above.[278] Sixteenth, the number of companies with nonunion appeal procedures is increasing.[279] And, last, the greater utilization of complaint procedures in the nonunion environment is one of the more encouraging trends in the field of human resources management.[280]

Who shall have the last word on the subject? That honor will go to Sharon L. Yenney and her excellent article entitled "In Defense of the Grievance Procedure in a Non-Union Setting." She states that in a nonunion organizational setting, "an effective grievance procedure goes beyond the provision of a mechanism for learning about and excising the reasons for employee dissatisfaction. The process opens honest avenues for discussion between individuals and their managers which often reveal that procedures and policies—not people and their actions—are the causes of dissatisfaction."[281] She also asserts that there are two purposes of a complaint procedure in a nonunion firm: "(1) to provide a reliable, observable mechanism to learn of and resolve individual employee dissatisfactions; and (2) to provide a mechanism for identifying practices, procedures, and policies that are causing employee dissatisfaction so that appropriate changes or resolutions can be considered by management."[282] Finally, Yenney concludes by saying that a complaint procedure in a nonunion company strengthens the role of human resource management specialists; identifies and resolves individual worker dissatisfactions; teaches supervisors and employees to confront their differences objectively and works toward creative and positive solutions to the company's problems; and provides a healthy and viable mechanism for diagnosing organizational practices and procedures.[283]

CONCLUSION

The purpose of this chapter was to be both an intensive and comprehensive review of the literature in the area of corporate nonunion complaint procedures and systems for the practitioner and/or scholar. Three major strategic issues were studied: the nature of nonunion grievance arbitration systems; the nature of internal tribunals and peer review systems; and the nature of open-door policies and philosophies, especially with formal appeals to higher level management. In addition, four major emerging issues were studied: due process for nonunionized employees; the relationship between the doctrine of employment-at-will and nonunion grievance procedures; the corporate ombudsman as a complement to the nonunion grievance procedure; and employer-employee relations in the nonunion setting—the role of the nonunion complaint procedure. Last, general principles vis-à-vis corporate nonunion complaint procedures were studied.

The study of the issues and principles surrounding the subject of nonunion complaint procedures leads to the conclusion that they are a sine qua non for sound and positive employer-employee relations and progressive human resources management.

NOTES

1. Peter Florey, "A Growing Fringe Benefit: Arbitration of Nonunion Employee Grievances," *Personnel Administrator* 30 (July 1985): 14, 16.
2. Ibid., 16.
3. Ibid.
4. Ibid.
5. Ibid.
6. Ibid., 18.
7. Robert Coulson, "An Informal Way to Settle Office Disputes," *Modern Office Procedures* (June 1980): 184. See also the American Arbitration Association, *Expedited Employment Arbitration Rules, As amended and in effect July 1, 1986* (NY: American Arbitration Association, 1986), 3–7.
8. Ibid.
9. Ibid.
10. Ibid.
11. Michael L. Wachter, "Comment," in *Arbitration 1986: Current and Expanding Roles, Proceedings of the Thirty-Ninth Annual Meeting, National Academy of Arbitrators, Philadelphia, Pennsylvania, June 2–6, 1986*, ed. Walter J. Gershenfeld (Washington, D.C.: The Bureau of National Affairs, 1987), 67.
12. Alfred G. Feliu, review of "Protecting Unorganized Employees Against Unjust Dismissal," by Jack Stieber and John Blackburn, eds., in *The Arbitration Journal* 39 (March 1984): 65.
13. Ibid.
14. Lawrence R. Littrell, "Grievance Procedure and Arbitration in a Nonunion Environment: The Northrup Experience," in *Arbitration Issues for the 1980s, Proceedings of the Thirty-Fourth Annual Meeting, National Academy of Arbitrators, Maui, Hawaii, May 4–8, 1981*, ed. James L. Stern (Washington, D.C.: The Bureau of National Affairs, 1982) 36.
15. Ibid., 35.
16. Ibid., 36.
17. Ibid., 37.
18. Ibid.
19. Ibid., 39.
20. Ibid., 41–42.
21. Ronald Berenbeim, *Nonunion Complaint Systems: A Corporate Appraisal* (NY: The Conference Board, Report No. 770, 1980), 17.
22. Ibid., 18–19.
23. Ibid., 18.
24. Ibid., 18–19.
25. Ibid., 19.
26. James J. Bambrick, Jr., and John J. Speed, *Grievance Procedures in Non-unionized Companies* (NY: National Industrial Conference Board, Studies in Personnel Policy, No. 109), 15.
27. Ibid.
28. Ibid.
29. Ibid.

30. Ibid., 16.

31. Alan Balfour, "Five Types of Non-Union Grievance Systems," *Personnel* 61 (March-April 1984): 75.

32. Ibid.

33. Daniel Quinn Mills, "Methods of Handling Communication and Grievances," in *Labor-Management Relations*, 2nd ed. (NY: McGraw-Hill, 1982), 149.

34. Larry Reibstein, "More Firms Use Peer Review Panel to Resolve Employees' Grievances," *The Wall Street Journal*, 3 December 1986, sec. 2, 29.

35. Ibid.

36. Ibid.

37. Ibid.

38. Ibid.

39. Ibid.

40. Ibid.

41. Ibid.

42. John D. Coombe, "Peer Review: The Emerging Successful Application," *Employee Relations Law Journal* 9 (Spring 1984): 659.

43. Ibid., 670.

44. Jonathan Tasini and Patrick Houston, "Letting Workers Help Handle Workers' Gripes," *Business Week*, 15 September 1986, 82.

45. Ibid.

46. Ibid., 82, 86.

47. Fred C. Olson, "How Peer Review Works at Control Data," *Harvard Business Review* 62 (November-December 1984): 58.

48. Ibid.

49. Ibid.

50. Ibid.

51. Ibid., 59.

52. Ibid.

53. Ibid.

54. Ibid.

55. Ibid.

56. Ibid.

57. Ibid., 62, 64.

58. Mary Jean Wolf, "Trans World Airlines' Noncontract Grievance Procedure," in *Arbitration 1986: Current and Expanding Roles, Proceedings of the Thirty-Ninth Annual Meeting, National Academy of Arbitrators, Philadelphia, Pennsylvania, June 2–6, 1986*, ed. Walter J. Gershenfeld (Washington, D.C.: The Bureau of National Affairs, 1987), 27–33.

59. Ibid., 28–29.

60. Ibid., 29.

61. Ibid.

62. Ibid.

63. Ibid., 28.

64. Ibid., 31.

65. Ibid., 30.

66. Harvey S. Caras, *Peer Grievance Review—A Proven Approach to Employee-Problem Resolution* (Washington, D.C.: CUE—An Organization for Positive Employee

Relations, National Association of Manufacturers, Number 41—Studies in Employee Relations, 1986), 2.

    67. Ibid.

    68. Ibid.

    69. Ibid.

    70. Ibid., 2–3.

    71. Ibid., 4.

    72. Ibid.

    73. Ibid., 8.

    74. Ibid., 12.

    75. Ibid., 13.

    76. Ibid., 14.

    77. Robert E. Bales, *Appeal System—A Different Approach to Resolving Employee Problems* (Washington, D.C.: CUE—An Organization for Positive and Progressive Employee Relations, National Association of Maufacturers, Number Nine—Studies in Employee Relations, 1981), 1–7.

    78. Ibid., 1.

    79. Ibid., 2–3.

    80. Ibid., 3.

    81. Ibid.

    82. Ibid., 5.

    83. Ibid., 7.

    84. Balfour, "Five Types of Non-Union Grievance Systems," 71.

    85. Ibid.

    86. Ibid.

    87. Ibid., 71–72.

    88. Bambrick and Speed, *Grievance Procedures in Nonunionized Companies*, 24.

    89. Ronald L. Miller, "Grievance Procedures for Nonunion Employees," *Public Personnel Management* 7 (September-October 1978): 311.

    90. Balfour, "Five Types of Non-Union Grievance Systems," 69.

    91. Ibid.

    92. Ibid., 69–70.

    93. Stewart Trisler, "Grievance Procedures: Refining the Open-Door Policy," *Employment Relations Today* 11 (Autumn 1984): 323.

    94. Ibid., 324.

    95. Ibid.

    96. Ibid.

    97. Ibid.

    98. Ibid.

    99. Paul Pigors and Charles A. Myers, "Complaints and Grievances" in *Personnel Administration: A Point of View and a Method*, 9th ed. (NY: McGraw-Hill, 1981), 236.

    100. Berenbeim, *Nonunion Complaint Systems: A Corporate Appraisal*, 11.

    101. Ibid.

    102. Ibid.

    103. Mary P. Rowe and Michael Baker, "Are You Hearing Enough Employee Concerns," *Harvard Business Review* 62 (May-June 1984):128.

104. Ibid., 129.

105. Ibid.

106. Everett T. Suters, "Hazards of an Open-Door Policy," *Inc.: The Magazine for Growing Companies* 9 (January 1987):99,102.

107. Sterling H. Schoen and Douglas E. Durand, "Effective Grievance Procedures," in *Supervision: The Management of Organizational Resources* (Englewood Cliffs, NJ: Prentice-Hall, 1979), 296.

108. Ibid.

109. Ibid.

110. Ibid.

111. David J. Cherrington, "Grievance Procedures in Nonunion Organizations," in *Personnel Management: The Management of Human Resources*, 2nd ed. (Dubuque, IA: Wm. C. Brown, 1982), 596.

112. Ibid., 586–87.

113. Edwin B. Flippo, *Principles of Personnel Management*, 4th ed. (NY: McGraw-Hill, 1976), 427.

114. A. W. J. Thomson, "The Structure of Procedures in Non-Unionized Companies," in *The Grievance Procedure in the Private Sector* (Ithaca, NY: New York State School of Industrial and Labor Relations, Cornell University, 1974), 11.

115. Lloyd L. Byars and Leslie W. Rue, "Discipline in Nonunionized Organizations," in *Human Resource and Personnel Management* (Homewood, IL: Richard D. Irwin, 1984), 372.

116. Stephen E. Catt and Donald S. Miller, "Handling Grievances in Nonunion Organizations," in *Supervisory Management and Communication* (Homewood, IL: Richard D. Irwin, 1985), 277.

117. Robert L. Mathis and John H. Jackson, "Nonunion Grievance Procedures," in *Personnel: Human Resources Management*, 4th ed. (St. Paul, MN: West Publishing, 1985), 595.

118. Judith R. Gordon, "Approaches to Resolving Grievances in Nonunion Organizations," in *Human Resources Management: A Practical Approach* (Boston: Allyn and Bacon, 1986), 557.

119. Michael R. Carrell and Frank E. Kuzmits, "Grievance Handling in Nonunion Organizations," in *Personnel: Human Resource Management*, 2nd ed. (Columbus, OH: Merrill Publishing, 1986), 489.

120. Randall S. Schuler, "Employer Strategies for Employee Job Security Rights," in *Personnel and Human Resource Management*, 3rd ed. (St. Paul, MN: West Publishing, 1987), 522.

121. Wendell L. French, *The Personnel Management Process: Human Resources Administration and Development*, 6th ed. (Boston: Houghton Mifflin, 1987), 7.

122. Ibid.

123. Ibid., 56.

124. Ibid., 145.

125. Fred Luthans, Richard M. Hodgetts, and Kenneth R. Thompson, "Employee Justice Systems," in *Social Issues in Business: Strategic and Public Policy Perspectives*, 5th ed. (NY: Macmillan, 1987), 314–15.

126. Keith Davis, "Grievance Systems," in *Human Relations in Business* (New York: McGraw-Hill, 1957), 439.

127. David W. Ewing, "Making Due Process a Reality," in *Freedom Inside the Organization* (NY: E.P. Dutton, 1977), 156.

128. David W. Ewing, "Due Process and Freedom of Inquiry," in *"Do It My Way Or Your're Fired!"*: *Employee Rights and the Changing Role of Management Prerogatives* (NY: John Wiley & Sons, 1983), 253.

129. Ibid.

130. Ibid.

131. Ibid.

132. David W. Ewing, "Due Process: Will Business Default?" *Harvard Business Review* 60 (November-December 1982): 120–121.

133. David W. Ewing, "What Business Thinks About Employee Rights," *Harvard Business Review* 55 (September-October 1977): 82.

134. Stephen R. Michael, "Due Process in Nonunion Grievance Systems," *Employee Relations Law Journal* 3 (Spring 1978): 526.

135. Ibid.

136. George A. Steiner and John F. Steiner, "The Rights Movement in Corporations," in *Business, Government, and Society—A Managerial Perspective: Text and Cases*, 4th ed. (NY: Random House Business Division, 1985), 517–18.

137. Fred Luthans, Richard M. Hodgetts, and Kenneth R. Thompson, "Dispute Resolution and Procedures for Employee Justice," in *Social Issues in Business*, 3rd ed. (NY: Macmillan, 1980), 137–38.

138. Alan F. Westin, ed., "New Management Policies and Procedures: The Inside Mechanism," in *Whistle Blowing: Loyalty and Dissent in the Corporation* (NY: McGraw-Hill, 1981), 150.

139. Manual G. Velasquez, "The Right to Due Process," in *Business Ethics: Concepts and Cases* (Englewood Cliffs, NJ: Prentice-Hall, 1982), 327.

140. Thomas M. Garrett and Richard J. Klonoski, "Due Process," in *Business Ethics*, 2nd ed. (Englewood Cliffs, NJ: Prentice-Hall, 1986), 32.

141. John D. Aram and Paul F. Salipante, Jr., "An Evaluation of Organizational Due Process in the Resolution of Employee/Employer Conflict," *Academy of Management Review* 6 (April 1981): 198.

142. Ibid., 203.

143. Michael Beer, Bert Spector, Paul R. Lawrence, D. Quinn Mills, and Richard E. Walton, *Managing Human Assets* (NY: The Free Press, 1984), 98.

144. Michael Beer, Bert Spector, Paul R. Lawrence, D. Quinn Mills, and Richard E. Walton, *Human Resource Management: A General Manager's Perspective—Text and Cases* (NY: The Free Press, 1985), 239.

145. Velasquez, "The Right to Due Process," 327–28.

146. Patricia H. Werhane, "The Right to Due Process," in *Persons, Rights and Corporations* (Englewood Cliffs, NJ: Prentice-Hall, 1985), 110.

147. Thomas A. Kochan and Thomas A. Barocci, "Due Process Procedures for Nonunion Employees," in *Human Resource Management and Industrial Relations: Text, Readings, and Cases* (Boston: Little, Brown, 1985), 384.

148. Mary P. Rowe, letter to Douglas M. McCabe, Spring 1987.

149. Richard T. De George, "Employment-at-Will: Rights in Hiring, Promotion, and Firing," in *Business Ethics*, 2nd ed. (NY: Macmillan, 1986), 204.

150. Master Printers of America, "Note," in *Due Process for Nonunion Complaint*

Procedures (Arlington, VA: Master Printers of America, A Division of Printing Industries of America, 1984).

151. Ibid.
152. Ibid.
153. Ibid.
154. Ibid.
155. Ibid.
156. Arthur A. Sloane, " 'Just Cause' Statutory Job Protection," in *Personnel: Managing Human Resources* (Englewood Cliffs, NJ: Prentice-Hall, 1983), 532.
157. Ibid.
158. John Hoerr et al., "Beyond Unions: A Revolution in Employee Rights Is in the Making," *Business Week*, 8 July 1985, 76.
159. Ibid.
160. Luthans, Hodgetts, and Thompson, "Employee Justice Systems," 314.
161. David R. Hiley, "Employee Rights and the Doctrine of At Will Employment," *Business & Professional Ethics Journal* 4 (Fall): 2.
162. Ibid., 8.
163. Ibid.
164. Sami M. Abbasi, Kenneth W. Hollman, and Joe H. Murrey, Jr., "Employment at Will: An Eroding Concept in Employment Relationships," *Labor Law Journal* 38 (January 1987): 30.
165. William J. Holloway and Michael J. Leech, *Employment Termination: Rights and Remedies* (Washington, D.C.: The Bureau of National Affairs, 1985), 153.
166. Andrew M. Kramer, "The Hazards of Firing at Will," *The Wall Street Journal*, 9 March 1987, sec. 1, 20.
167. Ibid.
168. Emily A. Joiner, "Erosion of the Employment-at-Will Doctrine," *Personnel* 61 (September-October 1984): 15–16.
169. Ibid., 16.
170. Thomas J. Condon and Richard H. Wolff, "Procedures that Safeguard Your Right to Fire," *Harvard Business Review* 63 (November-December 1985): 16.
171. Ibid., 16–18.
172. Stuart A. Youngblood and Gary L. Tidwell, "Termination at Will: Some Changes in the Wind," *Personnel* 58 (May-June 1981): 32.
173. Ibid.
174. Ibid.
175. Mary P. Rowe, "The Corporate Ombudsman," Draft Copy, Unpublished Paper (Cambridge, MA: Massachusetts Institute of Technology, 1986), 1. See also Mary P. Rowe, "Ombudsdman Sector Workshop," in *Bringing the Dispute Resolution Community Together, 1985 Proceedings, Thirteenth International Conference, October 27–30, 1985, Boston, Masschusetts, Society of Professionals in Dispute Resolution*, ed. Cheryl Cutrona (Washington, D.C.: Society of Professionals in Dispute Resolution, 1986), 363–65; and Mary P. Rowe, "The Growing Phenomenon of the Ombuds," *Alternatives to the High Cost of Litigation* 4 (October 1986): 3.
176. Ibid.
177. Ibid., 4.
178. Ibid., 6.
179. Ibid.

180. Ibid., 11.

181. Ibid., 16.

182. Kim E. Clark, "Improve Employee Relations with a Corporate Ombudsman," *Personnel Journal* 64 (September 1985): 12.

183. Ibid.

184. Ibid.

185. Ibid., 13.

186. J.H. Foegen, "An Ombudsman as Complement to the Grievance Procedure," *Labor Law Journal* 23 (May 1972): 289.

187. Ibid.

188. Ibid.

189. Ibid.

190. Ibid.

191. Ibid., 290.

192. Ibid., 293–94.

193. Deborah M. Kolb, "Corporate Ombudsmen," in *Bringing the Dispute Resolution Community Together, 1985 Proceedings, Thirteenth International Conference, October 27–30, 1985, Boston, Massachusetts, Society of Professionals in Dispute Resolution*, ed. Cheryl Cutrona (Washington, D.C.: Society of Professionals in Dispute Resolution, 1986), 401.

194. Michael Brody, "Listen to Your Whistleblower," *Fortune*, 24 November 1986, 77.

195. Ibid.

196. "Where Ombudsmen Work Out," *Business Week*, 3 May 1976, 114.

197. Isidore Silver, "The Corporate Ombudsman," in *Personnel Management Series, Reprints from Harvard Business Review*, No. 21145 (Boston: Harvard Business Review, 1968), 78.

198. Ibid., 84–85.

199. Henry L. Tosi, John R. Rizzo, and Stephen J. Carroll, "Ombudsmen," in *Managing Organizational Behavior*, (Marshfield, MA: Pitman Publishing, 1986), 494.

200. Edwin B., Flippo, "The Ombudsman or Ombudswoman," in *Personnel Management*, 6th ed. (NY: McGraw-Hill, 1984), 463.

201. Balfour, "Five Types of Non-Union Grievance Systems," 70.

202. Michael R. Carrell and Frank E. Kuzmits, "Ombudsman," in *Personnel: Management of Human Resources* (Columbus, Ohio: Charles E. Merrill, 1982), 595.

203. Fabius P. O'Brien and Donald A. Drost, "Non-Union Grievance Procedures: Not Just an Anti-Union Strategy," *Personnel* 61 (September-October 1984): 69.

204. Ibid.

205. Ibid.

206. Ibid., 67.

207. Ibid.

208. Ibid., 61.

209. Elmer H. Burack and Robert D. Smith, "Maintaining Nonunion Status," in *Personnel Management: A Human Resource System Approach* (NY: John Wiley & Sons, 1982), 334.

210. "The Antiunion Grievance Ploy," *Business Week*, 12 February 1979, 117.

211. Ibid.

212. Ibid.

213. Ibid.

214. Ibid.

215. R. Wayne Mondy and Robert M. Noe, "Union Free Organizations," in *Personnel: The Management of Human Resources*, 3rd ed. (Newton, MA: Allyn and Bacon, Inc., 1987), 607.

216. Ibid., 614.

217. Ibid.

218. Daniel Quinn Mills, "Methods of Handling Communication and Grievances," in *Labor-Management Relations*, 2nd ed. (NY: McGraw-Hill, 1982), 147.

219. Daniel Quinn Mills, "Nonunion and Union," in *Labor-Management Relations*, 3rd ed. (New York: McGraw-Hill, 1986), 171.

220. William H. Holley and Kenneth M. Jennings, "Characteristics and Policies of the Nonunion Employer," in *Personnel/Human Resources Management: Contributions and Activities*, 2nd ed. (Hinsdale, IL: The Dryden Press, 1987), 474.

221. Ibid., 474–75.

222. Louis E. Boone and David L. Kurtz, "Labor-Management Relations in Nonunionized Organizations," in *Contemporary Business*, 5th ed. (Hinsdale, IL: The Dryden Press, 1987), 313.

223. Thomas A. Kochan, "Management Strategies for Avoiding Unions," in *Collective Bargaining and Industrial Relations: From Theory to Policy and Practice* (Homewood, IL: Richard D. Irwin, 1980), 183.

224. Ibid., 185.

225. Fred F. Foulkes, "Large Nonunionized Employers," in *U.S. Industrial Relations, 1950–1980: A Critical Assessment*, Industrial Relations Research Association Series, ed. Jack Stieber, Robert B. McKersie, and D. Quinn Mills (Madison, WI: Industrial Relations Research Association, 1981), 151.

226. Ibid., 151–52.

227. Ibid., 153.

228. Ibid.

229. Fred K. Foulkes, "How Top Nonunion Companies Manage Employees," *Harvard Business Review* 59 (September-October 1981): 95.

230. Brian W. Gill and Daniel B. Loftus, *Union-Free Complaint Procedures—25 Samples* (Washington, D.C.: CUE—An Organization for Positive Employee Relations—An Educational Subsidiary of the National Association of Manufacturers, 1984), 1.

231. Ibid.

232. Ibid.

233. Ibid., 1–2.

234. Ibid., 2.

235. Ibid.

236. Ibid., 3.

237. Ibid.

238. Industrial Relations Department, National Association of Manufacturers, *Settling Complaints in the Union-Free Operation* (Washington, D.C.: National Association of Maufacturers, June 1982), 1.

239. Ibid.

240. Ibid., 1–2.

241. Keith Davis, "Grievance Systems," in *Human Relations in Business* (New York: McGraw-Hill, 1957), 435.

242. Ibid., 435–36.

243. Ibid., 439.

244. Ibid.

245. Sterling H. Schoen and Douglas E. Durand, "Characteristics of an Effective Grievance Procedure," in *Supervision: The Management of Organizational Resources* (Englewood Cliffs, NJ: Prentice-Hall, 1979), 292.

246. John S. Schauer, "Discussion," in *Industrial Relations Research Association Series, Proceedings of the Thirty-Second Annual Meeting, December 28–30, 1979, Atlanta*, ed. Barbara D. Dennis (Madison, WI: Industrial Relations Research Association, 1980), 184.

247. Ibid.

248. Miller, "Grievance Procedures for Nonunion Employees," 306.

249. Ibid.

250. Ibid.

251. Ibid.

252. Ibid., 307.

253. Ibid., 308.

254. Ibid., 311.

255. Pigors and Myers, "Complaints and Grievances," 239.

256. John M. Ivancevich and William F. Glueck, "Grievances," in *Foundations of Personnel/Human Resource Management*, rev. ed. (Plano, TX: Business Publications, 1983), 567.

257. Ibid.

258. Claude S. George, Jr., "How to Handle Discipline and Settle Grievances," in *Supervision in Action: The Art of Managing Others*, 3rd ed. (Reston, VA: Reston, 1982), 93.

259. Ibid.

260. Ibid., 94–95.

261. Gary Dressler, *Management Fundamentals: Modern Principles & Practices*, 4th ed. (Reston, VA: Reston, 1985), 337.

262. Ibid.

263. James P. Swann, Jr., "Formal Grievance Procedures in Non-Union Plants," *Personnel Administrator* 26 (August 1981): 70.

264. Reid L. Shaw, "A Grievance Procedure for Non-Unionized Employees," *Personnel* 36 (July-August 1959): 66.

265. Kenneth McCulloch, "Alternative Dispute Resolution Techniques: Pros and Cons," *Employment Relations Today* 11 (Autumn 1984): 315.

266. Ibid., 319.

267. Leo C. Megginson, "Handling Complaints in Nonunion Organizations," in *Personnel Management: A Human Resources Approach*, 5th ed. (Homewood, IL: Richard D. Irwin, 1985), 598–99.

268. R. Wayne Mondy, Harry N. Mills, Jr., Robert M. Noe III, and Arthur Sharplin, "Grievance Handling for Nonunion Employees," in *Personnel: The Management of Human Resources*, 2nd ed. (Boston: Allyn and Bacon, 1984), 539.

269. Ibid.

270. Ibid.

271. Ibid.

272. Ibid.

273. Lawrence A. Klatt, Robert G. Murdick, and Frederick E. Schuster, "Grievance Procedures," in *Human Resource Management* (Columbus, OH: Charles E. Merrill, 1985), 311.

274. Theo Haimann and Raymond L. Hilgert, "Handling Employee Complaints and Grievances," in *Supervision: Concepts and Practices of Management*, 3rd ed. (Cincinnati: South-Western, 1982), 396.

275. Fred K. Foulkes, "Grievance Procedures," in *Personnel Policies in Large Nonunion Companies* (Englewood Cliffs, NJ: Prentice-Hall, 1980), 315.

276. Ibid., 322.

277. Maurice S. Trotta and Harry R. Gudenberg, "Resolving Personel Problems in Nonunion Plants," *Personnel* 53 (May-June 1976): 58.

278. Ibid., 63.

279. Maryellen Lo Bosco, "Nonunion Grievance Procedures," *Personnel* 62 (January 1985): 64.

280. Donald A. Drost and Fabius P. O'Brien, "Are There Grievances Against Your Non-Union Grievance Procedure?" *Personnel Administrator* 28 (January 1983): 36.

281. Sharon L. Yenney, "In Defense of the Grievance Procedure in a Non-Union Setting," *Employee Relations Law Journal* 2 (Sprig 1977): 436.

282. Ibid., 436–37.

283. Ibid., 442–43.

PART II
CORPORATE NONUNION COMPLAINT/GRIEVANCE SYSTEMS: A PROCEDURAL ANALYSIS

This section is an analysis of the nonunion grievance procedures stipulated in the employee-relations policy manuals of some leading nonunion companies which are within the umbrella of the National Association of Manufacturers.

Chapter 3 studies the procedures of six nonunion grievance arbitration systems; Chapter 4 studies the procedures of 23 nonunion internal tribunals and peer review systems; and Chapter 5 studies the procedures of 49 open-door policies and formal appeals to higher management. Each chapter contains a requisite and comprehensive Integrative Analysis.

In the following pages, executives and human resource managers in the firms surveyed will have an opportunity, in the words of the Scottish poet, Robert Burns, "to see ourselves as others see us," a useful if not always pleasant experience.

3
Nonunion Grievance Arbitration Systems: A Procedural Analysis

INTRODUCTION

The words arbiter and arbitrator are derived from the Latin word *arbitrari*, meaning "to make a decision." An arbitrator is a neutral third party who renders a decision between two contending parties who cannot mutually arrive at a satisfactory resolution of their conflict.

A mediator, from the Latin *mediare*, meaning "to be in the middle," is a neutral third party who, while lacking authority to render a decision, assists the parties in achieving one of their own choice.

Arbitration and mediation have an honorable connotation. The biblical injunction, "Blessed are the peacemakers," is applicable to them. They are related in their purpose, which is to convert conflict into harmony, but different in their methods. It is necessary, if arbitration is to be meaningful, that it possess the attribute of finality, what is called "binding arbitration," in which the contending parties, however grudgingly, agree to accept the arbitrator's decision, preferring it to continuing conflict.

Mediation, on the other hand, inasmuch as it cannot render a decision, depends for its usefulness upon the mediator's ability, combined with the reasonableness of the contending parties, to steer them into their free acceptance of a decision proposed by one of them or by the mediator. A memorable example of mediation was President Theodore Roosevelt's invitation in 1905 to the parties in the Russo-Japanese War to meet with him at Portsmouth, New Hampshire, where, after a month of discussion, the parties signed a peace treaty. And in 1978 Pope John Paul II successfully mediated a territorial dispute which was threatening war between Argentina and Chile.

The obvious advantage of arbitration over mediation is the former's guarantee that a decision will be attained, while the obvious disadvantage is that the contending parties must relinquish their control over their own destinies into the hands of a third party. That disadvantage looms sufficiently large in the minds of some persons on both sides of the employer-employee relationship to weaken their enthusiasm for arbitration. Nevertheless, arbitration remains a sensible option which disputants should always consider. The speed with which it functions is a definite asset for both parties, and its low cost is very attractive in comparison with the expense of dragging a dispute through a time-consuming civil court suit.

However hopeful a party may be of obtaining a favorable arbitrated decision, there is always an element of uncertainty, and the choice is between it and having the dispute drag on indefinitely. Uncertainty exists because it would be unreasonable to expect that even professional arbitrators of equal ability and experience would all render identical decisions in a given case, a unanimity of opinion which it is difficult for judges in a multijudge tribunal to attain, split decisions being more common. In fact, it is the very element of uncertainty which makes arbitration feasible. No one would submit to it knowing the decision would be against him.

An important feature of arbitration is that the scope of the arbitrator's investigative authority and the facts to which he is limited in designing his decision are stipulated by the contending parties. For example, he may be instructed to determine whether an employee is entitled to remuneration because of hardship resulting from a factory being moved to a new location, while at the same time he is denied authority to consider the separate issue of whether the plant should be moved.

In general, the selection of an arbitrator is by mutual agreement of the parties, but in some instances management may reserve that prerogative to itself in a dispute with an employee. Legally, anyone may serve as an arbitrator, but it is "the better part of wisdom" to select a person who is a member of a professional arbitrators' association, because the essential characteristic of such an association is the indispensable attribute of impartiality. The association can be helpful by suggesting a few names of arbitrators experienced in the parties' type of dispute.

REPRESENTATIVE NONUNION ARBITRATION PROCEDURES

This section is an analysis of the arbitration procedures stipulated in the employee-relations policy manuals of some leading nonunion companies who are within the umbrella of the National Association of Manufacturers.

Company A

An employee may invoke arbitration only if the grievance is that of having been discharged, and only if the employee has at least two years of seniority. Arbitration may not be invoked if the cause of discharge was violation of rules regarding attendance and theft. The employee must tender a written request to management, or postmark it, within 48 hours after receiving a notice of discharge.

The arbitrator is selected by management, which requests three names from a "recognized" arbitration association and selects one "at random" within two weeks after receiving the three names.

The date on which the selected arbitrator will hold the hearing is agreed upon between the arbitrator and management. The arbitrator may direct that a transcript of the hearing be made, but its publication in summary form or otherwise requires the consent of both management and the employee. Persons not "directly involved" with the employee's discharge may not attend the hearing.

The employee "may" present evidence, summon and examine witnesses, argue the merits of his or her position, have prior access to his or her personnel file, and receive the assistance of a member of management in case preparation.

Management "shall" pay the arbitration costs, comply with the arbitrator's decision, and comply with the employee's "reasonable" requests for information and witnesses.

The issue before the arbitrator is whether the employee was "discharged for just cause," and in making the decision the arbitrator shall be governed by the plant's policies, rules, and disciplinary procedures as published, and call additional witnesses or conduct such other investigation as he deems necessary.

If the arbitrator determines that there was not a "just cause for discharge," an order of "reinstatement and/or back pay" may be given. Back pay is calculated by what the employee should have earned without discharge less income he or she earned, or could have earned "with reasonable diligence," since time of discharge.

The arbitrator's decision must be made without delay and within 30 calendar days of the hearing, with concurrent mailed notice to management and the employee.

Analysis of company A. The critical feature is that an employee may request arbitration only if the grievance is that of being discharged, but not if the discharge was for violation of attendance and theft rules.

Another feature is that management selects the arbitrator, doing so "at random" from a list of three persons suggested by an arbitration association.

A third important feature is that management pays the arbitration costs.

Company B

The plant manager may "invoke" arbitration and the employee may "request" it. The situation is that either the manager or the employee is appealing to arbitration from a recommendation for settling the employee's grievance which was made by a "peer group" in the company. If it is the employee who is initiating arbitration, it must be done within ten days of the "peer group's" recommendation.

The employee selects the arbitrator from a list provided by the American Arbitration Association.

The decision is binding. Only the employee, his or her supervisor, and "necessary" witnesses may participate in the hearing. There will not be a posthearing brief nor any stenographic record. Normally, the hearing should be completed in one day, but the arbitrator may, "in unusual circumstances and for good cause shown," hold a second hearing within five days.

Arbitration may proceed if a party who received due notice fails to be present, but an award shall not be made solely on the default of the party, and the arbitrator may require the attending party to submit supporting witnesses.

The arbitrator's decision is limited to questions involving the "application or interpretation" of the company policy at issue. The arbitrator will not judge its "reasonableness or propriety."

Unless the parties agree otherwise, the arbitrator's decision shall be made not later than 30 days after the hearing. It shall be in writing, mailed to the parties. The arbitrator's "opinion," if any, shall be in summary form, and it and the decision shall be made known only to management and the employee.

Management shall pay the arbitration expenses.

Analysis of company B. The interesting feature is that, although the company has established a "peer group," the members of which are employees, to settle employees' grievances, both management and an employee may appeal over the "peer group's" decision to arbitration.

Company A's arbitrator is selected by management but the employee makes the selection in company B.

An unusual feature is that arbitration may proceed if only one of the two parties is present. It would seem to be unlikely that management would fail to appear if it initiated the arbitration, and it would appear proper to cancel the arbitration if it was initiated by the employee and he failed to attend the hearing.

Company C

The headquarters of this very large, multiplant company issued a companywide employee-relations manual which includes provision for the arbitration of employees' grievances.

An employee may appeal to arbitration from the highest internal office in the company which reviews and decides employees' grievances. That office, which is staffed by three top executives in the division of the company in which the employee concerned works, is called a Management Appeals Committee. The employee must appeal from the committee's decision within five working days in writing, which is to be a clear, concise statement of the facts, "the issues to be resolved by an arbitrator," and the desired remedy.

The arbitrator is selected jointly by the company and the employee. If a selection is not agreed upon within 24 hours after the meeting held for that purpose, the company will request from "an appropriate source" a list of five arbitrators. First the employee will delete a name from the list, then the company will do so, after which the employee will delete another name, leaving two names from which the company will select the arbitrator.

The arbitrator's function is defined as determining whether company policies, practices, rules, or regulations have been complied with "in the case of your grievance." The arbitrator's decision is "conclusive and binding," and it will be limited to "the precise issue which is submitted for determination."

The arbitrator "may" interpret the various policies and rules, but does not have the power to change them or to limit in any manner management's authority to establish or revise such policies and rules.

The arbitrator is "requested" to render a decision within 30 days after the hearing is concluded and briefs, if any, are submitted.

Analysis of company C. It is the employee who lays out "the issues to be resolved by an arbitrator," and the latter is limited to "the precise issue which is submitted for determination." There is not necessarily a conflict in changing from the plural to the singular, but the inference is that only the employee may raise one or more issues. It is questionable whether, as appears to be the situation here, the company should waive its right to present issues deemed pertinent by it.

An axiom states that "Justice delayed is justice denied." The company may feel no urgency to settle an employee's grievance, but the 30 days which the company's arbitration rules allocated as a maximum for the arbitrator's decision may cause an employee serious hardship, especially if the decision is to be in his or her favor.

Company D

This company's employee-relations manual indicates that the prescribed arbitration rules apply specifically to hourly paid employees. Arbitration is permitted only in "cases not involving determinations in the general conduct of the Company's business." Employees have the option of a written request for an "impartial arbitrator."

An arbitrator is selected jointly by the company and the employee, and if they fail to agree on a choice they then jointly request the American Arbitration

Association to designate an arbitrator. Arbitration expenses are paid by the company. The decision is binding.

The arbitrator is provided with a written statement of the "issues to be resolved," signed jointly by the company and the employee.

Arbitration is not permitted regarding the company's retirement plan and the decisions of its medical director, although in the latter situation arbitration is provided in fact, even though not in name, by a third physician jointly selected by the company's doctor and the employee's doctor.

The company exercises caution in delineating the scope of an arbitrator's authority:

The arbitrator shall have jurisdiction and authority to interpret the written policies, rules, regulations and procedures of the Company as they apply to the case of the employee being reviewed. He may not consider or decide matters which are solely and exclusively the responsibility of the Company in the management and conduct of its business.

The arbitrator shall have no power to rescind, amend, alter or supplement existing written Company policies, rules, regulations, or procedures, including wage scales. The arbitrator shall, however, have the power to decide whether the application of such policies, rules, regulations, and procedures by the Company was arbitrary or discriminatory and, if so found, make his decision in conformity with such written policies, rules, regulations, and procedures of the Company.

The arbitrator may determine if a job description is properly written and rated.

Analysis of company D. The employee-relations manual quoted above can be read "between the lines" to reveal something of the company's attitude, even if not a conscious attitude, toward its hourly employees. It is a small point, but there is a tinge of condescension in informing employees that they may request an "impartial" arbitrator, as though there were any other kind and as though the employees do not appreciate the fact that the very purpose of invoking third party intervention is to achieve impartiality.

In addition, it is obvious that the company left it to the discretion of its attorney to draft the long quotation cited above regarding the scope of an arbitrator's authority, the result of which is to overwhelm with "legalese" diction the average hourly rated employee, for whom "rules, regulations and procedures" indiscriminately mean merely rules, while the word "change" would be less intimidating than, and just as meaningful as, "rescind, amend, alter or supplement." The intention here is obviously not to make the employees happy but only to make the company's attorney happy.

An employee-relations manual should be written by the human resources management department, which, among all the company's departments, can best be depended upon to exercise appropriate sympathy toward employees' problems.

It is proper for the draft of the manual to be reviewed by the company's attorney, but, in contrast with the sympathetic viewpoint of the employee-relations staff, his training in the legal system is more inclined to render his viewpoint controversial and adversarial.

Thus, while a member of the employee-relations staff will deem that he has earned his pay by informing the employees in a few utterly simple words that "an arbitrator may not change the company's rules," the attorney feels impelled to exhaust the dictionary, and also at least inadvertently intimidate the employees, by stating that "an arbitrator may not rescind, amend, alter or supplement the company's rules, regulations and procedures."

A similar defect in company D's manual is the statement that arbitration is permitted only in "cases not involving determinations in the general conduct of the Company's business." The company's attorney will undoubtedly be happy to explain, upon request, what that means, but this is of no help to a nervous employee who is reading and rereading the employee-relations manual at home in an agonized effort to determine whether he or she qualifies for arbitration.

It is interesting to note that, for an unexplained reason, company D has determined it advisable to single out job descriptions as a specific area of concern for arbitrators regarding whether they are "properly written and rated."

Company E

Arbitration is made available only to "Production and Maintenance employees" and only if their grievance is their dismissal from the company after having completed their probationary period of employment. Arbitration is permitted only after a discharged employee has exhausted "all appeals available through the company's complaint procedure." The written request for arbitration must be submitted within two weeks of the effective date of the discharge.

A statement of the grievance and a statement of the company's justification for the discharge are submitted to "a panel of three community residents" to determine if there is "reason for a full-scale hearing" (meaning arbitration).

If that panel recommends arbitration, the employee may make a selection from "a list of nationally known arbitrators."

The function of the arbitrator is to determine if the discharge was for "just cause." The company will accept the arbitrator's recommendation for retroactive pay.

The company pays the arbitration expenses, except that the employee is responsible for the fee of a counsel whom he or she retains.

Analysis of company E. A very important feature in company E's employee-relations manual is that arbitration is available only after the discharged employee has exhausted "all appeals available through the company's complaint procedure." Attention is here called to this feature because, while all companies do not make this specific statement in their manuals with respect to discharge and all other kinds of causes of employees' grievances, nevertheless the statement is certainly implicit in all employee-relations manuals. It is obvious that it is not proper procedure for a company to outline in its manual the "steps," a commonly used word, in the process of initiating a grievance and appealing from an unfavorable decision, if the selection of which "steps" the employee is to adopt are left solely to his or her own discretion. While various companies differ considerably in their appeal "steps," it is essential in each company that its published grievance procedure be adhered to, partly to achieve orderliness in the company and partly to achieve uniform treatment of all grievances.

A very unusual provision in company E's employee-relations manual is that the decision regarding whether an employee's request for arbitration shall be granted is left to the discretion of "a panel of three community residents" after they review "a statement of the grievance and a statement of the company's justification for the discharge." This is "tying a string" to an employee's request for arbitration which requires the employee, in effect, to struggle through not one but actually two arbitration proceedings. Furthermore, the official arbitrator, if the case gets to him or her, is faced with the inference that the "panel of three community residents" believes that the employee has an argument worthy of consideration.

Although the "panel of three community residents" is of major importance to employees who seek arbitration, there is nothing in the employee-relations manual to indicate the criteria by which the panel is selected by management. The panel is a hurdle over which an employee must leap on his progress toward arbitration, and a peculiar aspect of the overall situation is that management selects the panel, but if the panel favors the employee by recommending arbitration, management permits the employee to select the arbitrator. That is not necessarily an even trade if the panel rules against the employee.

Company F

This is a small company with 85 employees. Its employee-relations handbook states:

If you are not satisfied with the decision... you may ask that your problem be considered by an impartial arbitrator from outside the company. To do so, simply make your request in writing to the general manager within five (5) working days of receiving the... decision. Within ten (10) working days thereafter, the general manager will request, in writing, that the American Arbitration Association designate an impartial arbitrator to decide the matter. The arbitrator will investigate the matter in full, including interviewing you and any other employees involved in the case. If you need help presenting your position to the arbitrator, you may ask a co-worker or your supervisor to help you.

The arbitrator's decision must be based upon the company's policy as outlined in the employee-relations handbook, and it is binding on "both you and the company."

Arbitration expenses are paid by the company except that, if the decision favors the company, "your share will be $25.00 and the company will pay the rest of the cost."

This procedure is available for use by "all employees"—nonsupervisors as well as supervisors.

Analysis of company F. In this very small company of only 85 employees, it may be assumed that employer-employee relations are conducted on a first-name basis, with the president highly visible and internal affairs conducted with maximum informality.

It is not surprising, therefore, that, whereas the employee-relations manuals previously outlined herein rather impersonally discuss employees' rights in grievance cases in the third person—"the employee may or may not do such-and-such"—in this company's manual (called a handbook) the grievance procedures are discussed, in a refreshingly informal and friendly manner, in the first person: "If *you* need help presenting *your* position to the arbitrator, *you* may ask a co-worker or *your* supervisor to help *you*" (emphasis added).

The informal and friendly spirit of this company's employee-relations manual is uniform throughout. It is probable that, when an employee in one of the other companies reviewed above examines the arbitration procedure outlined in his or her employee-relations manual, one has the disturbing feeling of being annoying and even antagonizing management by requesting arbitration, but in company F the employee is told: "Simply make your request in writing to the general manager." It is almost as if management is putting its arm around the shoulder of an employee and saying: Grievances between you and us cannot be completely avoided, but when they arise let's not allow them to disturb our basic mutual friendship.

This informally managed company does not want any red tape in the selection of an arbitrator, and it leaves the selection to the discretion of the arbitrators' association.

It is interesting that this company permits arbitration in the case of management personnel at the supervisory level.

INTEGRATIVE ANALYSIS

This chapter is concerned exclusively with the use of arbitration as a means of disposing of employees' grievances in representative nonunion companies in the National Association of Manufacturers. In all cases in actual practice, as well as in theory, arbitration is the final step in those companies that permit arbitration.

Arbitration is an action that is performed *outside* of a company in neutral territory with respect to the relationship between employees and management. This fact is not impaired by the circumstance that, as a matter of convenience, the arbitrator uses a desk inside the company.

It is important to differentiate between arbitration and mediation. The universally accepted nature of an arbitrator's decision is that it is "binding" upon the two contesting parties. Having failed by their own effort to arrive at a mutually satisfactory solution of their problem, and sensibly desiring the problem to be resolved, they invoke the "good offices" of a neutral third party in establishing a solution.

Mediation, on the other hand, lacks the "binding" feature of arbitration, and is intended to assist the parties in arriving at something more desirable than a third party's decision, namely, the parties' own mutual decision. The function of a mediator is to cool minds, and to suggest helpful ideas to assist the parties in making their own decision.

It should be obvious that, if an arbitrator senses an opportunity to solve a case on which he is working by injecting a dose of mediation, he most certainly should make the effort before, as his last resort, rendering his binding decision.

The potential value of the arbitration function is very substantial. It is expeditious, and relatively inexpensive. Not only can it dispose of a dispute in a few weeks, in contrast with the year or more often required in a civil suit, but, moreover, it can do so at a fraction of the legal expense. It is obvious that arbitration, unlike civil suits, avoids the axiom that "Justice delayed is justice denied." All of these considerations are of interest to management, and arbitration offers an employee with a grievance the opportunity to have his case considered by an outside, neutral, and impartial tribunal in a situation in which it would be impracticable for him to utilize a court of law.

Professional arbitrators are frequently attorneys, and should be in cases in which the issues are involved with local or national laws, but such a qualification is not required in various other situations, one of which is the issue of whether an employee, or management in the opinion of an employee, has deviated from the officially published rules of a company.

It is noteworthy that those companies that permit employees' grievances to go to arbitration stipulate that an arbitrator must consider a company's rules "as written," that is, interpreting what they appear to state on the basis of impartial and reasonable judgment, but without authority to change them. An arbitrator should, of course, after rendering his decision, advise the company that a rule is subject to varying interpretations to a degree which renders it advisable for the rule to be more carefully written.

From the viewpoint of political philosophy, the justification for a company to insist that an arbitrator interpret a company rule "as written" is that it may be said that an implied contract exists between management and its employees, the essence of which is that management on its part and the employees on their part will adhere to the company's officially published rules. It is not surprising, therefore, that most of the six companies reviewed in this chapter permit an employee's grievance to go to arbitration only with the limitation which the employee-relations manual of company B stipulates as follows: "The arbitrator's decision will be limited to questions involving the *application or interpretation* of the company policy at issue. The arbitrator will not decide on the *reasonableness or propriety* of the policy itself" (emphasis added).

In other words, if the essence of an employee's grievance is that a company's policy or rule is itself inherently unfair, the grievance is not subject to arbitration even though in various other situations arbitration is permitted by a company having the above-quoted policy. Among the six companies reviewed in this chapter, only company E does not have the above-quoted limitation on an arbitrator's authority: company E's employee-relations manual states only that the arbitrator will determine whether the company had "just cause" for its action which generated the employee's grievance. It would be advisable for company E to clarify what it intends to say in its manual in this matter.

One of the very interesting features in the attitude of the six companies regarding the arbitration of employees' grievances is that two of them permit arbitration only if the employee's grievance is of being discharged from the company. A third, company D, permits arbitration only "in cases not involving determinations in the general conduct of the Company's business," a statement which may be interpreted to be sufficiently vague to allow the company to determine whether an employee's grievance is arbitrable.

Why were only six companies surveyed which provide for arbitration of employees' grievances? The fact is that of 78 companies' employee-relations manuals reviewed, only six, or less than 8 percent, permit arbitration. If the two companies that permit arbitration only in the case of an employee's discharge are subtracted from the figures, then only 5 percent of the 78 companies may be said to provide arbitration as a means for the resolving of employees' grievances.

What interpretation should be given to that figure of 5 percent? The first thing to keep in mind is that this research pertains only to nonunion companies.

One way to look at the six companies is to say they are the exception to the rule, but another way is to see them as the vanguard in a progressive trend in the area of employer-employee relations and human resources management. This latter view is supported by the fact that company C, which is engaged in scientific manufacturing of a highly technical nature, and which has a total of nearly 50,000 employees, accepts arbitration as a means for the settlement of employees' grievances and, moreover, does not limit it to cases of discharge.

The first page of company C's employee-relations manual, signed by both the chairman of the board and the president, states: "In its more than 45 year history_____has earned a reputation as a good place to work. This reputation is based upon challenging work, fair treatment of every employee, and *respect for the dignity of the individual*" (emphasis added). It may be that it was that "respect for the dignity of the individual" which caused company C, while retaining the privilege of final selection of an arbitrator, to recognize the stake of the employee in the selection:

If you and the company are unable to agree upon an arbitrator within 24 hours after meeting for that purpose, the company will request from an appropriate source a list of five persons from which an arbitrator will be chosen. The employee will delete the first person from the list of five, then the company, then the employee, leaving the company with the final choice between the two remaining persons.

To continue the discussion as to why only 5 percent of the 78 companies accept arbitration as a practical way to resolve employees' grievances, a few points should be considered. It is certainly not probable that the executives in those companies have been actively conscious of the availability of arbitration, have researched its pros and cons, and have arrived at the conclusion that it lacks value for their companies.

On the contrary, arbitration is like any other item which is available in the marketplace, in the sense that it requires selling effort, advertising, and sales promotion techniques. These tasks are perhaps the responsibility of the arbitrators, and, at least, specifically of their professional associations. It should be kept in mind that the particular market for the arbitrators' commodity which is here being examined is employees' grievances in nonunion companies, and in order to expand the arbitrators' participation in that market they should tailor their merchandising techniques specifically to it.

Arbitration has a long history as a reputable technique for resolving disputes involving persons and institutions. Before leaving the subject, it is appropriate to note that the state of Florida encourages apartment owners in a condominium to settle disputes among themselves or with the management of the condominium by means of arbitration. Rule no. 7D–50.04 of Florida's Division of Florida Land Sales and Condominiums states: "The intent of the arbitration process is to secure the *just, speedy* and *inexpensive* settlement of internal condominium disputes" (emphasis added). And Florida's statute no. 718.112 stipulates that the by-laws of a condominium "shall further provide, and if they do not, shall be deemed to provide for *voluntary binding arbitration* of internal disputes" (emphasis added). The state employs a full-time staff of arbitrators for this purpose and, because of the complexity of the state's laws and regulations pertaining to condominiums, requires these arbitrators to be attorneys.

The most notable feature of the arbitration rules of the six companies reviewed herein is their uniformity regarding three basic elements in the arbitration process: first, arbitration may be invoked by an employee only after he has exhausted the steps in the grievance procedure provided in the company's employee-relations manual; second, the arbitrator's assigned function is to determine whether the employee or management violated a published rule of the company, and he may not consider whether the rule is unfair or unreasonable, the obvious explanation for this limitation being that no company would consent to permitting an outsider to write or rewrite the rules under which it operates; and the third element is that the arbitrator's decision is binding on both parties, thereby finally closing the employee's grievance. By definition, it is the binding characteristic of arbitration that distinguishes it from the merely advisory function of mediation.

Five of the six companies pay the arbitration expenses, while company F, with only 85 employees, requires the employee to contribute $25 toward the expense if he loses the case.

The principal lack of uniformity in the six companies is in the methods prescribed for the selection of an arbitrator:

Company

A	Arbitrator selected "at random" by management from three names recommended by a "recognized" arbitration association.
B	Employee selects the arbitrator from a list provided by the American Arbitration Association.
C	Arbitrator selected jointly by the company and employee. If they fail to agree within 24 hours, company requests a list of five arbitrators from "an appropriate source." Employee strikes a name from the list, then the company does so, and then the employee does so again, with the company selecting an arbitrator from the two remaining names.
D	If the company and employee fail to agree on the selection of an arbitrator, they jointly request the American Arbitration Association to designate one.
E	After the employee requests arbitration, "a panel of three community residents" determines whether there is a "reason for a full-scale hearing," meaning arbitration. If the panel recommends arbitration, the employee selects an arbitrator from "a list of nationally known arbitrators."
F	The company requests the American Arbitration Association to designate the arbitrator.

The most peculiar system in the above tabulation is company E's "panel of three community residents." It is an extra hurdle that the company requires an employee to leap over in processing his or her grievance, and information should be provided in the employee-relations manual regarding what criteria are used by the company in selecting the members of the panel, and what criteria the company instructs the panel to use in determining whether the employee's grievance should be arbitrated. Moreover, no time limit is prescribed for the panel.

In general among the six companies it is the employee, and not management, who has the right to invoke arbitration. A plausible assumption in this situation is that the companies have confidence in their internal procedures for resolving employees' grievances. An exception is company B, and a plausible assumption to explain this company's asserting its right to initiate arbitration is that the company lacks confidence in the impartiality of the last step, prior to arbitration, in the procedure for resolving employees' grievances, which is a review by an employee's "peer group," namely, a panel of his fellow employees.

CONCLUSION

In closing this chapter, it is appropriate to refer again to the opinion of the state of Florida that arbitration is a "just, speedy and inexpensive" method of settling disputes. While Florida was referring specifically to condominium residents, the three adjectives undoubtedly can be applied to all disputes.

There is a natural tendency for individuals and organizations to be hesitant in relinquishing their destiny into the hands of a third party, including an arbitrator. A dispute is carried into a court of law only by a party who expects that the decision will be favorable. In the case of an employee who has carried a grievance all the way through his company's dispute-resolving procedure without securing the decision desired, it may be said that, if the company permits arbitration, the employee has "everything to gain and nothing to lose" by invoking it.

But what inducement is there for a company to permit its employees to invoke arbitration? The inducement is that arbitration is "just, speedy and inexpensive," and, beyond that, its availability should assure employees that their company is fair-minded to the degree of willingness to have their grievance settled on neutral ground. The final consideration is that an employee's grievance, even in the case of discharge, can be the proverbial monkey wrench in a company's otherwise smooth operations, especially if it affects the morale of other employees. Consequently, a company should leave no stone unturned in its efforts to dispose of employees' grievances promptly.

The essence of arbitration is its impartiality. Impartiality is the motto of the professional arbitrator. It is the only commodity that he or she has to sell to the public. It is the source of pride and sense of accomplishment. In that pride and sense of accomplishment the arbiter ranks equally with that other master of impartiality, a man who glories in the respect which the American people bestow on him even while they are threatening to "Kill him!": the professional baseball umpire.

4
Nonunion Internal Tribunals and Peer Review Systems: A Procedural Analysis

INTRODUCTION

The most formal system for the resolution of the grievances of nonunion employees is, of course, their resort to courts of law or, in certain situations prescribed by Congress, resort to a government regulatory agency, such as one pertaining to so-called affirmative action or to various forms of illegal discrimination.

The next most formal system is binding arbitration, which is the subject of Chapter 3, usually performed by a professional arbitrator, whose primary stock-in-trade is his impartiality. It is interesting to note that impartiality, while it is the keystone of arbitration, is not guaranteed in courts of law, in which judges and juries are free to render decisions that reflect their personal preferences regarding what the law should say, ignoring what it actually says.

We come now to the third most formal system, in descending order, in the resolution of the grievances of nonunion employees: internal tribunal systems. The plural term is used because of the wide variety of forms in which companies design their internal tribunals.

The word "tribunal" is used herein because, like a court of law and arbitration, the function is to render a decision in a dispute, in this case, a dispute between an employee and management, initiated by the former.

The word "internal" indicates that the persons who are the members of the tribunal are on the company's payroll. While there are numerous variations among companies in the composition of their internal tribunals, the favored type appears to be a tribunal whose members include both management personnel and one or more nonsupervisory employees.

The provision for one or more nonsupervisory employees in a tribunal which has the function of rendering a decision regarding an employee's grievance against management, has its roots in political philosophy. In the Middle Ages one of the rights that the common people developed for themselves was that, in criminal court cases, they should have decisions regarding their guilt or innocence rendered by a group of persons chosen from among their own kind, instead of such decisions being the prerogative of government officials. The underlying philosophy was that justice required that the decisions regarding defendants be rendered by their "peers," that is, their equals in the sociopolitical system. That is the origin of today's jury system in criminal cases.

This concept of trial by one's peers has been accorded at least token acceptance by the managements of those companies that provide internal tribunals for the settlement of the grievances of nonunion employees. By token acceptance is meant that, although the general practice is for a majority of the members of an internal tribunal to be management personnel, it is also a common practice for one or more nonsupervisory employees to be members.

Unquestionably, the employee with a grievance feels more comfortable if the internal tribunal before which he appears contains one or more of his peers. On the other hand, a cynic may suggest that the presence of peers in a tribunal in which management holds majority control is merely a psychological gimmick intended to lull the grievant into a false sense of security. Such a cynic is unjustly accusing the management members of an internal tribunal of indifference to the demands of justice in rendering their decisions.

Contrariwise, a cynic may suggest that the peers in an internal tribunal will invariably vote in favor of their fellow nonsupervisory employee, but such a cynic is unjustly maligning the integrity of the peers. An anecdote is appropriate here regarding peers in a tribunal of any kind. During World War II, a friend of mine was the president of a courts-martial board at an Army Air Force base. The members of the board were all commissioned officers. On one occasion my friend was discussing the Army's judicial system with a few enlisted men, and he asked them a question which had been puzzling him: "If you were to be tried by a courts-martial board, would you want its members to be officers or enlisted men?" The answer was that officers would be preferable to the enlisted men's peers. My friend asked why, and the answer was that the peers would be more strict in judging and sentencing an enlisted man than officers on courts-martial boards were. It is beyond the scope of this book to determine whether that situation may prevail in the internal tribunals of nonunion companies, but it is certainly a possibility, at least if this thesis is correct that the so-called "common people" in our nation, the people who staff the nonsupervisory jobs in business and industry, "common people" who, Abraham Lincoln declared, God must have loved because he created so many of them—the thesis that those people possess an intense sense of justice and that it is enhanced by the sense of responsibility inherent in service on a tribunal.

What is here being discussed is, in its broadest aspect, an honored and very highly respected institution: the approximately 800-year-old Anglo-American jury system.

There is not a standardized name in companies' employee-relations manuals for their internal tribunals. Some of the names which will be encountered in this chapter are Roundtable, Appeal Board, Appeals Board, Board of Review, Right of Review Board, Advisory Committee, Grievance Panel, and Ad-Hoc Committee. It is this diversity that necessitates titling this chapter with a generic term: internal tribunal system.

It should be noted that it would be improper to describe one of these tribunals as performing "peer review" of an employee's grievance except in the case, if any, in which nonsupervisory employees constitute at least a majority of the tribunal's members, and, strictly speaking, the phrase "peer review" should be limited to a tribunal consisting solely of nonsupervisory employees.

The word "peer" identifies a type of person, and it has absolutely nothing at all to do with how that person would be expected to vote in an internal tribunal. The entire system would be vitiated if there were even a hint or insinuation that an employee in a tribunal would vote "as an employee," or that a member of management in a tribunal would vote "as management." If there is any unanimity among the companies reviewed herein which provide internal tribunals for the resolution of employees' grievances, it is the desire of their top managements that the members of the tribunals perform their work with the impartiality and objectivity which are the foundation for justice in the jury system.

In the reading of this chapter, an internal tribunal should be thought of as comparable with a court of appeals in the judicial system, in the sense that an employee with a grievance "appeals" to the tribunal, if there is one in the company, over the decisions of various levels of management regarding his case.

It requires a certain degree of courage for the management of a company to relinquish the control of its affairs into the hands of an arbitrator or an internal tribunal, but very likely the need for courage is minimized by the intense desire to do everything possible to achieve harmony between management and its employees.

This chapter analyzes the 23 nonunion companies, out of the total of 78 reviewed in this book, which provide for an internal tribunal for the settlement of employees' grievances.

REPRESENTATIVE NONUNION INTERNAL TRIBUNAL AND PEER REVIEW PROCEDURES

This section is an analysis of the internal tribunal procedures stipulated in the employee-relations manuals of some leading nonunion companies who are within the umbrella of the National Association of Manufacturers. (*Note*:

"A" and other letter designations in this chapter do not refer to the companies so identified in Chapter 3.)

Company A

This company's internal tribunal is called an Employee Problem Solving Group. If an hourly employee with a grievance appeals over a management decision regarding his case to the Group, which is not a permanent establishment but is recreated for each individual case, the employee randomly selects the names of 12 hourly employees. In the order selected, management contacts each person, without identifying the employee and his problem, to ask the person to serve in the Group. This process continues until six persons have agreed to serve. The employee then selects a member of the personnel department to serve as chairperson, who will vote only for the purpose of breaking a tie vote among the six members of the Group if they fail to achieve a majority vote after three attempts.

The employee may appeal over the decision of the Group for a decision by the plant manager and, following that, may invoke arbitration and the plant manager has the option, instead of rendering a decision, of invoking arbitration.

Analysis of company A. This company has a unique system for resolving employees' grievances, and it may even be described as peculiar, in the sense that it is radically different from the more customary systems.

There is an even number (six) of voting members in the internal tribunal, necessitating that the nonvoting chairperson have tie-breaking power.

Insomuch as the voting members are all nonsupervisory employees, this Employee Problem Solving Group could be classified as an example of the rare true or pure peer review, that is, judgment of the plaintiff's case solely by his equals, except for the fact that the tie-breaking chairperson is a member of management.

This company departs from a customary procedure, which is that decisions regarding an employee's grievance must be rendered by both lower and higher management before the employee may appeal to the internal tribunal. In this company that appeal may be made from a decision by lower management, and, if the employee is dissatisfied with the tribunal's decision, an appeal may be made to higher management, namely, the plant manager.

It is interesting to note that in this company the plant manager may waive the right to make the final decision by invoking arbitration. A plausible advantage of this is that it forestalls the employee from voiding a decision of the plant manager by invoking arbitration, but it can expose the plant manager to the criticism of dodging a task by "passing the buck" to an arbitrator.

Company B

If the grievance of a nonsupervisory employee, a title which includes hourly and salaried personnel, is not settled to his or her satisfaction at the highest authorized management level, which is the decision of a so-called administrative officer, the employee may within five working days appeal to the Management Appeals Committee, which consists of a division officer (this is a large company), the division's senior industrial relations executive, and the corporation's vice president of industrial relations, or their designees.

The Committee will consider the employee's appeal "as soon as practical," and issue its decision in writing within 15 working days of its meeting. The appeal is a written notice of appeal prepared by the employee with the assistance, if desired, of the employee-relations department. The employee is encouraged to appear in person before the Committee, but in any case his or her viewpoint as stated in the notice of appeal provides the basis for the Committee's decision.

The employee may appeal over the decision of the Management Appeals Committee to arbitration.

Analysis of company B. The most important difference between company A and company B is in the composition of the internal tribunal. In the former company only the petitioning employee's peers, that is, his or her fellow hourly employees, serve in the tribunal, whereas in the latter company only management personnel serve in the tribunal, and they are at a high management level. As will be seen in this chapter, between those two extremes are companies in which both peers and management personnel serve in a tribunal.

Company C

This company's internal tribunal is called the Roundtable. This is an extremely small company with only 85 employees. An employee with a grievance may process it up, step by step, through the several layers of management, including the president, and at any step in the process, or after review of the case by the president, may appeal to the Roundtable.

Despite the very small size of the company, its internal tribunal is tailored to the employee having the grievance. In all instances two of the three tribunal members are from management and, more specifically, from the employee's department (production, office, or outside sales force), and the third member is an employee of that department.

All employees are given what the employee-relations manual calls "an opportunity" to serve in his or her department's "Roundtable," this membership being on a rotating basis among the available employees, each serving for a term of three months.

Analysis of company C. In comparison with the titles of the internal tribunals of many companies, the word "roundtable" has a warm and pleasant connotation, reminiscent of the fabled King Arthur and the Knights of his Round Table and denoting an intimate and friendly environment rather than the cold impersonality implied by the title Appeals Board. It is obvious, furthermore, that, in a company with a total payroll of 85 persons, the provision of a separate Roundtable for each of the company's three small departments must necessarily result in the two management personnel and the one employee in a Roundtable being generally on very friendly terms with the employee who has a grievance. It is also interesting to note that, in this extremely small company, a Roundtable has authority to overrule a decision by the president regarding an employee's grievance.

Company D

If an employee is dissatisfied with his or her department's decision regarding a grievance, an appeal may be made within five working days to the Appeal Board, which will render a decision by a majority vote within ten days after concluding its investigation.

The personnel representative serves as a nonvoting chairperson of the Board, the members of which are the plant manager, the manager of the employee's department, two employees chosen by the employee who has the grievance, and an employee chosen by unanimous consent of the four other members.

A member of the Board may not be a relative of the appealing employee, should have at least five years' seniority, should be familiar with the appealing employee's department, and should be objective, fair, and not afraid to ask questions. An employee may refuse to participate on the Appeal Board.

Analysis of company D. The grievance step prior to the Appeal Board is a decision by a management committee which includes the manager of the appealing employee's department, and it may therefore be stated that there is a conflict of interest inherent in the fact that that manager is a member of the Appeal Board.

The interesting feature of this Appeal Board is that a peer group of three of the appealing employee's fellow employees constitutes a voting majority of the Board. They may be expected to have a certain amount of mature judgment due to the provision that they have five years' seniority in the company.

Company E

If the employee is dissatisfied with the management decision regarding his or her grievance, an appeal may be made within seven days to a Board of Review. The request is made to the director of human resources, who will decide within two weeks whether a lack of fairness or accuracy in the management decision justifies convening the Board. If so, the director appoints a chairperson who does not have any supervisory relationship with the employee but is knowledgeable in the area of the grievance and has the ability to administer the Board.

There are two additional members of the Board. One is selected by the chairperson from a list of three employees submitted by the appealing employee, and the other is selected by the appealing employee from a list of three employees submitted by the chairperson.

A representative of the human resources department sits with the Board as a nonvoting member to "facilitate administration." The decision is rendered within seven days after the hearing.

"The Chairperson of the Board of Review and its members will be given specific instructions with respect to the proper, ethical and expeditious handling of the hearing. They will help be responsible for assuring that all pertinent facts are considered and an appropriate decision is made for the fair and equitable treatment of the parties involved."

Analysis of company E. Of the three voting members of the Board of Review, two are the appealing employee's fellow employees, giving this peer group majority control of the Board.

An exceptional feature of this company is that the director of human resources may exercise a veto over whether the employee may appeal to the Board of Review, by virtue of that director's power to decide whether there was "a lack of fairness or accuracy" in the management decisions regarding the grievance. In practical effect, therefore, the employee's appeal is not directly to the Board of Review but only to the director of human resources, with the employee hoping that the director will permit the matter to go to the Board.

The last paragraph in the company E description was inserted as a direct quotation because of its peculiarity. The company's Board of Review has the status, like all the internal tribunals reviewed herein, of a judicial body. It is a principle in political philosophy that a judicial body must be independent from all outside influence and that its members must be immune from personal hazard resulting from their decisions. Company E violates this principle by rendering the members of the Board of Review "responsible for assuring that all pertinent facts are considered and an appropriate decision is made." Moreover, the employee-relations manual which contains this provision fails to stipulate who in the company will review the work of the Board, determine whether "all pertinent facts are considered and an appropriate decision is made," and impose pertinent penalties on the Board members for failure to act properly.

Company F

An employee may appeal from a management decision to this company's Right of Review Board, which consists of the director of human resources and three vice presidents as voting members and a vice president of the employee's choice as a nonvoting member. The three vice presidents are selected annually by the vice president and general manager. A majority of the voting members is decisive.

If significant financial impact on the company is involved in the employee's grievance, the Right of Review Board has the option of submitting a recommendation to the vice president and general manager for his final decision.

Analysis of company F. This organization, which actually is a large division of a very large company, is interesting because of the tight grip that management maintains over decisions involving employees' grievances. The employees do not have any peer group members on the internal tribunal. It is also interesting that the three voting vice presidents on the tribunal may pass the buck for a decision involving a "significant financial impact on the company" to the vice president and general manager, although the general principle regarding internal tribunals in the companies surveyed in this research is that the tribunal has the authority to override a decision by top management. It should be noted, however, that employee-relations manuals as a rule ignore the special situation of an employee grievance's "significant financial impact on the company." After all, both management and the tribunal can say no in the matter and let the employee pursue the matter in a court of law. This organization is the only one surveyed which recognizes in its employee-relations manual the possibility that the grievance may be a demand for financial remuneration of "significant" size. Many manuals are so worded as to imply that the only type of grievance is one against some form of disciplinary action imposed on the employee. Many manuals, in addition, stipulate the scope of authority of an internal tribunal, and none in the survey provide for a tribunal to award a financial benefit of a kind which would jeopardize a company, the authority being limited generally to such situations as granting back pay or correcting an improper fringe benefit.

Company G

This company's employee-relations manual provides for a job applicant's or an employee's appeal to an Advisory Committee when the complaint is of discrimination related to "race, color, sex, religion, national origin, age, marital status, veteran's status, or handicap."

The basic composition of the Advisory Committee is a management representative, a representative of the personnel department, and a third person who may be management or nonmanagement. When a case comes before the Committee, three additional members are added. The complainant may disqualify one member of the committee, in which instance the chairperson will appoint a replacement.

The Committee will render its decision within 30 working days after it is established, and the chairperson will review the decision with the complainant within 5 working days after it is rendered.

If the complainant is dissatisfied with the decision of the Advisory Committee, he or she may appeal to the company's director of affirmative action, who will render a decision within 20 working days.

Throughout the processing of one of these discrimination-type grievances, strict confidentiality is maintained, an allegation of discrimination being deemed by its nature to be confidential.

Analysis of company G. The notable feature of this company's process of disposing of employees' and job applicants' grievances based on charges of discrimination is that the appeal for review of a case by the Advisory Committee may be followed by an appeal from it to the director of affirmative action.

An unsatisfactory situation is the time element. The 30 days allocated for the Advisory Committee's decision, 5 days to notify the employee of that decision, and 20 days more if the Committee's decision is appealed to the director of affirmative action total nearly two months, which exhibits the principle that "Justice delayed is justice denied."

Company H

An employee who is dissatisfied with lower management's handling of a grievance has the option within two working days of an appeal to the plant manager or an Appeals Board, the decision in either case to be final. It must be rendered within ten days. An employee's working day is defined as a day on which one is scheduled to work.

The Board is conducted by a nonvoting moderator, who determines that the hearings are conducted pursuant to company policy but without influencing the Board's decision.

The employee and his or her supervisor each select an employee to be a member of the Board, and then those two selectees jointly select three additional members. The two original members are selected before the hearing, but they do not select the three additional members until the time of the hearing, and they must be available within an hour. The Board members are not selected to "represent" the employee or supervisor. As soon as the five Board members have assembled, the moderator will see that they read and understand the employee-relations manual's policy statement regarding the Board.

The Board may not render a decision contrary to the letter of plant or department policies, nor contrary to federal, state, and local laws. It may decrease any disciplinary action imposed on the appealing employee, but not increase it. The decision is by secret ballot. The ballots are counted one at a time until three ballots, representing a majority of the Board, are the same, at which time the counting will stop. However, the written decision will be signed by all members of the Board as assurance that the decision conforms with company policy.

After the decision is made, the Board decides whether disciplinary actions should be reduced and whether it should recommend means for avoiding the cause of the grievance in the future. Decisions do not set precedents for future cases.

No record is made in the personnel file of the employee or of a Board member regarding the appeal. A summary of the appeal will be written and copies given to the employee, the affected supervisor, and the employee relations manager.

Analysis of company H. Although this is a large company with 30,000 employees, the procedure outlined above pertains only to one plant, which has 500 employees. The procedure was prepared by "a task force of employees" at that plant.

A unique feature is the option that an employee has of obtaining a final decision regarding his or her grievance either from the plant manager or from the Appeals Board.

Whatever the overall quality of the procedure is, it is evident that careful thought was given to its preparation. For example, while the plant's working days are Monday through Friday, it is painstakingly defined that the appealing employee's working days are those on which one is scheduled to work. Another example is the lengthy instructions that are read out of the employee-relations manual by the Appeals Board moderator to the Board members and which contain such worthwhile statements as this: "No one on the Appeals Board has rank. One member, one voice, one vote, and the simple majority rules."

The nonvoting moderator of the Appeals Board is an important feature, required to provide the Board with maturity in the guidance of its proceedings, inasmuch as the Board is merely an ad hoc committee assembled hurriedly to review only the single grievance, with probably most, if not all, of the five voting members not having had previous experience on the Board.

A weakness in the procedure is very likely the requirement that the two originally selected Board members do not jointly select the three additional members until the Board's hearing convenes, with the necessity that those three members be available within an hour, and no provision is made for an employee declining for any reason to serve on the Board.

A peculiar feature is that all the votes in the Board's secret ballot are not counted, the counting stopping as soon as three examined votes, constituting a majority, are seen to be the same, and even more peculiar is the requirement that, although one or two of the votes which were not counted may represent a minority opinion, all Board members must sign the decision as an assurance that the decision conforms with company policy. That assurance, it would appear, is something which only the Board's moderator, and not the hurriedly selected and assembled members of the Board, is qualified to provide.

This plant of company H is exceptional in that, unlike companies in general, it recognizes the fact that the supervisor of an employee who has a grievance may develop an emotional problem if his or her decision to reject the grievance is overruled by the Appeals Board. A letter written by the plant's employee-relations manager states: "We approach an Appeals Board hearing from the aspect that if the Board does reverse a supervisor's original decision, we tell him ahead of time that it will not reflect on his capabilities and that management will continue to support him."

Company I

An employee may request an Appeal Board, which will meet within ten days after it had been formed, and the employee will be notified of any delay, such as vacations and work schedules.

Company policy is not appealable, but its application is. A nonvoting moderator will ensure that questions asked of the employee by the Board are reasonable and responsible.

The Board consists of the personnel manager, a member of management from the employee's department, two employees selected by the employee, who are usually friends but not relatives, and a fifth member chosen by the four other members half an hour before the meeting of the Board. The fifth member must have at least six months of seniority in the company. The decision of the Board is mailed to the employee within seven days.

Analysis of company I. Special attention should be accorded the statement in this company's employee-relations manual that "Company policy is not appealable, but its application is." This concept, variously stated in company manuals and certainly implied when not specifically stated, is one of the few universally accepted principles of grievance administration.

The statement that the employee selects as members of the Appeal Board two employees who are usually friends but not relatives is explained by the fact that this is a very small company with 150 employees. It is a reasonable assumption that, even in much larger companies, the employees will, whenever given the opportunity, select friends rather than other employees to serve on internal tribunals.

Company J

An employee forfeits his or her right to have a grievance processed through the company's complaint and appeal system if the matter is taken to court or to a government agency. The company's Appeal Board handles only cases "involving a charge of policy violation or claim of unjust treatment in which written disciplinary action has been taken." The employee may appeal the justification for the disciplinary action or the severity of the action. The plant manager makes the final decision regarding "complaints involving management decisions other than policy violations." Grievances regarding equal employment opportunity and sexual harassment are settled by the employee-relations manager. A request for an Appeal Board by a discharged employee must be made within seven working days after discharge.

The Appeal Board consists of the employee-relations manager, who is the chairperson; two employees selected by the appealing employee who are not the latter's relatives and are familiar with the complainant's department; the employee's department head; and a fifth member chosen unanimously by the four other members.

The Board may not change company policy or programs; it may reduce a disciplinary action in response to mitigating circumstances. The decision, which is final, is by majority vote, with the chairperson deciding whether the ballot will be secret. The decision is rendered within five working days.

Copies of the Board's decision are given to the employee and his or her supervisor and are confidential, one copy being kept in a special appeal case filed in the employee-relations department for record purposes, and a copy is not placed in the employee's personnel file.

Analysis of company J. This company is exceptional in stipulating in its employee-relations manual that an employee loses the right to process a grievance inside the company if the matter is taken to court or to a government agency. Probably all companies agree with that, even though the subject is not discussed in their employee-relations manuals. If an employee were to take his or her case to court or to a government agency, and later invoke the company's internal grievance resolution process, there would be a serious question as to where the final decision in the matter lies, a question only a court of law could settle.

It is interesting to note that, like a previously reviewed company, the decision of this company's Appeal Board is confidential, and a copy of the decision is not placed in the employee's personnel file. The obvious justification for not having a record of the grievance in the employee's personnel file is the management policy, which is general in business and industry, of encouraging employees freely and without fear of retribution to air their grievances, settle them, and forget them.

The Appeal Board consists initially of two management personnel and the two employees selected by the appealing employee. Obviously in the interest of impartiality the fifth member is selected "unanimously" by the four other members. That stipulation sounds simple, but in the minds of the two management members and the two employee members the question undoubtedly is whether the fifth member should be from the ranks of management or of the employees of the company, and, if this decision is to be made with proper objectivity, either the two employee members must have strength of character comparable with that of the two management members, or the latter must circumspectly avoid unduly influencing the judgment of the two employee members.

Company K

An employee may appeal his or her grievance for a final decision of the company's president if it involves pay, employee benefits, or company policy. In other cases an appeal may be to the Grievance Panel. The employee draws the names of four panelists who are peer fellow employees and then discards one, and the employee-relations director selects two panelists, providing five members for the Panel. Its decision is final, and is issued within three working days after the hearing.

Analysis of company K. The essential feature of the above briefly stated appeal procedure, in a company of 300 employees, is that the members of the Grievance Panel are the employee's peer group, at least the majority of three members.

Companies L, M, and N

These companies are all parts of the same large hotel chain. Company L is actually one of its regional offices, not a single hotel, and its employee-relations manual contains only the very brief statement that, if an employee is dissatisfied with a decision regarding his or her grievance which has been rendered by the regional human resources director, an appeal may be made within seven days to the region's Complaint Review Board, which will render a decision within 15 days.

A 1–800 telephone hotline number is provided for an employee's initial contact with the regional human resources director.

Companies M and N each have an internal tribunal called a Board of Review. A member on each of the two Boards is a management representative from a department other than that in which the appealing employee works, selected from an approved list by the Board's chairperson; one of the Boards has as a member an employee-relations counselor while the other has an equivalent called a human resources department representative, and this member serves as chairperson of the Board; finally company M has a member from the requesting employee's department, while company N more specifically has "an elected Employee Representative from the requesting employee's department."

A decision of a Board is final and is reported in writing to the company's vice president. Company M stipulates a maximum of 30 days within which a Board will meet after the date it was requested. In both companies a majority decision of two of a Board's three members is "considered unanimous."

The "Boards of Review" in the two companies have the following identical authority:

Reinstate employees who have been unjustly terminated or suspended, and authorize back pay if necessary;

Modify or reduce disciplinary action, or uphold the action of the disciplining department;

Recommend wage adjustments within the limits of the wage and salary program;

Recommend department transfers;

Recommend a change in company policy or procedure;

Recommend corrective action when a company policy or procedure was not followed; and

Recommend investigation of any alleged practice which may be detrimental to the company.

The personnel department of company M prepares a bulletin board notice of the Board of Review's decision. The personnel department of Company N has that same responsibility and, in addition, obtains on the notice the signature of the top executive and has the following responsibilities:

Assures that the Board's decision and recommendations are properly carried out and without discrimination towards the employee or witnesses; and

Arranges payment for the elected Employee Representative if off duty when the hearing is held. The elected Representative will be paid a minimum of four hours if the Board is held off his or her shift. Such time will be considered as time worked in computing overtime.

In both companies, a nonemployee may not be a witness unless the Board makes an exception, for example in the case of a doctor's testimony.

Both companies do not tolerate reprisal against a person because of participation in a Board of Review. The policy of company N is stated in the greater detail:

If the employee, a witness or a member of the Board of Review is discharged within 90 days following a Board of Review, the terminating supervisor must report and substantiate such action to this top department management level and to the Director, Human Resources. If the reasons for the discharge appear to have violated our philosophy of fair treatment to employees, an investigation by Human Resources will be conducted and corrective action taken as necessary.

The employee-relations manual of company N is considerably more detailed than that of company M, containing the following exclusive provisions:

Witnesses called by Management will receive payment for the time spent at the Board of Review hearing. An employee's witnesses must testify on a voluntary basis only and do not receive payment . . .

Presentation of the Department's position shall be made only by that level of supervision directly involved in the action resulting in the Board of Review request, unless other managerial levels are requested to testify by the Board of Review.

No member of Management: Director, Assistant General Manager level or above, shall volunteer to appear as a witness at a Board of Review.

Supervisors may request a Board of Review under the same conditions required of nonsupervisory employees. The supervisor selects three supervisors of equal level, one of whom will be appointed by the Vice President or Assistant General Manager over the supervisor's department to serve in place of the elected Employee Representative.

When a Department Manager requests a Board of Review, the Board shall be comprised of the Director of Human Resources, a Vice President or Assistant General Manager without jurisdiction over the requesting Manager, and a representative appointed by the Senior Vice President from three nominees specified by the requesting manager.

Both the employee and the manager involved must represent themselves before the Board. No attorney or outside spokesman is permitted.

Analysis of companies L, M, and N. What is here called company L is unusual in that it is not, like the two others, an individual hotel; it is a regional office of the hotel chain and the internal tribunal, called a Complaint Review Board, is at that regional level for that particular region, complete with a telephone hotline number so that employees can quickly appeal to the Board.

The next thing to be noticed is that, although companies M and N are members of the same hotel chain, they have their own individual employee-relations manuals, which, although based on a single source, differ in various details, one of which is that, while company M has an employee-relations department, the equivalent department in company N is called human resources. A peculiar feature, common to both companies, is that a majority decision by a company's three-member Board of Review is "considered unanimous," a phrase that the two companies obviously copied from a single source without scrutinizing its appropriateness.

These are companies in which, while providing for a peer employee of the appealing employee to sit on the Board, the Board's majority membership is from the ranks of management. As is the case with some other companies which are being reviewed herein, company M raises the issue of "Justice delayed is justice denied" by providing a maximum of 30 days within which to hold a Board hearing.

The space provided in the employee-relations manuals of companies M and N regarding their Board of Review is exceptionally lengthy and detailed in contrast with most such manuals. They are quoted extensively above to emphasize the fact, which these two companies exemplify, that in practice, as these two companies have endeavored to anticipate, the establishment and operation of a company's internal tribunal can be a much more complex situation than the author of a company's employee-relations manual may imagine, especially if he or she has not had personal experience with any internal tribunal. It is noteworthy that the manual of company N, which is the more complex of the two manuals, concludes with this cautionary statement: "Inasmuch as no policy can anticipate every question or every eventuality, the Board is empowered to make decisions which are not contrary to this written policy or which are not specifically proscribed by this policy."

Additional evidence of the desire of the managements of companies M and N or at least of the authors of their employee-relations manuals, to be exhaustive in anticipating as many problems as possible, is the fact, of which company N is the better example, that, while most companies content themselves in their employee-relations manuals with stating that there is to be no discrimination against anyone participating in an internal tribunal, these two companies establish an actual procedure for detecting such discrimination, stipulating that an investigation must be made of any participant in a Board of Review, including a Board member, who is discharged from the company within 90 days of a Board's decision. This is the critical differences between merely having a policy and actually stipulating a procedure for its implementation.

Unlike some companies that keep their grievance decisions confidential, these two companies post the decisions on bulletin boards. In what appears to be a discriminatory policy, in company N management's witnesses are paid for their time in a Board hearing, whereas the appealing employee's witnesses do not receive payment, although all witnesses are employees except in such cases as a doctor's testimony.

A feature worth noting in company N is that not only nonsupervisory employees but also supervisory employees and even management personnel up to the level of a department manager may submit their grievances to a Board of Review.

Company O

Although this is a plant of 8,000 employees in a company totalling 80,000 employees, the plant's employee-relations manual only very briefly outlines the plant's internal tribunal, called an Ad-Hoc Committee.

The members of the Committee are a peer chosen by the appealing employee, a member of the employee-relations staff, a supervisor or higher level manager from a "related department," and a peer of the appealing employee chosen by the three previously mentioned members, and with a fifth member who is the manager either of the employee-relations staff or the human resources staff, with this member having a vote only in the event of a tie. A quorum of the Committee consists of three of the four voting members.

An appeal to the Committee must be made within 30 days of the event which caused the grievance, the Committee will convene within 7 days of its being invoked, and it will render its decision within 10 days after the completion of its investigation. The decision is final.

Employees serving on the Committee will not suffer a loss of wages.

Analysis of company O. This company's briefly written procedure for appeal to an internal tribunal contrasts sharply with the voluminous details in the procedures of companies M and N, especially the latter.

A maximum of 47 days is allocated for the Ad-Hoc Committee to be convened and render its decision. Even if the appealing employee is willing to wait the 30 days allotted to initiate an appeal, it is questionable that it is in the best interests of the company to permit a grievance to smolder that long.

A peculiar feature of this company is that its internal tribunal has a "quorum" provision whereby three of the four voting members suffice to hear the case and render a decision. This provision enables the chairperson of the tribunal to determine, based on his or her prerogative of setting the date of the hearing while knowing that a member of the tribunal must be absent, whether the quorum of three voting members will consist of two management members or two peers of the appealing employee, obviously a matter of major importance to that employee.

Company P

This company's internal tribunal, called a Peer Review Panel, is available only to a salaried production employee whose grievance is one of being discharged, and who has been employed 90 days or more.

The company's manual states: "Confidentiality is of utmost importance. All discussions, meetings and correspondence related to these procedures will remain confidential."

Employees who desire to volunteer as members of the Peer Review Panel must complete six hours of training, "after careful thought and attention to the important responsibilities." The training takes place after working hours.

The discharged employee randomly draws four names among peer employees from the list of trained panelists, and then selects one name to be discarded. Next, the employee draws three names of management personnel from the list, and selects one to be discarded. The five remaining names constitute the Panel, with the personnel manager moderating it. The decision is determined by a majority of the five members, and is final.

The company's manual states: "Most other companies do not provide for such an extensive participatory procedure as peer review."

Analysis of company P. Although this company's internal tribunal is called a Peer Review Panel, it is not one in the true sense because only three of the five members are the appealing employee's peers, the two others being management personnel, and, if one of the peers votes with the two management personnel, that majority decision may not be called a decision by the employee's peers. Strictly speaking, the title of Peer Review Panel would be proper only if all five members of the Panel were the appealing employee's peers. And therefore, strictly speaking, this company should include itself in the "most other companies" which, as its manual states, "do not provide for such an extensive participatory procedure as peer review."

This company should be complimented on its requirement that persons serving on the Peer Review Panel receive six hours of training. It was observed regarding some companies previously reviewed herein that they permit an employee to be summoned without training, and even with only an hour's advance notice, to serve on an internal tribunal.

Company Q

The company is actually a plant of 300 employees, to which the following procedure applies, in a company totalling 30,000.

This company's internal tribunal is called a Membership Rights Committee (the company calls its employees "members"). The Committee is composed of two managers and three employees. One of the managers is the vice president, who serves as chairperson and, for each appeal case, selects at random a department manager as the second management representative. The three employees on the Committee are selected by the appealing employee at random, excluding employees from his or her department. No employee will serve twice on the Committee until all employees have had an opportunity to serve once. The employee-relations department monitors the functioning of the Committee, and a member of that department is assigned to assist the employee in preparing his or her appeal.

The Committee's decision is by secret ballot "to permit each Board member the opportunity to express their true feelings regarding this issue without any negative repercussions." A member may not abstain from voting, and a majority rules.

In cases involving dishonesty or offenses resulting in discharge, the Committee determines innocence or guilt. In all other cases, it upholds or reverses the original management decision. The Committee does not have authority to adjust any penalty that had been imposed.

Analysis of company Q. It is not unusual, as in this example, for a small subdivision of a large company to have its own special grievance procedure, undoubtedly a reflection of a policy of decentralization in large companies.

The notable features of this company are that voting in the internal tribunal is by secret ballot to protect the tribunal members from "negative repercussions," a majority of the tribunal's members are the appealing employee's "peers," and the tribunal may not adjust any penalty imposed by the original management decision, although some companies examined above were seen to permit an internal tribunal to reduce an imposed penalty but not to increase it.

Company R

This company is exceptional in having not one but two internal tribunals, a Board of Review followed by an Appeals Board. Air transportation is a major element in the company's business, and the grievance resolution procedure is designed to provide very careful handling of the grievances of flight personnel, which can involve highly technical matters. The employee-relations manual states:

Attorneys or other agents will not be permitted to appear on behalf of the Company or otherwise represent employees or ex-employees.... Attorneys or other such representatives shall be directed to contact the Legal Department in connection with such matters. No third party shall be permitted to participate in any manner.

Within seven days of the occurrence of the situation that generated an employee's grievance, he or she may request a Board of Review, but only the senior vice president of the employee's division may make the decision whether to convene the Board of Review, which he must do within seven days. Before the vice president grants a Board of Review he must consult the legal department regarding the company's possible liability, for example, in the case of a grievance involving the documentation of required professional flight licenses or certifications.

A Board of Review consists of a nonvoting chairperson, a nonvoting representative of the personnel department, and five voting members. Relatives and persons who could personally gain from a decision of the Board may not serve on it.

The division's senior vice president appoints a chairperson who has no supervisory relationship, directly or indirectly, with the complainant. The chairperson must hold a valid applicable FAA license if the complainant holds one and the exercise of its privileges is involved in the grievance.

The complainant selects three potential voting members from among coworkers of equivalent job title or higher grade within the work area or division, and the chairperson selects three of these nominees to serve on the Board of Review. The chairperson then selects four names, with the complainant designating two of them to serve on the Board.

When the senior vice president is deciding whether to convene a Board of Review he or she has three options: uphold the decision made in the case by management, overturn that decision, or initiate a Board of Review. From the date on which the vice president makes a decision, a Board will have a maximum of 30 days in which to perform its investigation and, beyond that, a period of 10 calendar days in which to render its decision in writing, signed by each member of the Board. Apart from the decision regarding the grievance, the Board may recommend "relief action" to the senior vice president of the division.

The senior vice president of the division will generally initiate a Board of Review if:

There is a substantial question as to the fairness and/or accuracy in management's handling of the grievance.

The latter concerns substantial loss of pay, promotion opportunity, or termination in cases in which there is a substantial disagreement regarding facts.

Disciplinary action could result in loss of status as an FAA-licensed employee.

The vice president may deny the complainant's request if: In the case of a non-FAA-licensed employee, there is no question of fact as established by corroborating sources or by the complainant.

In the case of FAA-licensed employees, the complainant has admitted blatant, willful, and intentional violation of corporate policies or federal statutes of such a severe nature as to subject the company to loss of its flight-operating certificates or damage claims for negligence in protecting the public safety had the disciplinary action against the complainant not been taken.

In the case of senior management personnel or officers, the disciplinary action resulted from willful and deliberate violations of leadership principles, management responsibilities, or the special trust and confidence accorded such personnel.

The role of the representative of the personnel department is that of an observer and a consultant on personnel policy.

The complainant is given the privilege of an opening statement, a rebuttal, and a closing statement, and may call witnesses, whose names are to be submitted to the chairperson five working days prior to the convening of the Board of Review.

Management is represented during a Board of Review by the complainant's immediate manager or, if not able to attend, by the manager's superior.

All of the five voting members of the Board must vote, which is done by secret ballot with the majority ruling. "Confidentiality of these hearings is of utmost importance. The Board should discuss the case only among its members and should not discuss it beyond the confines of the meeting room."

All expenses of the Board, including transportation, meals, and lodging, are paid by the complainant's department.

The decision of the Board of Review is final, except that an appeal may be made from it to the Appeals Board, within seven calendar days of the Board of Review's decision, and the decision of the Board of Review remains final if not overturned within seven calendar days after the Appeals Board receives the case.

If the senior vice president of the complainant's division refused the latter's request for a Board of Review, the complainant may request that the grievance be heard by the Appeals Board, which will do so within 14 calendar days of receiving the request. The Appeals Board consists of the CEO, the COO, and the senior vice president of personnel, except that, if the complainant is a member of the personnel division, the senior vice president of personnel will not participate and the CEO will designate another senior vice president of the company as a substitute.

When an Appeals Board receives a case in the situation in which the complainant's request for a Board of Review was rejected by the division's senior vice president and the complainant thereupon invoked the Appeals Board, the latter Board has the option of hearing the case or of requiring it be heard by a Board of Review, and in this case its chairperson is appointed by the Appeals Board instead of by the senior vice president of the complainant's division.

Analysis of company R. A recapitulation of the involved appeal procedure of this company is appropriate as a clarification, as follows: If the employee is not satisfied with the decision of management regarding a grievance, he or she may request the senior vice president of his or her division to convene a Board of Review; if the employee is not satisfied with that Board's decision or if the vice president refused to convene that Board, the employee may take his or her case to the Appeals Board, which has the option of convening a Board of Review or hearing the case itself; and finally, if the Appeal Board convenes a Board of Review instead of hearing the case itself, the employee may appeal from the decision of the Board of Review to the Appeals Board.

This company is a special case, inasmuch as its objective is not merely the simple one of providing an internal tribunal for the settlement of employees' grievances, but rather the more complicated objective of conforming with the need to provide exceptionally cautious treatment to those employees who hold FAA flight licenses, a situation in which not only internal company policies in the area of employee relations but also the regulations of the FAA and related federal laws must be taken into consideration. The company's desire to be extremely cautious in this matter is evidenced by the presence on the Appeals Board, a situation not seen in the other companies reviewed herein, of top management: the chief operations officer (COO), the senior vice president of personnel, and, most surprising of all, the chief executive officer (CEO), a case of a company attacking the problem of employee grievances with its "heavy artillery." Stated differently, it is a case of top management deeming a problem to be too important for the authority to make decisions regarding it to be delegated to middle management.

However, top management sensibly reserves its heavy artillery for situations of last resort. That is, when an employee appeals to it in its form as the Appeals Board, without first having asked for a Board of Review, it reserves the right, in preference to hearing the appeal itself, of referring the case to the Board of Review, which is a peer group of the employee's fellow employees, top management's hope being that the matter can be disposed of at that lower level.

The fact should be stressed that the five voting members of the Board of

Review are the complainant's fellow employees "of equivalent job title or higher grade within the work area and/or division," two selected by the complainant from a list of four proposed by the Board's chairperson and three selected by the chairperson from a list of six proposed by the complainant. This may be described as "democracy at work," as fair and reasonable as the jury system in courts of law.

The popular expectation undoubtedly is that the Board of Review, consisting of the complainant's fellow employees, will render a decision more favorable to the complainant than will the Appeals Board, consisting of top management people who may become irritable when a grievance develops in their company. However, there is evidence that that popular expectation is a myth. Early in this chapter reference was made to the finding of this writer's friend that at least some enlisted men in the Army Air Force in World War II would rather be tried by a courts-martial board consisting of officers than of enlisted men. And in this company top management says, in effect, to its employees: When you think that your fellow employees in the Board of Review have treated you too severely, you may appeal to us in our capacity as an Appeals Board.

This company's Board of Review, with members who are the complainant's peers, essentially resembles the internal tribunals of the companies being reviewed herein, whereas the Appeals Board, which has authority to overrule the Board of Review, is automatically constituted, its members being the company's three top management officials. While it would be wrong, in the absence of evidence, to suggest that those three officials lack impartial integrity, nevertheless it is obvious that their Appeals Board represents management and therefore does not conform with the definition of a tribunal.

A feature of the Board of Review which deserves comment is its legalistic procedural structure. Companies' internal tribunals are generally informal activities in which the emphasis is on obtaining and interpreting facts, whereas in this Board of Review procedure is paramount, with the complainant being accorded what the employee-relations manual classifies as the privilege of presenting an opening statement, a rebuttal of management's statement, and a closing statement, and also the calling of witnesses. It is questionable whether this should be classified as a privilege rather than as a right. And it is also questionable whether the average employee, with the services of an attorney not being permitted in a Board of Review, is adequately competent to defend his or her case when strapped in the mental straightjacket of having to think within the constraints of an opening statement, rebuttal, and closing statement.

Company S

In order for an employee to appeal the decision of management regarding a grievance, he or she must have been employed for at least three months. Equal employment opportunity (EEO) grievances are handled separately from the appeal process outlined herein. "Performance reviews may be appealed, but are difficult to review, because the immediate supervisor is in the best position to evaluate an individual's performance. The Appeal Board may vote to inform the employee that it is in no position to evaluate performance and to hear the appeal further."

The Appeal Board may uphold or reduce the discipline that the employee is appealing, but not increase it. A majority vote rules.

The company's application of its policies is appealable, but the policies themselves are not. Within seven working days after management's decision regarding the grievance, the employee may submit to the employee relations manager a request for review by the Appeal Board, and within three working days the employee-relations manager determines whether the employee is appealing a policy itself rather than its application, and if not, forwards the case to the Appeal Board, which meets within ten working days thereafter, and renders its decision within seven working days of the hearing.

The employee-relations manager prepares a summary of the hearing and its decision, with copies forwarded to the employee, his or her supervisor, and the department manager, but a copy is not placed in the employee's personnel file.

The Appeal Board consists of the personnel manager, who serves as chairperson, the manager of the appealing employee's department, two employees who are selected by the appealing employee and who agree to serve, and a third employee who is selected unanimously by the four other members of the Board and who is not from the appealing employee's department.

Analysis of company S. It is noteworthy that equal employment opportunity (EEO) grievances are handled separately from this company's appeal process.

The provision that an employee may appeal the application of company policy, but not the policy itself, is standard practice in most if not all companies, as is the requirement that the Appeal Board may change, but not increase, discipline which was imposed on the employee.

The feature of a majority of the Appeal Board being the peers of the complainant is typical of a substantial percentage of such boards.

In general, this small company's appeal procedure, briefly stated though it is, exhibits the basic feature of many such procedures reviewed herein.

Company T

"Company policy is not appealable, but the application of the policy is."

"An employee cannot be given additional discipline through the appeal procedure."

"An employee shall be expected to comply with the decision, orders, circumstances and situations until the complaint, problem or disagreement is resolved or finalized by management or through the appeal process."

An Appeal Board is established for each individual employee request, except that an existing Board may be used if both parties agree to it. A majority of the Board rules.

The complainant may select one person, either an hourly employee or a member of management, to assist in the preparation of his or her presentation to the Board, but this person may not be present during the Board's hearings unless authorized by the plant manager in unusual circumstances.

The request for an Appeal Board must be made within five days of management's decision regarding the grievance, and the Board must hold its hearing within five days after the complainant's request for it.

Two of the five members of the Board are selected by management and two by the complainant, and these four members select the fifth member on the day of the hearing. The complainant's selectees and the fifth member may be the complainant's friends, but not his relatives. Selectees may decline to serve on the Board. The fifth member is selected by drawing a name at random from a group of names submitted by one of the management members of the Board, names continuing to be drawn until one is found who does not refuse to serve, whereupon the hearing begins immediately. One of management's selectees serves as chairperson. Voting is by a raising of hands. All members of the Board and the complainant sign the decision of the Board, the signatures of the members not indicating their agreement or disagreement with the decision "but rather that the report accurately reflects the proceedings."

After the Board concludes its work, its members should answer the following questions: "Did you reach your conclusion of your own free choice?" "Do you think the appeal process is fair?" "If you felt an injustice were done to you would you use the appeal process to resolve it?"

Analysis of company T. This is an extremely small company, with 600 employees. The reader may be conscious of the interesting circumstance that some of the phraseology in this company's employee-relations manual is taken verbatim from the manual of company I reviewed in this chapter, although the two companies are widely separated geographically and in different industries. Despite the verbatim feature, however, this company's appeal process differs in various respects from that of company I.

An unusual requirement, not found in the other appeal procedures reviewed herein, is that the appealing employee must comply with management's decision in his or her case while that decision is being appealed.

At this point in this review of internal tribunals serving as appeal boards, it is possible to note that an area of major diversity in the appeal processes of the companies being reviewed is the manner of selection of board members.

A unique feature of this company is the questionnaire submitted to the Board members after they complete their work. It is not that evident simple yes/no answers to the questions are informative for management, although thoughtful comments can be helpful.

Company U

This company defines a grievance as "an employee allegation of an improper or incorrect interpretation or application of the Administrative Manual or Employee Handbook."

The internal tribunal is called a Grievance Committee, which is convened within four days of the employee's appeal to it. The manager of human resources is the chairperson of the Committee and the department head is a member. A third member is a manager or supervisor selected by the complainant from outside the chain of supervision concerned with the grievance. Four additional members are "peer group" fellow employees of the complainant, selected at random from his or her shift one work day before the Committee is schedule to meet, with exclusion of an employee who has an "obvious self-interest" in the grievance. The Committee will hear the case during the complainant's shift.

"As the use of a committee has been adopted to benefit employees, employees are expected to serve on the committee when determined by random selection."

The complainant has the option of limiting the membership of the Grievance Committee to his or her department head and the manager of human resources.

"The committee meeting is designed to be informal." The decision is by secret ballot, with a majority ruling, within two working days of the hearing.

If the Committee cannot reach a majority decision, the case is referred to the executive vice president or president, who will hear the testimony of the parties and witnesses and render a decision within four work days after receiving the case.

"Operational policies and management decisions that are not part of the established policy or procedure are not subject to the grievance procedure. Items such as policy establishment, size and direction of the workforce, product line, cafeteria, or any other matter beyond the area of interpretation of an existing policy are not grievable." Provision is made for employees to submit nongrievable matters to management through what the company calls its "Industrial Relations Council."

Analysis of company U. Emphasis should be placed on this company's definition of an employee's grievance because, although it conforms with the general concept extant in business and industry, it is unusual in being carefully spelled out in what may be described as classic diction: "an employee allegation of an improper or incorrect interpretation or application of the Administrative Manual or Employee Handbook." However, there is a deficiency in this otherwise excellent definition, namely, the absence of the phrase "by management in its treatment of the employee" following the word "application." It does not suffice to say that that phrase is implied. The entire definition is implied generally in business and industry, and the requirement, in the interest of precision, is to reduce it to a universally accepted written form. Universally, employees are saying to management: "You wrote the rules of your relations with us, we accepted them by accepting employment with you, and if you violate them we have a legitimate grievance."

There is something to be said in favor of this company's calling its internal tribunal a Grievance Committee rather than the more common term of Appeal Board. Appeal of what from what? Titles should be self-explanatory, but at the same time brief. Probably a generally useful title would be Grievance Appeal Board, although it has not been encountered in the research.

This company is another example of the widespread, but certainly not universal, policy of management in business and industry of establishing a "democratic" procedure of the resolution of employees' grievances by means of "peer group" representation in the voting members of an internal tribunal, namely, providing for a majority of those members to be the grievant's fellow employees selected by him or her, even though it is common practice for management to have some voice in the selection. However, this research is finding that true or pure peer group representation, that is, an internal tribunal in which all of the voting members are the grievant's fellow employees, is a rarity.

A feature not seen in the employee-relations manuals of the companies previously reviewed is the stated business philosophy of this company that employees have an obligation to serve on the Grievance Committee because it was established "to benefit employees." Other companies, looking at the situation from a different perspective, stress their preference that such service be voluntary. This company is emphasizing employees' duty, while other companies emphasize their freedom to do as they please. It is my opinion that duty transcends freedom.

This is the only grievance procedure encountered thus far in this research in which the employee has the option of waiving the presence of his "peer group" fellow employees in the internal tribunal and limiting its members to the two management representatives, a reminder of the previous discussion regarding some Army Air Force enlisted men preferring to have officers instead of their peers as members of courts-martial boards. In this company management appears to be saying to its employees: You may have the majority of the members of the Grievance Committee be your fellow employees, but if you dislike placing your destiny in their hands, we will not insist upon it. This company is also unique in providing that, if a majority decision of the Grievance Committee cannot be obtained, the grievance will be placed for decision before the executive vice president or president, who will examine the parties' testimony and witnesses.

The meeting of the Grievance Committee "is designed to be informal." This is quoted as contrast with the arrangement in the last company reviewed above for the complainant to make an opening statement, a rebuttal, and a closing statement, a system taken from courts of law.

Company V

In this company a grievance is defined as "anything at work which you feel is unjust, wrong, or unfair. When an employee takes the problem to the supervisor to get it solved, it becomes a grievance."

The company's internal tribunal is called an Arbitration Panel. Its members are the industrial relations manager, who is the only permanent member, a person appointed by the division manager, and three of the complainant's "peer group" employees, four of whom he or she selects at random from an approved list, after discarding one of the names.

That brief description of the Arbitration Panel is expanded in one of the company's documents, a talk given by the vice president of employee relations:

We established a system of Peer Review.... Now what is Peer Review? An arbitration panel, made up of three employees and two managers, and this panel has final authority to reverse management's decisions in a number of grievance areas, including discipline and discharge cases.

All employee panel members are volunteers, who take a sixteen-hour training session, on their own time, where they learn about employment law, consistency, fair decision making and listening skills.

So, what are we doing here?... What we're really doing is that we're willing to give up some authority in order to gain what?... What we're trying to do here is gain credibility and an improved perception of fairness on the part of all employees about how people are treated in our company.

We had to pay a price for that. The price we had to pay was the willingness to be reversed in some individual cases where we thought we were right.

Now interestingly enough, in the first cases with the pilot program, we've found the employee-members of the panels to support management's position more stridently than the management-members of the panels.

And if reversal does occur, there's another interesting phenomenon: when management has been reversed, it was because additional facts came out in the investigation, and management in general has agreed with the panel's decision to reverse. Now that's better than we expected.

The Arbitration Panel has authority to review such issues as discipline, promotion, discrimination, overtime assignment, application of company policies and procedures, improper actions of management (such as favoritism, abusive language, and inconsistency), and unsafe working conditions. Other issues may be submitted to the Panel if the industrial relations manager, who is the permanent member of the Panel, determines that they are within the

Panel's authority. In special cases requiring technical knowledge of a situation involving a grievance, the industrial relations manager may authorize the selection of panel members from a particular division or job classification.

The decision of the Panel is by majority vote, and is final. A written decision is provided the employee within five days. Information presented to the Panel, and statements and votes of its members, must be kept in the strictest confidence.

The following are a few of the numerous items covered in the comprehensive training sessions in which volunteer employees qualify to serve as members of an Arbitration Panel:

Always ask: Could, in any way, management's decision regarding the grievance be viewed as arbitrary, unfair, or discriminatory?
Ethics: The standards of conduct and moral judgment...
Legal considerations: Can you ask the grievant if he ever used drugs?...
Case studies of fictitious grievance cases.
Precedents: Actions by the Panel should be consistent with similar cases.

A selected Panel member may disqualify him or herself from serving on the pending case or be disqualified by the industrial relations manager because of a personal interest in the case.

If the grievance has not been resolved when it has reached the level of the division manager, at this point the grievant has the option of appealing to a higher level of management or of invoking an Arbitration Panel.

Analysis of Company V. This is a small company with 2,000 employees. It is obvious that top management has gone all out, definitely so in comparison with most of the companies reviewed herein, in its project to design an internal tribunal capable of maximum efficiency. The standard for measurement of that efficiency was stated in the talk by the vice president of employee relations: "What we're trying to do here is gain credibility and an improved perception of fairness on the part of all employees about how people are treated in our company."

An interesting feature of the project, which was not stated above, is the initial establishment of the Arbitration Panel project on a "pilot plant" basis so that the company could benefit by learning while doing, with active search for opportunities for refinement of the project over time.

As was the case with the previous company reviewed, the company's definition of a grievance is subject to improvement. It is inexact to state that initially an employee has a "problem" but that it becomes a "grievance" when taken to the supervisor. Formally, of course, that is true from the company's viewpoint, but the more important viewpoint—more important because of its impact on employees' morale—is that of the disturbed employee, who cannot discern the subtle distinction, if any, between a problem and a grievance, and who is a potentially serious monkeywrench in the gears of the company as long as that discontent is kept bottled up inside him or her. If there is any unanimity in the employee-relations manuals being here reviewed, it is the pleading of management that employees promptly and calmly refer to supervision their causes of discontent with confidence that their act of coming forward will not result in any retribution.

The company's title for its internal tribunal, Arbitration Panel, may be criticized as a deviation from the commonly accepted definition of arbitration as a decision imposed upon two contending parties, with their permission, by an impartial third party external to them. The two management members and three peer group members of this company's internal tribunal lack the critical attribute of externality, and it is questionable whether they can achieve the fullness of impartiality characteristic of a professional arbitrator. The internal tribunals' title previously recommended is Grievance Appeal Board.

As has been seen to be characteristic of other companies reviewed herein, this company classifies its internal tribunal as peer review, defined as "made up of three employees and two managers." The good-intentioned but obviously strained definition in many employee-relations manuals of peer review as consisting of a majority of an internal tribunal's members being the complaining employee's peers despite the fact that the minority members are management personnel is amusing. The point is that, in the customary panel of five voting members, if one of the employee's three peers votes with the two management members, the decision cannot properly be called a peer review even if the decision is in favor of the employee. The predilection of employee-relations departments for the phrase "peer review" is undoubtedly a corollary of their emphasis on the desideratum of a democratic spirit in their companies, certainly a very laudable objective.

The vice president of employee relations in this company is to be commended for his statement, in his quoted talk, outlining the philosophy underlying the establishment of the company's Arbitration Panel. It is undoubtedly the philosophy motivating all companies that provide internal tribunals to which grievants can appeal their cases after management has rendered its decisions. The vice president stated that, in order to achieve "an improved perception of fairness on the part of all employees about how people are treated in our company," the company "had to pay a price for that," and that price is "the willingness to be reversed in some individual cases where we thought we were right."

Two paragraphs in the vice president's talk deserve to be repeated here verbatim, partly because they are contrary to popular expectations and partly because they are encouraging to companies which are considering installing internal tribunals:

Now interestingly enough, in the first cases with the pilot programs, we've found the employee-members of the panels to support management's position more stridently than the management-members of the panels.

And if a reversal does occur, there's another interesting phenomenon: when management has been reversed, it was because additional facts came out in the investigation, and management in general has agreed with the panel's decision to reverse. Now that's better than we expected.

The first of these two paragraphs is additional evidence supporting the previously discussed finding that some Army Air Force enlisted men in World War II preferred the members of courts-martial boards to be officers rather than their peer group of enlisted men.

The most important contribution that this company is making, by example, to the growing concept of internal tribunals for the final settlement of employees' grievances is its emphasis on the need for intensive training for the volunteer members of the Arbitration Panels. The program of training installed in this company is by far the most comprehensive of those examined. It exhibits a high degree of professionalism in the area of employee relations by its recognition of the fact that integrity and impartiality are the basic, but not the only, attributes desirable in persons who sit in judgment over their fellow employees.

There is an apparent conflict between the policy of confidentiality in an Arbitration Panel and the requirement on the other hand that actions by the Panel should be consistent with similar cases. Confidentiality prevents knowledge regarding a Panel from being known by subsequent Panels, unless the only permanent member, the industrial relations manager, reveals the information. It would become his or her function to implement the policy of being "consistent with similar cases." The industrial relations manager would, in effect, have to present previous cases as precedents and, moreover, present them not only as precedents in the sense of previous decisions deserving to be given due consideration but actually as previous decisions which should replace the independent judgment of members of subsequent Panels in order to achieve the objective of consistency. It may not be predicated that the decision in the first of a series of similar cases has privileged status, and it may not be predicated that consistency has priority over justice independently meted out in individual cases. Finally, the management policy that "Actions by the Panel should be consistent with similar cases" in beyond the capability of management to enforce.

Company W

This company's Board of Review, as described in the employee-relations manual, is copied, substantially verbatim but in much briefer form, from the Board of Review procedure of the three hotel-chain companies which were reviewed above as a unit, the probable explanation being that this company is a hotel. One of the items copied verbatim is the peculiar one that the binding majority vote of the members of the Board is "considered unanimous."

Analysis of Company W. In view of what is stated above, an analysis of this company would be repetitious. However, a statement in its employee-relations manual which is not in the manual of the hotel chain should be noted:

The Board of Review is an invaluable tool for both employee and supervisor. From the findings of Board hearings, recommendations are often made which assist the supervisor in performing his duties more effectively. In addition, the supervisor who views it in a positive manner can better promote the values and benefits of the Board of Review to his employees.

That subject is controversial. As has been seen, some companies desire the decisions, and also recommendations for changes in company policy and procedure, to be made public knowledge within the company, whereas other companies consider confidentiality to be, as one company states, "of utmost importance." Confidentiality caters to the complainant, while openness of information caters to the company's desire to improve itself. The two viewpoints are incompatible. The answer is that the potential benefit of open information to the company overrides the potential harm to the employee—and, anyhow, it is probably no easier to prevent the "leaking" of information in a company than it is in government offices in Washington, D.C.

INTEGRATIVE ANALYSIS

I will resist the temptation, which is generated by the knowledge accumulated in this chapter, to draft the format of an ideal grievance appeal board, which is my recommended title for the internal tribunals described herein.

The recommended title has the virtue of describing the function of the internal tribunal, namely, an appeal board concerned with employees' grievances. It is not always easy for a newcomer in a company, and even an employee with some seniority, to become familiar with, and clearly understand, all the terminology used in a company, including such phrases encountered in this review regarding internal tribunals as employee problem solving group, management appeals committee, roundtables, appeals board, appeal board, board of review, right of review board, advisory committee, ad-hoc committee, peer review panel, membership rights committee, grievance committee, arbitration panel, and even, in one company, a board of review which is followed by an appeals board.

Two things are evident from a glance at that list. First, it is obvious that there is no collusion in violation of the antitrust laws in companies' selections of titles for their internal tribunals. And second, standardization is apparently not a virtue in this matter. One businessman at a convention has to say to another: "Our Employee Problem Solving Group, which, by the way, is the same thing as your Ad-Hoc Committee...."

The advantage of self-descriptive titles is indicated by the following anecdote. Upon joining a division of the General Electric Company, a friend of mine was assigned the task of modernizing a complicated, multicopy paper form called a Works Order. Following the copies as they circulated through the division, he asked many persons, "What is a Works Order?" No one could tell him, although each person who handled a copy could explain his or her action regarding it. Upon completing his analysis, he said to top management: "The Works Order is an authorization to ship something, or to bill a customer for something, or both. Let's change the title to Shipping-Billing Authorization." Top management said, "Do it."

Now, then, why do I refuse to draft a recommended format of an ideal grievance appeal board procedure to be incorporated in companies' employee-relations manuals? In the first place, that would be standardization for standardization's sake, which is not a good motive because the business philosophies of companies in the area of employee relations are sufficiently different to require pertinent procedures to be tailored to an individual company. The most obvious example among the companies reviewed herein is the degree of control that top management maintains over the selection of the members of an internal tribunal; some companies are willing to let peer group selectees of the complaining employee have majority control in a tribunal, while other companies assign that control to management's selectees from the ranks of management personnel. Another example is that some companies want the deliberations and decisions of a tribunal to be kept strictly confidential, while others desire the information to be disseminated freely. A third example is the special case of the company whose roster includes flight personnel subject to FAA regulations, regarding which the members of the internal tribunal must be familiar. And some companies find the phrase peer review attractive in situations in which only the majority of the members of an internal tribunal are the complainant's peers, whereas true peer review requires that all the members be his or her peers, inasmuch as one of the three peers voting with two management personnel to provide a majority vote certainly is not peer review. Finally, some large companies prefer to avoid standardization among their decentralized divisions, favoring instead maximum local autonomy and initiative, as is indicated by the following memo to this writer from the manager, Corporate Human Resources Practices, of one such company:

(This) is a very decentralized company and thus has a variety of different Complaint and Grievance Procedures.... Incidentally, they all seem to work effectively, since (local) Human Resource Management has not seen the need to change or revise their procedures in the last six to seven years.

It is noteworthy that one of the divisions of that company has an internal tribunal, which is called a Right of Review Board, while others do not. Standardization for the sake of standardization is not a policy of this company.

The internal tribunal provides a forceful example in the area of employee relations of the difficulty of drafting the format of an ideal procedure, widely acceptable in business and industry, for the resolution of employees' grievances. Where pragmatism is the fundamental principle, the peculiar principle that there are no governing principles in human affairs, unanimity of thought and action is as impossible in the economic sphere as it is in the political sphere.

Is there a governing fundamental principle underlying the concept of companies' internal tribunals? Apparently not, if importance is assigned to the fact that, among the 78 companies or divisions of companies reviewed in this research, only 26, or one-third, have installed internal tribunals. But there is at least one of those 26, actually not a company but only a division of a company, which recognizes a governing fundamental principle. Its employee-relations manual informs an employee who has a grievance that "You have a right to be heard," and it is interesting that this division's internal tribunal is called a Right of Review Board. Human rights are based not on arbitrary pragmatic considerations but only on recognized fundamental principles. The point here is that, while it is an obvious fundamental principle that an employee who has a grievance has a right to be heard, it is not at all a settled principle, generally accepted, that that employee has a "right" to carry his or her grievance past the management decisions unfavorable to him or her into what this research calls an internal tribunal, staffed by the employee's peers and/or management personnel and empowered to reverse or modify the previously rendered management decisions in the matter.

However, to deny that employees have a "right" as a matter of principle to access to an internal tribunal does not close the subject of internal tribunals. There is a fundamental principle at work which keeps the subject very much alive, namely, the ethical obligations of management to do everything possible to achieve the imperative objective of a harmonious, peaceful environment for the growth and maintenance of justice in the relationship between management and its employees. If evidence develops in a company that the installation of an internal tribunal will achieve an improvement in employee relations, then that evidence assumes the status of a governing fundamental principle which transcends a management viewpoint of take it or leave it pragmatism.

The most important feature of a company's internal tribunal is its membership composition. Here again the matter of a governing fundamental principle is vital. Is there a principle dictating that the majority of the tribunal's members be the complainant's peers, defined as fellow employees of at least approximately equal level with him or her in the hierarchy of job responsibilities? There is certainly no such principle independently existing solely in the employee-relations corner of the world of economics; if such a principle operates in that corner, it does so only by extension, that is, by extrapolation, from the world of civil and criminal law's dictum that a defendent is to be judged by a jury of his peers. In law, that actually means only that a person is to be judged by a jury of his fellow citizens instead of one composed of government officials. A corporation president accused of embezzlement may be tried by a jury consisting of janitors and ditch diggers, although his peers are corporate presidents. The probability that the janitors and ditch diggers have more integrity and therefore are better able to render just decisions is beside the point.

No fundamental principle has been discerned in this research which dictates that judgment by one's peers must, or even should, be an intrinsic feature in the resolution of employees' grievances. At best, the use of what various companies call "peer review," but which is not true peer review because the internal tribunals include members who are management personnel instead of exclusively the complainant's peers, is dictated not by a mandating fundamental principle but only by the desire of management to be "democratic" in the hope thereby of enhancing the goodwill of employees toward their companies. That hope is, of course, very legitimate and should be encouraged.

The absence of a mandating fundamental principle is also evident in the general lack of uniformity among companies in the various details of the establishment and operation of internal tribunals. In one company a complainant may waive an appeal from middle management's decision to top management and, as an option, appeal immediately to the internal tribunal, whereas another company requires a top management decision prior to the tribunal being invoked. One company surveyed herein places majority control of a tribunal in the members selected from among management personnel. Some companies desire tribunal proceedings and decisions to be confidential, and others desire them to be published. One company, apparently more or less blindly copying the employee-relations manual of another verbatim, requires the majority vote of the tribunal's members to be "considered unanimous," whatever that may mean. Another company, clearly denying the concept of another company reviewed herein that complainants have a "right of review," grants discretion to its director of human resources to decide whether a particular complainant may have the internal tribunal consider his or her case. One company desires the proceedings of its tribunal to be "informal," while another requires the complainant to present his or her case in the stilted form of a law court, that is, as an opening statement, a rebuttal of management's testimony, and a closing statement. One company pays its management personnel, but not its employees, for time spent as tribunal witnesses. And the rules of companies differ regarding who, and to what extent, persons may assist a complainant in his or her case, although there is a generally excepted rule that such persons must be employed by the company and not be, for example, an outside attorney. That generally accepted rule is evidence that management, while very graciously offering its employees access to an internal tribunal, as it is described herein, for the resolution of grievances in one-third of the 78 companies surveyed, nevertheless reaches the point where it says "enough is enough" in its generosity, and closes its doors against invasion of a company by outside attorneys, who, as management very likely has good reason to fear, would be troublemakers, at least in the sense of converting the internal tribunal into a legal battleground in which management would have to mobilize its own attorneys for a counterattack. An employee should be able to see the wisdom of management's desire to keep a family squabble inside the family, and, if an employee feels that justice can be obtained only by the extreme action of retaining an attorney, and if the issue is commensurately important, the forum for that attorney should be a court of law and not the company's internal tribunal.

The previous lengthy paragraph is not presented as an argument against internal tribunals based on the wide lack of uniformity among companies in the details of their tribunals. On the contrary, it is merely an argument supporting my claim that I should not endeavor to draft the format of an ideal grievance appeal board, as I prefer to call an internal tribunal. Such an endeavor would serve no purpose other than to make a fetish out of uniformity. Many years ago, as the story is told, an American farmer was amazed to hear that in Denmark the emphasis on uniformity was so intense that, when pigs on a farm were assembled with their noses touching a wall, a string touching the tips of their tails would be a perfectly straight line. That would not improve the flavor of pork, and standardization only for the sake of standardization has no place in economics and least of all in the complex relationships between management and its employees.

There is diversity in the training provided to members of internal tribunals. Some companies provide no training at all, and, in fact, that appears to be the general rule, with only one of the companies surveyed having what could be called a professional program, consisting of 16 hours of intensive study. While it is true that jurors in courts of law are selected without any training, their deliberations are closely monitored by the judges, sometimes with very intensive "charges to the jurors" by judges to assure that they do their work properly. It is obviously with a similar purpose in mind that a number of companies stipulate that the manager of employee relations or someone with a corresponding title be a member, and usually also the chairperson, of the internal tribunal. In some cases that person is a voting member; in other cases does not vote, or votes only to break a tie.

There is also diversity in the composition of internal tribunals. At one extreme among the companies surveyed herein, one tribunal consists solely of the complainant's peers, and at the other extreme one tribunal is composed exclusively of high level management personnel. Between those extremes, the most common composition of internal tribunals is two management personnel, generally from middle management, who are usually permanent members, and three of the complainant's peers, who are selected to handle only his or her particular grievance.

There is variation in the manner of selecting the complainants peers, with wide acceptance among companies of the principle in courts of law that the contending parties should have some say in the selection of jurors. The manner of management's participation varies considerably among the companies surveyed, as does the freedom accorded complainants to designate peers of their own choice. There are so many variations in the companies surveyed, some rather complex, that it would be difficult to reduce them here to brief tabulated form.

If a formula can be designed from the companies surveyed, it will be substantially as follows: an internal tribunal consisting of five voting members, two of them selected by the complainant from a small list of peers which was selected by complainant at random or by management at random, and one of his or her peers selected by management from a small list of peers which complainant selected at random.

That formula is actually a description of one of the internal tribunals surveyed, and it is presented as most representative, in the sense of an "average," of the tribunals. Its complexity is typical of the caution exercised by management in granting some latitude, but not complete freedom, to a complainant in the selection of his or her peer members on a tribunal. It is also typical of the desire of companies to have not only peers of the complainant but also management personnel as tribunal members.

To complete that formula, there should be added a member of the employee-relations department, either as one of the two management voting members of the tribunal or as a nonvoting chairperson, for the purpose of assuring that the deliberations of the tribunal conform with its proper purpose and with pertinent company policies.

An important characteristic of internal tribunals is that their decisions are final, and binding on both the complainant and management. However, four exceptions are present in this survey: a company in which the employee, having appealed from a decision by middle management to the internal tribunal, may appeal from the tribunal's decision to the plant manager; and three companies in which the employee may appeal from the internal tribunal to outside arbitration.

Is service as a member of an internal tribunal a "duty" of nonsupervisory employees? Its purpose is to provide complainants, as is the case in courts of law, with a jury of one's peers, and it can be argued, at the level of philosophy, that such service is indeed a duty of employees in companies that have internal tribunals. However, management generally stipulates in employee-relations manuals that this service is voluntary, and only one of the companies surveyed argued forcefully in its manual that the service is a duty which should not be shirked by employees.

It is worth noting that some companies, probably reflecting the viewpoint of all companies but exceptional in incorporating the matter formally in their employee-relations manuals, insist that there shall be no recrimination by supervisory or managerial personnel against an employee who carried his or her grievance to an internal tribunal, or against anyone who served as a member of the tribunal or as a witness. An internal tribunal, like a court of law, is sacrosanct. In a few companies, if one of these persons is discharged within a stated period of time after the tribunal was held, a report must be made to the employee-relations department, which then must initiate an appropriate investigation.

Finally, some of the larger companies tailor the composition of their internal tribunals to fit more appropriately, in individual cases, the voting members to the type of complainant, such as nonsupervisory, supervisory, or managerial, but with preservation of the principle of some members being the peers of the complainant. An exception is the company in which, when the complainant is from the ranks of management, the members of the internal tribunal are the three top executives of the company.

CONCLUSION

There are two paramount questions a company must answer when it is drafting the Grievances section of its employee-relations manual.

1. Should provision be made for an internal tribunal to which an employee may appeal from management's decision regarding his or her grievance?
2. If so, how many voting members shall there be in the tribunal, what type of employee shall each member be, and what shall be the procedure for selection of that member?

A company can have two unrelated motives for installing an internal tribunal. One is its psychological value as a symbol of management's desire to be known as "democratic" in its relations with its employees, evidenced by the peer review feature common to the tribunals, and the other is a felt need for a means for double-checking management's decisions regarding employees' grievances as insurance against improper decisions. It is doubtful that management's confidence in the quality of its decisions is so dubious that there is a felt need for a means for double-checking them. The psychological motive is the more likely one, and it was best expressed by the previously quoted vice president of employee relations who wrote: "What we're trying to do here is gain credibility and an improved perception of fairness on the part of all employees about how people are treated in our company. . . . We had to pay a price for that. The price we had to pay was the willingness to be reversed in some individual cases where we thought we were right."

There is the justification for a company to install an internal tribunal based on "an improved perception of fairness on the part of all employees about how people are treated in our company." Among the various intangible aspects of a business firm, as military officers acknowledge regarding armies, the most important is the morale of employees.

The importance of morale is more evident to military officers than to business executives, because in the case of the former its absence is more quickly and more dramatically noticed, but business executives dare not ignore it. The bottom line, therefore, in this research is that, if a company has reason to believe that an internal tribunal will contribute meaningfully to employees' morale, serious consideration should be given to installing it. The size of a company is apparently not pertinent, as the companies observed in this research to have internal tribunals vary from 85 to 30,000 employees.

The remaining question concerns the form of the internal tribunal, and the method for the selection of its members. Its single indispensable feature, copied from the legal system, is that the tribunal is a jury of one's peers, that is, fellow employees of the complainant instead of management personnel. It is precisely this feature which provides "an improved perception of fairness on the part of all employees about how people are treated in our company." It is a popular practice among the companies that have internal tribunals to describe them as performing "peer review" of an employee's grievance.

This writer is disappointed that he has not found a single company which espouses peer review in the pure, perfect form implied by the legal system's phrase, "a jury of one's peers." On the contrary, in every internal tribunal surveyed in this research, there is at least one member who is taken from the ranks of management personnel. Even though it is the honest intention of top management that that person or persons vote his or their conscience without reflecting management's thinking, nevertheless the presence of at least one person taken from the ranks of management is a compromise in top management's acceptance of the legal principle of "a jury of one's peers." In other words, top management welcomes the opportunity to describe its internal tribunal as "peer review," but hedges itself by attaching a string to the situation by stipulating that at least one member of the tribunal be taken from the ranks of management. The closest approach to pure peer review in this survey is the company in which there are six voting members in the tribunal all selected from the ranks of employees, but with top management attaching a string in granting that a nonvoting member selected from the ranks of management has the authority to break a tie vote among the six members, pure peer review existing only if four of the six voting members agree in arriving at a decision.

The most common form of internal tribunal is one with an odd number of voting members, which avoids the problem of a tie vote, with three of the members being the complainant's peers and two being selected from management. It is obvious that this very common format cannot properly be described as peer review when one of the peers votes with two management members in achieving the decisive majority decision. Unlike the legal system, in which the decision of a jury must be unanimous, companies recognize the impracticability of requiring such a decision and accept a majority decision.

The method of selecting the peers and the management members of a tribunal differs considerably among companies, even among companies which have the most common arrangement of three peers and two management members. The prevailing principle is that, as in a court of law, both parties, namely, the complainant and management, share in the task of selecting the tribunal's members. The details of this act of sharing differ among companies, but a generally accepted principle is observable: The complainant should select his peers from a list of employees selected at random by management, but with management designating the members from its ranks without participation by the complainant. Management usually designates as a tribunal member, with or without voting authority, a member of the employee-relations department, the advantage being that this person, who is customarily the chairperson of the tribunal, is knowledgeable regarding company policies and procedures pertaining to employees, can guide the deliberations of the tribunal accordingly, and can prevent the deliberations from wandering off into irrelevancies.

Numerous detailed variations from the above described general method of selecting the members of an internal tribunal are recorded in the preceding pages. To restate them here would be repetitive. A reader who has the responsibility of establishing a selection method for his or her company's internal tribunal members will most profitably refer to the preceding pages, at the same time being aware that the examples provided do not exhaust the possible methods. Much of practical value can be gleaned from the preceding pages, but, in the last analysis, any method which is to be submitted to a company's top management for approval should be tailored to that company's specific circumstances. For example, while it is exceptional, it is sometimes advantageous to grant the complainant the privilege of selecting from a list at least one of the tribunal members who are to come from the ranks of management. Another very special case is a grievance against a company initiated by a member of management, the internal tribunal possibly to consist partly of his peers in management with one or more persons from the ranks of top management.

To summarize, 26 companies have been reviewed which, out of a total of 78 surveyed, have internal tribunals to which an employee can appeal from a decision by management regarding his or her grievance, a percentage of one-third of the total. There seems to be a general pattern which, although there may be exceptions in top management thinking, I would like to categorize and dignify as an employee-relations principle, best expressed by the vice president of employee relations quoted above who stated:

What we're trying to do here is gain credibility and an improved perception of fairness on the part of all employees about how people are treated in our company. . . . We had to pay a price for that. The price we had to pay was the willingness to be reversed in some individual cases where we thought we were right.

That vice president said something else worth emphasizing here:

Now, interestingly enough, in the first case with the pilot program, we've found the employee-members of the panels to support management's position more stridently than the management-members of the panels.

And if a reversal does occur, there's another interesting phenomenon: when management has been reversed, it was because additional facts came out in the investigation, and management in general has agreed with the panel's decision to reverse. Now that's better than we expected.

One additional argument in favor of internal tribunals, which has nothing to do with the peer review principle, is stated in the employee-relations manual of the hotel chain analyzed in this survey: "The Board of Review is an invaluable tool for both employees and supervisor. From the findings of Board hearings, recommendations are often made which assist the supervisor in performing his duties more effectively."

Should every company have a grievance appeal board which, based to a greater or less degree on the peer review principle, will render a decision binding on both an employee and management when the former is dissatisfied with the results of management's consideration of his or her grievance? No, not every company, but what this research obviously recommends is that every company familiarize itself with the potential benefits of a grievance appeal board and weigh them against any potential detriment applicable to the particular company. This writer is not aware of detriments existing in general.

5
Nonunion Open-Door Policies and Formal Appeal Systems to Higher Management: A Procedural Analysis

INTRODUCTION

It is universally recognized by business executives that it is inevitable that the complexities of human relations in a company will generate employees' grievances. Consequently, good business practice requires suitable arrangements to systematize a company's handling of the grievances. It is axiomatic that the internal health of a company requires that its employees possess high morale, and this in turn requires that grievances, which are very destructive of morale, be dealt with as quickly as possible, and, of course, as satisfactorily as possible from employees' viewpoints. The very first requirement, therefore, is the maintenance by management of a company environment which encourages employees to reveal their grievances to management instead of keeping them hidden.

In view of such considerations, it is not unexpected to find, as found in a survey of 78 companies within the umbrella of the National Association of Manufacturers, that a so-called *open-door policy is a basic ingredient in companies' employee relations*. The evidence for that is the customary practice of companies of emphasizing in the introductions of their employee-relations manuals a very specific statement of their open-door policy.

It is also typical of employee-relations manuals that their introductions are addressed to new employees, welcoming them to the company, stating management's hope that the newcomers will enjoy being associated with the company, and assuring the newcomers that, if they have "a problem or a question"—the disagreeable word "grievance" is inappropriate in the introduction of the manuals—the doors of the managerial personnel are "open" to the employees for appropriate discussions.

It is necessary here to provide a definition of the phrase "open door." The phraseology in some employee-relations manuals can easily be interpreted by a new employee as meaning that he or she is invited to visit the manager of his or her choice at any level of management, including the president and even the chairperson of the board of directors, without the formality of first consulting the immediate supervisor and members of middle management.

That is a simple and clear definition of the phrase "open door." It was best expressed, among the 78 companies I examined, not in one company's employees-relations manual but in a handwritten note in a copy provided to me: "Employees can talk to anyone at anytime about anything."

That is certainly an ideal policy in the area of employee relations. However, there is a problem with ideals, namely, the fact that they are seldom, if ever, achieved. It is probably exceptional for an ideal of any kind to be even half-realized in practice. Picture the complete realization of the open-door policy, in a large company, with employees talking "to anyone at anytime about anything," including the president. It would be natural for employees to find it most satisfying to talk with the president rather than with subordinate managers. The president would not have time to do any work other than talk with employees, especially when it is considered that the open-door policy applies not only to employees' grievances but also to their other "problems and questions," a phrase used in various employee-relations manuals.

It is obviously impractical for the ideal of a fully operational open-door policy to be achieved except in a company of a very few employees in which the managerial staff, including the president, are on a first-name basis with the employees. It is obvious, moreover, that, if too many employees in a certain group too frequently bypass that groups' supervisor by consulting with higher levels of management, this situation is evidence that that supervisor is not doing his job properly. It is interesting, regarding that potential situation, that many employee-relations manuals state that their companies have an open-door policy and then assert in the next statement a belief that most employees will find that their problems can be disposed of satisfactorily in discussions with their immediate supervisors. That is equivalent to stating that a company has the doors of its higher managerial personnel open to employees but that it is expected that relatively few employees will take advantage of the system. In that quite common situation, the policy of an open door at higher levels of management has both psychological value and practical value in the area of employee relations.

The reader will be correct at this point in anticipating that this discussion is leading up to a statement that the managerial doors in the businesses studied are open to employees. However, no sooner do the manuals describe the open-door policies than they go into considerable detail regarding what management obviously prefers, namely, more or less rigidly structured procedures for formal appeals by employees to higher management after discussions with immediate supervisors leave the employees dissatisfied.

A quick example is the manual discussed above in which my copy contains the handwritten explanation that "Employees can talk to anyone at anytime about anything," together with these words: "We stress an open door policy." However, note the formal system for processing employees' grievances which is stipulated in the printed portion of that manual, which is silent regarding an open-door policy:

The first step in the procedures is for you to talk with your supervisor. If you feel your supervisor hasn't satisfactorily answered your problem, you are encouraged to discuss the subject with his or her supervisor directly.... Additional steps... are available if you do not agree with the decisions of your supervisor's supervisor.... You may think that the answer you receive is not correct. If you feel this way, an appointment will be made for you to talk with the Plant Manager.

Does that company have an open-door policy for the handling of employees' grievances? It is true that an employee may contact the plant manager, but his door is open only after the employee has dealt with his or her supervisor and middle management. The answer to the question depends on the definition of open door. In this writer's opinion, at least when endeavoring to look at the situation from the viewpoint of an employee rather than from management's viewpoint, the managerial doors of the company are at best only half open, and even that is debatable inasmuch as the employee is strictly limited to going through channels to reach middle and top management. A truly open door is one in which an employee, on the spur of the moment, can approach a member of middle or top management who is walking through the company or seated in his office, and say: "Mr. Smith, I'd like to discuss a problem with you."

That, however, is obviously not the definition of "open door" which is standard in business and industry, so far as I've been able to determine. The standard definition is this: *An open-door policy is one in which management is motivated by a desire for employees to feel comfortable, and without fear of retribution, in going over the heads of their immediate supervisors in search for satisfying answers to personal problems, but, inasmuch as management deems it impractical for all its doors to be open at all hours and under all circumstances to employees, a more or less formally structured system is prescribed for an employee's appeals upward through management to the highest level authorized in the employee-relations manual.*

In short, management's doors are open to employees but only under very limiting conditions, which differs from company to company as will be indicated below.

One of the very important differences among companies is the matter not of the rules for an employee to carry a grievance upward step-by-step through channels in management, but the matter of an employee's appeal over management's decision at its highest level. Among the 78 employee-relations manuals surveyed, 6 provide for an employee who is dissatisfied with top management's decision to appeal to arbitration by an outside professional arbitrator. In addition, 23 of those companies provide for appeal to an internal tribunal of the company staffed by employees serving as a quasi-jury, with differences among these companies regarding the types of employees serving on the tribunals, that is, the number selected from the ranks of management and the number who are the complaining employee's peers, more or less equal to him or her in status in the company. These internal tribunals have differing names among the companies; the name preferred by this writer is grievance appeal board. Among the 6 companies mentioned above which provide for appeal to arbitration, an employee may first appeal to the internal tribunal provided in 3 of those companies and then, if desired, to arbitration.

To recapitulate the figures quoted above, out of the 78 companies surveyed, 26, or one-third of the total, provide for an internal tribunal or arbitration or both, indicating that the employee-relations concept of providing employees with the privilege of appealing over a decision of top management enjoys substantial popularity in management circles. Those 26 companies were analyzed in Chapters 3 and 4.

The remaining two-thirds of the surveyed companies, in which top management's decisions in grievance cases are final, will be reviewed in detail below for the purpose of comparing their structured systems for formal appeals to higher management, and to determine which of the procedural details have the most common acceptance.

At the same time, data will be provided regarding statements, if any, in each company's employee-relations manual pertaining to open-door policy as a means for nurturing a friendly employment environment.

REPRESENTATIVE NONUNION OPEN-DOOR POLICIES AND FORMAL APPEAL PROCEDURES TO HIGHER MANAGEMENT

This section is an analysis of the open-door policies and formal appeals to higher management stipulated in the employee-relations policy manuals of some leading nonunion companies who are within the umbrella of the National Association of Manufacturers.

Company A

"We will provide an atmosphere in our plants where open two-way communications is practiced and there is no fear or concern about retribution. ... Your grievance procedure provides you the formal vehicle for your part of the communication process."

"Management encourages you to use the grievance procedure.... If you are not satisfied with the answer, you are urged to take your grievance to the next step." The "steps" are the presentation of the grievance in sequence to the employee's supervisor ("Experience has shown that most grievances can be resolved by discussion between you and your supervisor."), the plant manager, the region manager, and, finally, the corporation's employee relations department.

Analysis of Company A. This company professes to have an open-door policy, described by the phrase "open two-way communications." However, it is evident that employees are expected to process their grievances, as distinguished from other types of problems, through the formal procedure stipulated in the employee-relations manual.

Company B

"This procedure will be followed whenever an employee has any complaint, problem or criticism regarding his/her employment or condition of employment." The steps are the employee's supervisor, the supervisor's manager, the facility's manager, who will consult with the corresponding vice president and the employee relations department, and finally with the appropriate member of the corporation's executive committee. "The intent of this procedure is to involve successfully higher-ranking management members in the review process and do so with no more than four steps." If there are more than four levels of management above the employee, some steps will be combined. If there are less than four levels, the mandatory levels are the supervisor and the member of the executive committee. A special case is a suspension or discharge, with the grievance being initiated with the facility's manager instead of lower management.

Analysis of Company B. It is obvious from the stern tone of voice of this company's employee-relations manual that an employee's "complaint, problem or criticism" must be processed in a very structured, formal manner and with emphasis on the company's welfare rather than the employee's welfare. This is not to imply any unfairness on the part of management, which emphasizes that "In no case will employees experience reprisals for using the Formal Complaint Procedure." However, the requirement that the employee's first step always be with his supervisor instead of a higher level of management is contrary to the practice of most companies, which grant employees the discretion of bypassing their immediate supervisors if they feel more comfortable in doing so. It is easy to think of such situations, one being a grievance caused by a personality conflict with a supervisor.

Company C

An employee's grievance is defined as "a legitimate complaint concerning pay, hours of work, length of service, or any other matter relative to employment," and a "specified procedure" is provided for processing the grievance. "Each employee should clearly understand this complaint procedure." The first step is consultation with the employee's supervisor, the second with the department manager, and the final step, if the employee is still dissatisfied, with the division president. The personnel manager may advise and assist the employee.

Analysis of Company C. Its definition of an employee's grievance was quoted to draw attention to the fact that some companies state in their employee-relations manuals that grievances will be heard by management only when they pertain to subject matter listed in the manuals. This company's stipulation that the personnel manager may advise and assist employees in processing grievances is a very common practice in business, but the permitted assistance is limited to the employee's preparation of his case. The generous offering of the helping hand of the personnel manager or one of his assistants may or may not be a genuinely altruistic gesture by management toward employees, at least if the fact is taken into consideration that the members of the personnel department are the most suitable representatives of management for counseling employees in grievance matters, with such counseling very likely disposing of frivolous or otherwise improper grievances and improving the businesslike format in which grievances will be submitted to management. Unlike the custom in some European companies, most American companies do not favor placing an ombudsman in the human resources management department—that is, a person paid by management to represent employees' interests vis-à-vis management, and companies are averse to authorizing employees with grievances to be represented in meetings with management by other employees or by lawyers. Whatever informal assistance an employee may receive in preparing his or her grievance, the complainant customarily must be his or her own unaided spokesperson in formal meetings with management at all levels.

Company D

"Under no circumstances will an employee be penalized for using the complaint resolution procedure." A complaint is defined as "an employee's expressed feeling of dissatisfaction concerning conditions of employment or treatment by management or other employees." Examples: Application of company policies; unfair treatment such as coercion, reprisal, harassment, intimidation, or discipline; civil rights discrimination; and improper or unfair administration of employee benefits or conditions of employment.

The requirement that an employee submit his or her grievance first to the immediate supervisor is waived if it would create an awkward situation, the second step in the complaint resolution procedure being referral of the complaint to the department head. If the employee remains dissatisfied, the grievance will be considered by a representative of top management for a final decision, but prior to that decision the situation will be examined by the employee-relations department and its appraisal submitted to top management, and after the decision is made a copy of that appraisal will be given to the employee at his or her request.

Strict confidentiality will be maintained, with information regarding the grievance and its resolution being known only to persons involved in disposing of the grievance.

The following statement is unique with this company: "Management decisions on complaints will not be precedent-setting nor binding on future complaints unless they are officially stated as Company policy."

Analysis of Company D. This company is careful to define as well as possible the subject matters which may form the basis of grievances. One of them, namely, the application of company policies, is often listed in employee-relations manuals as a legitimate subject for grievances, but unlike this company other such manuals contain the additional statement that the policies themselves, as distinguished from their application, may not be the subject of grievances.

The liberality of this company in permitting an employee to bypass his or her supervisor in "an awkward situation" is more common than the mandatory inclusion of the supervisor in the grievance procedure of one of the companies examined above.

A unique aspect of this company's procedure is the situation where a grievance is taken by an employee all the way to top management. First, top management will not make the final decision until it has in its hands an appraisal by the employee-relations department of the grievance. Second, the stipulation that the grievance be processed and a decision rendered not by a member of top management designated in the employee-relations manual by job title, which is the customary practice in companies, but by "a representation of management," leaves the employee uncertain as to whose hands hold his destiny.

Company E

"First, discuss the problem with your supervisor. In most cases, he or she is the person best qualified to help you." If that fails after two working days, the employee may approach the personnel department, which, if it cannot settle the matter to the employee's satisfaction within five working days, will assist the employee in preparing a written grievance, which he or she jointly with the representatives of the personnel department presents to the department manager. If the manager does not satisfy the employee within five working days, the latter may appeal to the next higher level of management, which will review the case jointly with the corporate director of personnel. After that, the final appeal is to "the appropriate corporate official who, in his position, reports directly to the President."

"Employees are strongly encouraged to use this procedure when they have a grievance with the company. Under no circumstances shall any employee be criticized or adversely affected for using this procedure."

Analysis of Company E. This company has employees in different locations totalling 7,000. The initial statement above—regarding most grievances going first to the complaining employee's supervisor as this is "the person best qualified to help you"—is the general thinking among business managers, but, as has previously been discussed, some of them make allowances in their employee-relations manuals for the exceptional case in which it would be awkward for some reason for an employee to tender the grievance to his or her supervisor.

It should be noted that included in the description of this company are the maximum number of days between the various steps of the grievance resolution process. Most employee-relations manuals stipulate this information, but it is excluded from this study as statistically unimportant inasmuch as individual companies tailor these time elements to suit their particular circumstances rather than following the guidance of other companies. In some instances too much time is permitted between the steps in the appeal process because the very nature of a grievance and its detrimental effect on morale are such that time is of the essence, and therefore a grievance should be disposed of as quickly as possible. The short time elements in this company's procedure are obviously intended to accomplish that desideratum.

Company F

The scope of this company's employee-relations manual is "all U.S. units" of the company. At levels of management above the complaining employee's supervisor, the grievance and all recommended resolutions of it should be reduced to documentation. At all levels the employee may obtain the assistance of the human resources department in resolving the grievance. The employee's supervisor "should research policy and practices applicable to the complaint."

If the supervisor's decision is unsatisfactory to the employee, he may appeal to the "second management level," and if its decision is also unsatisfactory, to the "third management level," the manager of which conducts fact-finding, reviews the grievance and his proposed solution with the human resources department and the "next higher management level," and makes a written report.

If the employee still remains unsatisfied, the matter may now be pursued with the human resources department, which "initiates necessary fact-finding, policy-practices review and any other useful action." The results, with "potential alternative solutions," are reported to the division head, who issues a written decision. If the employee is still not satisfied, an appeal may be made to the human resources office at the corporate level. Its decision is issued by the "Corporate Senior Vice President-Human Resources" after any required fact-finding and consultation with management at lower levels.

This company's formal grievance procedure was established in 1982, and in 1985 a bulletin to management was issued which is here quoted in part:

Ongoing communication and honesty between a supervisor and worker are essential to the success of a dispute-resolution procedure... primarily through face-to-face dialogue.... Getting problems out into the open quickly can create new perspectives on a troublesome situation.... If a problem is not remedied by these informal discussions, employees can use the procedure's more formal steps.

One of the main obstacles to successful resolutions of complaints and concerns is employee fear of management retaliation. All employees have the right to present complaints to management without concern for prejudicial treatment for having done so. The grievance-handling procedure is "absolutely confidential."

Recommendations for employees:

Make certain that your problems fits the definition of "work-related."

Ask for a private meeting with your boss.

Write down your complaint, and include all valid documentation.

Wait for anger to subside. Emotional flairups are not productive.

Identify your problem-resolution expectations before you start.

Recommendations for managers who have been approached by an employee:

Act immediately, and assure the employee of confidentiality.

If the problem relates to your on-the-job actions, treat it as work-related, not as a personal attack.

Be an active listener. Ask questions to get to the heart of the matter.

Seek a prompt solution, but don't give an off-the-cuff answer if you need time for research of the issues.

Recommendations for both employees and managers:

Take notes during discussions.

Use discussion time to solve the problem, not to make additional accusations.

Be honest and frank in discussion. Don't assume anything or jump to conclusions.

At the end of the meeting, review what was discussed and make certain the problem is understood by both parties.

Analysis of Company F. The employee-relations manual states that it is applicable to "all U.S. units" of the company. In contrast with that policy, it should be noted that the principle of decentralization is practiced in many medium-sized and large-sized companies. The result is that their individual plants or divisions often have employee-relations manuals that are designated at those local levels without coordination with other local units or corporate headquarters. An important feature of this situation is that, if the manual pertains only to a particular unit of a company, an employee's appeal of a grievance to higher management cannot go higher than the management of that unit, whereas a manual issued by corporate headquarters for use by the entire company will sometimes stipulate that the employee may appeal finally to corporate headquarters, as is the case with company F, the appeal being to the corporate senior vice president for human resources. It is stipulated that that official will engage in any required fact-finding and consultation with management in the local unit. What is at issue here is a management principle, namely, the question whether justice both to the employee and to the company is best served by a decision of local management or of corporate management. If the principle of decentralization has validity, it may be argued that there is something wrong with the management of a plant or division if it cannot control its own affairs without employees appealing their grievances to corporate headquarters.

The recommendations both to managers and employees regarding their participation in the resolution of grievances was quoted extensively from the company's bulletin to management because it is obvious, although the employee-relations manuals of many companies ignore the matter, that both managers and employees need training in this activity, just as they need training in all their other activities.

The grievance-handling procedure in this company is "absolutely confidential." It has previously been noted that some companies prefer that practice, whereas others desire a grievance and the decision regarding it to be known throughout a company. This writer is disinclined to attempt to determine a solution for this controversial subject in the absence of evidence that an imperative basic principle exists which impels all companies to handle the matter identically.

Company G

The procedure in this company for an employee's appeal steps through higher management is this sequence: the employee's supervisor, the supervisor's manager, the department head, the employee-relations manager, the director of employee relations, and the vice president of human resources.

Analysis of Company G. There are five steps of appeal over the decision of the supervisor, an unusual number. Another way to look at the situation is that, by the time a grievance reaches the vice president of human resources, the complaining employee has failed five times to obtain a decision that satisfies him. Another interesting, as well as very unusual, feature of this company's appeal procedure is that the first three decisions are rendered by operating on "line" management, while the last three decisions are rendered by nonoperating or "staff" personnel. While a number of the companies surveyed by this writer provide for a decision at one of the appeal steps by an official in the human resources department, the general rule is that an appeal over the head of that official may be taken by the employee to a high level operating or "line" manager, such as the plant or division manager or the company's president.

Company H

If the supervisor does not satisfy an employee regarding the latter's grievance in an informal, verbal discussion, the employee may "seek counselling" with the employee-relations department. If still dissatisfied, the employee may obtain the assistance of that department in preparing a written statement of the grievance and in presenting the grievances to the employee's department manager. The employee may make his last appeal to the plant manager.

Analysis of Company H. The appeal procedure described above, which is applicable to a plant of 700 employees in a company totalling 8,000, has the advantage of injecting the employee-relations department into the appeal process at its earliest stage, that is, upon the employee becoming dissatisfied with his supervisor's decision. It is at that early phase that a neutral third party trusted by the employee, as a member of the employee-relations department should be, can best assist both the employee and the company in reaching a proper decision and doing so in minimum time, which is highly desirable, and with minimum emotional trauma on the part of the employee.

It is notable that the employee-relations department not only assists the employee in the case preparation but also in "presenting" it to the employee's department manager, a situation which comes close to the representative of the employee-relations department serving as an ombudsman, that is, paid by management but representing employees' interests.

Company I

"Grievances are broadly defined as work-related complaints, problems or situations which an employee feels are unfair or need correcting."

"It is an employee's right to make his grievances known . . . with the guarantee that in so doing he will in no way place his standing or job in jeopardy."

"Personnel Department staff is available upon request by the employee to assist in presentation of complaints or handling of problems at any step."

The appeal steps in the grievance resolution procedure are:

Employee's supervisor
Supervisor's manager
Department or plant manager as applicable
Applicable vice president
Senior vice president
President

The official at each level meets separately with the next lower official and the employee, and then jointly with them, "to gather all facts." If the grievance reaches the senior vice president and is not resolved to the employee's satisfaction, the former refers the case in writing to the personnel department. The personnel department then interviews the employee "to further define the complaint and requested solution," and submits all information to the president, who renders a final decision after discussing the matter with each member of management who reviewed the grievance, including the employee's immediate supervisor, and with the employee being the last person interviewed by the president.

Two alternatives are available to the employee. First, in an unusual case of a personal nature, the employee may discuss it directly with the personnel department, which will keep it confidential if the employee does not want to pursue the matter with management. And second, in a case of a "very" personal nature, the employee may deal exclusively with the president.

Analysis of Company I. This is another example of numerous appeal steps, the first three with management within a plant and the second three with officers of the company. It is exceptionally generous on the part of this company's management to assign two vice presidents and the president as steps in the employee's appeal process. Inasmuch as the above-described appeal procedure has been in effect for eight years in this 3,500-employee company, it would be interesting to see a special study of the company's experience, the principal question being why the company apparently has seen no need to modify the procedure, especially with regard to the participation by three officers.

Company J

Like many companies, this one's procedure for formal appeal to management rather vaguely defines the permissible subject matter, namely, "suggestions, problems or complaints." Also, like many companies, an employee may bypass the immediate supervisor if the problem is personal. Like some companies, the employee may proceed to the supervisor's manager if the supervisor does not quickly respond to the grievance, in this company within two working days. The third appeal step is to the employee-relations manager, and the last step to the general manager.

Analysis of Company J. The most interesting feature of this company is the expeditiousness with which the appeal procedure functions, in contrast with some companies in which the procedure drags on for a month or even longer. The supervisor is allotted two days, the supervisor's manager three days, the employee-relations manager three days, and the general manager three days, a total of eleven "working days."

Company K

This very large company of 60,000 employees is decentralized and has many different procedures for resolving employees' grievances. The following one is described by the corporate director of employee relations as "typical." Its title in the employee-relations manual is *Communications and Problems Solving*, and the subtitle is "Complaint and Open Door Policy," which is here quoted in its entirety:

Most of us have a question or complaint at some time. If you do, remember we can only answer your question or solve your problem if you tell us about it. If you have a question or complaint, talk to your Supervisor about it. Your Supervisor knows more about you and your job than any other member of your management, and he is in the best position to handle your work problem properly and satisfactorily. Your Supervisor will do his best to satisfy you, and in most cases will be able to solve your problems. If you don't get a prompt answer, or if you aren't satisfied with the answer you get from your Supervisor, you may request assistance from the Industrial Relations Manager or Plant Manager. If you are still not satisfied, you may appeal directly to the Vice President of Industrial Relations, Executive Vice President of Operations or the Division President. Your management strongly supports and encourages the use of our "open door" policy.

Analysis of Company K. The door in that "open door" policy is only partly open, in contrast with the permission that employees have, as an option, to bypass their immediate supervisors. In this company it is mandatory to approach them before dealing with other management personnel. This company also contrasts with the many companies that provide for employees to take a grievance informally at any time to the personnel department. A third unusual feature, especially in a company of this very large size, is that the employees have the option, after dealing with their immediate supervisors, of avoiding appealing to higher levels of so-called "line" management by appealing supervisors' decisions to the industrial relations manager. Then, if desired, they can appeal to the vice president of industrial relations, thereby denying the supervisors' managers any participation in the grievance resolution process. It is probable, of course, that the industrial relations personnel will informally consult with the higher managerial levels, but the point here is that such advisable consultation is not a mandatory provision of company policy.

Company L

"While the handling of employee problems and misunderstandings is a line responsibility, it shall be the responsibility of the Corporate Personnel Department to provide assistance as needed and to provide information on applicable laws, regulations and/or Company policies to the responsible member of management."

The steps in an employee's formal appeal to management are: the foreman, the foreman's supervisor, department manager, and division manager.

Employees are urged to use the above "step" procedure. "They may, however, also contact the Personnel Department or any officer of the Company, including the President or Chairman of the Board."

Analysis of Company L. This procedure is applicable to a States-side plant with 2,000 employees of a multinational oil company, and it has been in effect since 1971 under the written policy title of *Employee Complaints, Problems and Misunderstandings.*

The interesting features are that only three formal appeal steps over the decision of the employee's foreman are authorized.

Furthermore, inasmuch as employees have the option of bypassing the step procedure and directly approaching either the personnel department or "any officer of the Company, including the President or Chairman of the Board," it is arguable that this company has an open-door policy regarding employee complaints, problems and misunderstandings. However, under the subheading of "Basic Policy," the employee-relations manual stipulates that "Employees should be urged" to use the formal "step" procedure, not the informal options, which is equivalent to saying that employees should be discouraged from taking advantage of the open doors.

The grievance procedure described above has been in effect for 16 years without amendment, an indication that it is functioning satisfactorily regarding its detailed provisions.

Company M

In the meeting between the complaining employee and the supervisor, either party may request the presence of the personnel manager to assist in solving the problem. If that fails, the employee may appeal to the plant manager and finally to the operations manager. A grievance which is "personal or embarrassing" may be taken directly to the personnel manager instead of to the supervisor. Management members will act in as timely a manner as is practical.

Analysis of Company M. This extremely brief procedure in a medium-sized company has the virtue of simplicity, and its best feature probably is the presence of the personnel manager very early in the processing of the grievance, that is, in the meeting between the employee and the supervisor. In some companies the personnel department is not called into the appeal procedure until a rather high level of management has been reached, although its intervention early in the procedure as a neutral third party and moderating influence would have maximum effectiveness.

Company N

"We want you, our employees, to know and feel that you are the most important asset of the company."

"If you do not receive what you consider a satisfactory answer from your Supervisor, or if the problem is of the type you cannot discuss with your Supervisor, state that you would like to see someone in the Personnel Department about a 'personal matter.' "

If the personnel representative is unable to satisfy the employee, the former will assist the employee in presenting the case to the supervisor's manager. "Thus, the Personnel Representative will serve as a spokesman or advocate for you."

A higher appeal may be made, with the assistance of the personnel representative, to the division manager, and finally, "in the case whereby the Personnel Director or the employee does not feel that the solution is fair, the Personnel Director shall make arrangements for the problem to be discussed with the President."

Analysis of Company N. It is standard practice for a company to state in the introduction of its employee-relations manual that it is management's hope that the employees will enjoy their association with the company. However, this company is exceptional in acknowledging its acceptance of the principle that employees are a company's "most important asset."

This company is also exceptional in adopting the ombudsman principle, that is, a management official paid by the company to represent employees' interests. Numerous companies, if not all companies, arrange for employees' access to the human resources department for varying amounts of assistance in the processing of grievances through appeal to higher levels of management. However, this company goes much further than most companies by making it a responsibility of the personnel director—if he or she considers a high-level management decision in a grievance case to be unfair—to "make arrangements for the problem to be discussed with the President." That is an excellent example of ombudsmanship, because the employee-relations manual mandates that, if an employee appeals to his supervisor's manager, "the Personnel Representative will serve as a spokesman or advocate for you."

Another exceptional feature of this company's manual is that it contains a section regarding the relationship between management and employees which has the rare title of "Human Relations," with obvious emphasis on the adjective.

Company O

1. Company policy shall not be subject to grievances, but the application and administration of company policy can be.
2. The Company has a specific procedure for handling of questions, problems or grievances.
3. The Industrial Relations Supervisor at each plant has been given the specific responsibility of serving as the employee's representative in the Grievance-Problem Solving Procedure.... If you so desire, he or she will help you formulate your grievance, reduce it to writing, go with you in person and represent you through the various steps.
4. The appeal steps involve the standard management levels observed in this writer's survey, with a final decision by the plant manager.

5. In cases of unusual plant-wide situations or "personal" problems you may not want to discuss the problem directly with your immediate supervisor. In such cases, you may take your problem directly to the Personnel Department."

Analysis of Company O. This company's procedure has been very briefly outlined because it is quite typical of the generality of procedures examined. Many employee-relations manuals stress item 1 above. Item 2 is typical in enumerating not only grievances but also "questions, problems" as subjects for an employee's appeal over his supervisor to higher management. Item 3 is typical in providing access of an employee to the human resources department, but it is exceptional, as was discussed above regarding another company, in providing for the industrial relations supervisor to perform the ombudsman function of "representing" the employee in appeals to higher management levels. It is common for companies to provide for human resources personnel merely to accompany an employee without the responsibility of speaking on his behalf.

Item 5 is of interest because it is a verbatim copy of a paragraph found in the manual of another company located in a different industry in a distant state. The point here is that this survey of 78 companies has revealed so little, rather than so much, uniformity in the provisions of employee-relations manuals regarding management's processing of employees' grievances. In other words, there appears to be minimum coordination among companies on this subject, and sometimes even between the plants or divisions of a single company.

Company P

"Generally, satisfactory solutions to any problems employees may encounter are not found by discussing them with fellow employees of other members of this staff."

The employee's supervisor will provide an answer to the grievance within 24 hours, with the supervisor and employee thereupon jointly preparing a written record of the discussion.

If the supervisor fails to respond within 24 hours or his decision is not acceptable to the employee, the latter may appeal to higher management with the personnel department assisting in the preparation of a written presentation, first to the department manager, then to the general manager, who will hold a meeting if advisable with the employee, supervisor, and department manager. Further appeals may be made to the director of employee relations, who has authority to render a decision in the matter, and finally to the president.

Analysis of Company P. This company is unique in discouraging employees from discussing their problems with "fellow employees or other members of the staff" based on the argument that "satisfactory solutions . . . are not found." If the word "staff" is intended to include the employee-relations department, then this company is at variance with the practically universal principle in business that employees are encouraged to consult informally with that department regarding their problems.

It is an unusually strict rule to give a supervisor only 24 hours to respond to an employee's grievance or other problem, which is a time limitation of only 8 working hours.

This is one of the relatively few companies which assigns authority to the head of a human resources department to render a decision in a grievance case, especially when it overrules a decision of such high management officials as the department manager and the general manager, with only the president authorized to overrule the human resources department.

Company Q

"Your supervisor is the first person to contact when you have problems, questions, and concerns that are work-related. The success that you and the Company enjoy together depends upon your willingness to discuss your problems and concerns with your supervisor. Your suggestions on how to improve your job are also welcome. Your ideas might prove to be the best yet!"

An employee's presentation of a grievance to his supervisor is classified as informal. If the employee is dissatisfied with the answer, he notifies the supervisor that a "formal complaint" is being initiated, which requires a meeting of those two individuals with the department manager, whose decision may be appealed to the industrial relations office and, finally, to the president.

Analysis of Company Q. Sometimes persons say the same thing in different ways, depending on what features are to be emphasized. For example, the previously discussed company and this company agree that the proper procedure is for an employee to initiate a grievance with his or her supervisor, but the former company places the emphasis on not discussing it with "fellow employees or other members of the staff," while this company's emphasis is to provide both concepts in a single statement, because designating the supervisor as the "first person" does not necessarily indicate that even an off-the-record discussion with a fellow employee should be avoided—at least, of course, from management's viewpoint.

Company R

"Grievance—a condition which any employee feels is unjust or inequitable. There is no limitation as to what may be considered a grievance. . . . This procedure does not allow a supervisor to be bypassed. . . . If an employee prefers, he or she may take the matter to Personnel rather than the supervisor." The employee may appeal to the supervisor's manager, in which instance the personnel department or the supervisor will help the employee fill in the grievance form. The final appeal is to the president, who will reply in writing within two working days.

Analysis of Company R. Inasmuch as this company's Grievance Procedure was issued in 1972 and revised in 1986, the revision could have been prepared with greater clarity regarding the supervisor not being "bypassed" and yet the employee being permitted to "take the matter to Personnel rather than the supervisor," with the next step being appeal to the supervisor's manager. Employee-relations manuals, precisely because they are guides for employees, should be phrased with great care.

Many manuals stipulate the types of problems which may be classified as grievances but in this company "There is no limitation," a circumstance which probably is not improper inasmuch as this is a small company with only about 600 employees. Possibly, that is the reason why the president apparently does not find it difficult to reply to a grievance "within two working days."

Company S

The grievance procedures of three plants of this company were studied, obviously written independently. The appeal steps in the first plant are through the employee's supervisor to the department head and finally the plant manager. The second plant has a similar procedure except that the employee may appeal one step higher to the general manager and, in a discharge case, may begin the grievance with the plant manager and appeal finally to the general manager. In the third plant the process is through the supervisor to the department head and finally the plant manager, but employees who "feel you cannot take your complaint to your supervisor or department head" may go to the employee-relations department and, in a discharge case, the employee goes initially to that department, which arranges for the appeal to be heard only by the plant manager.

Analysis of Company S. The fact that three plants in a large company have independently written grievance procedures, with substantial differences in the appeal steps, is proof that the principle of decentralization of employee-relations functions is practical, but it is not proof that varying employee-relations procedures are equally good. The principle of decentralization in large companies is acceptable because of its advantages, and not because it could be expected in all cases to produce the very best results. As long as the decentralized plants or divisions of a company are functioning with satisfactory efficiency, it could do more harm than good for the corporate headquarters to force its opinions upon them.

Company T

This company of 19,000 employees has about 15 divisions, one of which has its independent grievance appeal procedures, while the other divisions are covered by a single procedure. In all the divisions the procedures here reviewed pertain only to hourly paid employees.

In the division that has its own separate procedure, the appeal steps are through the supervisor to the foreman, the department superintendent, the group superintendent, the division director, and "the member of General Management who shall be designated by the president for this purpose." In the other divisions, the appeal over a decision of the division director is to "the President, Chairman of the Board, or, if the employee prefers, the Director of Relations Services."

This company is not decentralized with respect to its grievance appeals to higher management, the only deviation from standard procedure being the single division in which the highest appeal is to an official designated by the president. All the divisions have the following identical provisions:

Aggrieved employees will be paid for all the time spent in discussing their grievances when the time falls within the employees' working hours. Employees who represent aggrieved employees in the presentation of grievances are not to be paid for the time spent in these discussions.

If, at any step, appeal is not made within the time limit specified, the grievance shall be considered settled on the basis of the last answer given, unless it is otherwise agreed. The circumstances set forth in the grievance must... have arisen within thirty (30) days prior to the time the grievance is presented (to the supervisor).

The term "decision" shall include either (1) settlement of the grievance or (2) an agreement as to how the grievance will be settled after further necessary investigation or research or (3) an agreement on an extension of time within which to handle the grievance.

Analysis of Company T. An unusual feature of this large company of 15 divisions and 19,000 employees is the fact that, except for one division, an employee may appeal beyond the division management to the corporate headquarters. In addition, the employee may have the choice of dealing with the president, chairperson of the board, or the director of relations services, each of whom, because of the geographical dispersion of the divisions, may be expected to have some inconvenience in ascertaining the facts required for a decision regarding the grievance.

The centralized nature of this company's grievance resolution procedure contrasts with the principle of decentralization discussed above regarding some other companies. The choice between centralization and decentralization depends on a number of factors, one of which is the personalities of the top management, and a company must make the choice most appropriate for it.

Company U

This company's grievance procedure is here quoted in its entirety:

You should feel free to discuss with your Foreman any questions or problems that you might have. If you are not completely satisfied with your supervisor's answers, feel free to discuss the issue with your Plant Superintendent or the Personnel Manager. If you are still dissatisfied, you may bring the problem to the General Manager who will further investigate, then make a decision on the matter. In presenting your problem or dissatisfaction to management you may have another employee accompany you to help present your case.

Analysis of Company U. This is a small company totalling 160 employees in four extremely small plants located in three states. It should not be assumed that the extreme brevity of the grievance procedure is a reflection of the diminutive size of the company. The document actually contains all the essential features of an appeal of an employee's grievance to higher management. More complex procedures contain worthwhile features, but what is being emphasized here is the distinction between what is essential and what is optional.

Company V

This company of 50,000 employees maintains "an open line of communication" for employees' contacts with management. There are three phases.

Phase 1. The supervisor is contacted. If his decision is unsatisfactory, he "will arrange interview(s) with additional levels of your management, including the top company official of your department or location."

Phase 2. This phase is for "privately" raised matters not resolved in Phase 1, and for matters "too touchy to go through your supervisor." This phase is "strictly confidential" with the company providing a "coordinator" to process the employee's problem (the word "grievance" is not used, the company speaking only of "work-related concerns"), and "Only the coordinator will know your identity if you choose."

Phase 3. This is the final step, with "direct access to the Head of your Operating Group" by means of a letter fully stating the issue, with a copy to the coordinator.

Analysis of Company V. This is a peculiar procedure for resolving an employee's grievance, in the sense that it differs substantially from most procedures. The employee-relations manual speaks of "an open line of communication" between employees and management, but the procedure which is prescribed strictly limits contacts above the level of supervisors, in one instance by working confidentially through a "coordinator" and after that by appealing "by means of a letter" to the local manager.

Company W

In this very small company of 140 employees the appeal of an employee's grievance is from supervisor to "your Department Manager, the Personnel

Manager, or to the Plant Manager." "Although the foregoing procedure has been established for an orderly handling of problems, this does not prohibit any employee from presenting a matter of serious personal concern to management at any time on an informal basis."

Analysis of Company W. The inference here is on informality of the so-called open-door type, further evidenced by the absence of formal appeal steps when one employee prefers to approach his or her supervisor and then higher management. Instead of steps upward in an orderly manner through higher levels, the employee has the choice of appeal from the supervisor to the department manager, personnel manager, or plant manager for a final decision. It is logical to assume, especially due to the small size of this company, that whichever manager the employee selects will coordinate the decision with one or both of the two others.

Company X

A letter to this writer from the corporate-level manager of human resources of this very large company of 90,000 employees states that it is "a very decentralized company and thus has a variety of different Complaint and Grievance Procedures. Incidentally, they all seem to work effectively, since local Human Resource Managers have not seen the need to change or revise their procedures in the last 6–7 years." The following is the procedure of one of the company's divisions for appeals of employees' grievances to higher management, the procedure's title in the employee-relations handbook being "Employee Problem Solving."

Although initial discussion is encouraged at the immediate supervisory level, management assures the individual employee the right to discuss any problem or complaint at any management level . . . in writing or in an informal discussion. . . . Written reports will be filed in the employee's personnel folder only upon the employee's request.

Managers have the obligation to listen to the employee . . . and to help to refer the case to the next higher level of management should the employee so desire. Employee Relations will be notified by the immediate supervisor that the matter is being moved to a higher management level. If the problem was presented in writing, the original letter is used through the various levels of review and is, at the conclusion and resolution of the problem, returned to the employee or, if so requested, placed in the employee's personnel folder. A problem . . . may be appealed through each level of management up to and including the Vice President and General Manager of the division. If the nature of the problem is such that the employee does not wish to discuss it with the immediate supervisor, the employee may contact a higher level of management or Employee Relations directly. However, the employee should recognize that eventual problem resolution may require the involvement of immediate and/or higher level management.

Analysis of Company X. This division of the company follows the practice of many companies of not using the word "grievance" in its employee-relations manual, using the phrase "problem or complaint" instead. A few of the companies which use the word "grievance" define it by listing the types of situations covered, and some of the companies which use the word "problem" define it similarly, some by the brief requirement of "work-related." Some companies include employees' "questions" in the procedure of appeal to higher management.

Like companies which have varying degrees of an open-door policy, this division offers free access by employees to managers at all levels but urges the use of the formal appeal procedure as management's preference. Unlike such companies in general, this division specifically warns employees that their "problems" may ultimately require "the involvement of immediate and/ or higher level management," a situation which should be obvious.

Unlike a number of companies, this division does not provide a form for an employee's presentation of his case, being satisfied with a "letter."

A subject which occurs occasionally in this research is the matter of centralized versus decentralized management in the case of large companies, and the evidence which is accumulating herein is that, in the area of human resources management, both forms of management have their proponents. However, it should be noted that, as is the case in company X, which has decentralized employees relations at the division level, there is customarily a coordinating employee-relations office at the corporate headquarters of decentralized companies.

A notable difference between various decentralized companies is that some, but not all, permit an employee's appeal from the level of the plant or division manager to an official at the corporate headquarters, sometimes to the president.

Company Y

The employee-relations manual states: "A constant and direct line of communication is open between you and all levels of management."

After rhetorically asking whether an employee has any questions, the manual states "If so, let us know! Here's how." The manual then lists four steps from the supervisor to the department head, the head of employee relations, and finally, if the employee is still unsatisfied, the plant manager.

An exception to the formal procedure is authorized: "There may be instances when you prefer to skip step one or even step two and take your problem directly to the employee relations manager or the plant manager."

Analysis of company Y. That is the procedure of appeal to higher management of a division of a company totalling 3,000 employees. The initial statement regarding "a constant and direct line of communication" implies a so-called open-door policy. But here, as in most of the companies thus far reviewed, it is evident that the primary policy is the four formal appeal steps outlined in the manual, with the open-door feature of secondary importance in management's intent—that is, in the category of an exception to a general rule.

Company Z

The employee-relations manual of this company of 15,000 employees states:

When you have a problem, discuss it first with your immediate supervisor. If you feel you cannot, go directly to your Industrial Relations Department.

If you and your immediate supervisor cannot resolve the problem, you should discuss it with your Industrial Relations Department, and if not resolved here, talk to the plant manager. In the event you disagree with your manager's decision, you may appeal to the Resource Committee of the Employee Relations Department.

This procedure also applies to termination.

Analysis of Company Z. This company is exceptional in that there is no appeal step to middle management personnel between the supervisor and the plant manager.

An appeal of a termination of employment is handled as indicated above, whereas some but not many companies have a separate procedure for appealing a termination.

Company AA

The employee-relations manual of this small company of 200 employees has a section titled "Communications" with the statement that "Good communications is the key to mutual understanding." A subsection titled "Open-Door Policy" establishes the following system.

"This policy offers you the opportunity to discuss the matter with everyone all the way up to the President if you feel that is necessary. The first discussion can take place between you and your supervisor or the Personnel Manager." If that fails, the employee may ask for a meeting with the supervisor and the department head, with a further appeal in a meeting with the personnel manager and the department head, and a final appeal to the president.

Analysis of Company AA. This is another instance of the very common practice of companies to speak of their open-door policies but stipulate a formal procedure for an employee's presentation of a grievance, or problem as many companies prefer to say, to various levels of management.

This company places considerable emphasis on the role of the personnel manager. An employee may approach him or her instead of the supervisor. Furthermore, if the second step in the appeal process fails in the employee's meeting with the supervisor and the department head, the third step is a meeting of the employee with the personnel manager and the department head, ignoring the supervisor. It is nearly a universal practice for employees to have access to the human resources management department as a step in formal appeal procedures, but this company is exceptional in requiring an employee to meet jointly with the personnel manager and the department head instead of solely with the personnel manager. Of course, it is reasonable to assume that an official at any level of an employee's appeal procedure will informally discuss the matter with various other officials before making a decision, and particularly with the personnel manager inasmuch as his or her expertise is in the area of employee relations.

Company BB

This medium-sized company's Management Availability Policy states that an employee "shall first discuss the matter with his-her supervisor." The first appeal step is to the department manager, then the personnel manager, who "will attempt to resolve the matter to the mutual satisfaction of the employee and the company," and finally, if the employee desires, the plant manager.

Analysis of Company BB. Far from having a so-called open-door policy, this company states that an employee "shall," which means "must" and not "may" according to the dictionary, take the grievance first to the supervisor.

An interesting feature of this company is its definition of the function of the human resources department as a participant in the grievance appeal process—namely, "to resolve the matter to the mutual satisfaction of the employee and the company." Most companies which provide for a formal appeal to that department undoubtedly intend that it "resolve the matter" itself rather than serve merely as a counselor of the employee and then let the employee appeal to higher management. However, this company is wise in emphatically spelling out the department's responsibility to try to keep the problem from going to higher management, which is sufficiently busy without it.

Company CC

Under the heading of Employee Problem Solving, this large company of 35,000 employees enunciates a policy of "open and free exchange of information, problems and complaints," adding that "unusual problems or complaints can be resolved between an employee and the supervisor in the normal course of their day-to-day relationship." A more detailed presentation of company policy is then provided as follows:

In some cases though, a personal problem, a policy interpretation, or disagreement should be taken to a higher level of supervision. If an employee wants to talk to a higher level of management, or to Employee Relations, the employee should feel free to do so, and it is the policy to encourage this.

No supervisor or manager should discourage employees from discussing their problems in any way with a higher level of supervision or from seeking a review of any decision at a higher level, either at the Division or the Corporate level. Supervisors should advise each employee of this policy and encourage them to seek a review of any decision which the employee feels is improper or unfair.

The problem may be presented in writing, but a particular form is not provided.

With or without first approaching the supervisor, an employee may take a grievance to "any higher level of management the employee chooses in the employee's division, or any Personnel Representative in the Employee Relations Department." The next higher appeal is to the Personnel Director, and the final appeal is to:

the Vice President, Personnel, who will direct a review of the matter with the Management Review Committee consisting of the Vice President, Personnel, the member of the Operations Committee responsible for the organization to which the employee belongs, and Mr. _____, retired Executive Vice President.

Analysis of Company CC. This company is interesting for several reasons. First, it not only claims an open-door policy in employee relations but also, unlike some companies, does not contradict that stated policy by injecting restrictions into the prescribed formal appeal procedure regarding an employee's freedom to present a grievance to a management level of his or her choice. This company's formal procedure has an exceptionally wide open door in its permission to an employee—even without first approaching the supervisor—to go to "any higher level of management the employee chooses in the employee's division, or any Personnel Representative," whereas most companies prescribe formal steps through higher management which do not permit the skipping of management levels.

Second, this company's open-door policy, in its sense that—in both its informal and its formal procedures regarding employees' grievances—an employee may have direct initial access to "any higher level of management," raises the question of the advisability from a management viewpoint of such a practice. The basis for this question is the fact that levels are established in the management of a company to accomplish a more efficient control over internal affairs, whereas an open-door policy contravenes the purpose of the levels by ignoring them. An example of this dilemma is a member of middle management who is bypassed by an employee and later learns that higher management has rendered a decision in the matter. It would appear appropriate for that member of middle management to complain to his or her superiors that they took an action which was more properly within the scope of his or her own authority and responsibility. The practical solution to this problem is most probably that the higher management approached by the employee should consult with the bypassed member of middle management and, by the same logic, with the employee's supervisor.

Third, the company's formal procedure is confusing in the form in which it is drafted because, although it permits an employee to initiate a grievance at "any higher level of management," the employee may interpret later provisions in the procedure—if they are studied carefully—as exempting the president from being approached by the employee.

Company DD

This small company of 600 employees states that its "philosophy" is that "open communication is very important for the success of this company," and that therefore an employee has the option of discussing a grievance with "someone outside of your normal reporting relationship" or of following the formal procedure: an appeal from the supervisor to the next level of management and finally the general manager. In both options, the employee may be assisted by the human resources department.

Analysis of Company DD. The small size of this company contributes to informality in employees' dealings with management.

Company EE

For 40 years this very small company of 400 employees has had what it calls "a very impressive and effective communications vehicle...under a rather casual atmosphere which encourages the employee to come forth and present his or her problems."

"A Cooperative Committee of employees representing the various departments meets monthly with the employees and the plant manager" to review a number of subjects. "Many times, a personal or individual problem will surface at committee meetings, is addressed briefly, and is referred to management for further study."

Separately from the Committee's activity, employees are encouraged to discuss problems with their supervisors. "The ones that seem too complicated will be referred to the Plant Manager."

Analysis of Company EE. This company has a very interesting and very unique grievance resolution procedure, the critical feature of which is a committee of employees—a committee, therefore, which can be relied upon to be sympathetic toward employees, to which employees can informally present their problems, and with the committee exercising the initiative of forwarding the problem to management when advisable. As an option, an employee may deal directly with the supervisor, with complicated cases referred to the plant manager.

Company FF

This is a division with 300 employees in a company with a total of 20,000. "All employees are free to talk with any member of management about a problem or complaint. Action, however, can be taken only through the normal channels," as follows.

If an employee is dissatisfied with the supervisor's decision, an appeal may be made to the department head, whose decision will include consultation with the employee-relations department. The final appeal is to the plant manager, acting in consultation with the employee-relations department.

Analysis of Company FF. This company is more specific than most in differentiating between informal and formal grievance resolution procedures, stipulating that informally an employee may merely consult with higher management, with action on the employee's grievance being taken only through the formal procedure, beginning with the supervisor.

Other divisions of this company have different procedures—for example, see Company MM.

Company GG

This company of 2,500 employees "believes most matters will be satisfactorily resolved between individuals and their supervisors, but... he or she is completely at liberty to bring the matter to the attention of anyone in management." In addition:

Any employee who is subject to supervisory retaliation for expressing problems or concerns to management representatives should contact either their Plant Personnel Manager or the Corporate Human Resources Department. Supervisors who retaliate against employees, in any manner, will subject themselves to disciplinary action up to and including discharge.

This company has several plants, each of which is required to draft its own local procedure for resolving employees' grievances, subject to the corporate level policies stated above and also the following, which is under the heading of Corporate Receipt of Complaints.

Employee complaints received by the corporate office will be reported to the manager of the employee's plant and "investigated by the next higher level of management" in that plant. The plant manager prepares a response to the complaint for the signature of the corporate staff member handling the matter. A copy is forwarded to the vice president of human resources. In all cases both the employee and his or her supervisor are interviewed. "In cases where the Corporate Staff member feels that the complaint has not been satisfactorily investigated, or in cases which have Corporate-wide implications, or are extremely serious in nature such as alleged discriminatory treatment or unjust dismissal, Corporate Human Resources will directly investigate the complaint."

Analysis of Company GG. This company has an exceptionally wide open-door policy regarding employees directly approaching higher levels of management of their choice, including also exceptionally, initial contact directly with the corporate offices. In addition, the corporate management is acutely sensitive to employees' complaints which have "Corporate-wide implications." Although this company has only 2,500 employees, it has seen fit to have its corporate human resources department decentralize its activities into individual plant personnel departments, including the in-plant handling of employees grievances.

Company HH

This should be called not a small, but rather a tiny, company as it has only 160 employees. Under the heading of Open Door Policy, the employee-relations manual states that "every member of management is accessible to every employee according to the procedures outlined below," namely:

The employee should communicate first with the supervisor. . . . However, should the supervisor not respond promptly, or not provide an answer satisfactory to the employee, the employee may make an appointment through the supervisor to see the department manager.

If the department manager's answer does not satisfy the employee, the employee may make an appointment through the department manager to see another member of the management staff, such as the operations director, the vice president of technical services, or the human resources director.

If the employee is still not satisfied, the human resources director will be informed, and the item will be discussed at the next president's staff meeting.

All employees are to follow these procedures to utilize the Open Door Policy. Although the ultimate answer may not totally satisfy the employee, the Open Door Policy assures the employee that questions and problems are thoroughly and objectively investigated and responded to.

Analysis of Company HH. This company provides an opportunity for a brief consideration of the phrase open door. Its definition is controversial or, more correctly stated, differs in various companies. Paradoxically, in most companies, instead of an employee having the privilege of consulting with any manager he chooses at any level, open door means merely that an employee may appeal from a decision of the supervisor to higher management, with the doors of higher management not being open until after the employee's supervisor has rendered a decision, and even then only according to specified steps.

In this writer's opinion, the first half of this company's sentence describing its open-door policy, namely, "every member of management is accessible to every employee," is contradicted by the last half of the sentence, "according to the procedure outlined below," which restrict employees to dealing first with supervisors and with restrictive appeal steps.

The feature in the area of employee relations which this research indicates has universal acceptance is that an employee's immediate supervisor must not have the final word in responding to an employee's grievance, including what many companies call "problems, complaints, or questions." Consequently, every company surveyed has been found to have a system for appealing from supervisors' decisions. However, when examining a particular company, care must be exercised in determining that company's definition of the phrase open door. Rarely are the doors of management wide open at all levels, especially in the sense of an employee skipping levels in search of a satisfactory decision. Generally, management uses the phrase open door for its psychological value in making employees feel comfortable, but without any intention that employees should indiscriminately take their grievance to any management officials they prefer. In fact, most employee-relations manuals insist that most employees' problems can and should be settled by immediate supervisors. After all, that is what supervisors are hired to do. The acceptable inference is that, if supervisors do their jobs correctly, the system of appeals from their decisions will be of relatively minor importance.

Company II

This is one of the smallest companies surveyed, with 100 employees. An appeal may be made from a supervisor's decision to the department manager, at which stage the human resources manager will coordinate a decision in meetings jointly or separately with the employee, the supervisor, and the department manager, and the employee may appeal that decision to the president. This is called an Open Communications Procedure.

Analysis of Company II. As with the previous company, the word "open" here means no more than that a formal system is prescribed for appeal over the decision of a supervisor. The central position of the human resources manager in facilitating a decision at the middle management level is typical of many companies, and to some extent it is comparable with the activity of military chaplains in mediating complaints of soldiers against their officers.

Company JJ

This medium-sized company has a simple procedure:

If you believe you have been treated unfairly, please see your supervisor. If the matter has not been resolved, you may request a meeting with the Superintendent. If the matter still has not been resolved, you may request either a private meeting with the Personnel Manager or a joint meeting with the Superintendent, Personnel Manager and Manager of Manufacturing.

Analysis of Company JJ. The last sentence in that procedure is unsatisfactory because it does not clearly inform an employee as to who makes the final decision. It would be the manager of manufacturing if the employee selects the joint meeting with him or her, but "a private meeting with the Personnel Manager" as an option for the employee does not imply that that official may overrule the superintendent's decision.

Company KK

This is a small division of a company totalling 1,000 employees. The brief procedure is to consult the supervisor, after which an appeal may be made to the supervisor's manager and, following that, to the plant manager.

If an employee does not want to deal initially with his or her supervisor, the manager of personnel may be contacted.

Analysis of Company KK. Like many companies, the role of the personnel manager is not specifically described. Strictly speaking, it is an advisory role, inasmuch as employee relations is a "staff" function, not a "line" or "operating" function, unless designated as having decision-making authority over employees' grievances.

Company LL

This is a division of 400 employees in a company totalling 27,000.

An employee may appeal from the supervisor's decision to the superintendent and, above him, to the department manager, and finally the general manager. The human resources manager will assist, if desired by the employee, in presenting the case to the general manager.

"If your problem is broader than your own department or you are not sure who (sic) to talk to, you should call the Human Resources Department."

"As long as your supervisor is aware that you intend to talk to one of his supervisors about your problems, your job status will not be affected."

Analysis of Company LL. The last paragraph above is unique. This writer has not encountered any other employee-relations manual in which an employee is threatened with having his or her job status "affected" if he or she discusses a grievance with higher management without first notifying the immediate supervisor.

Company MM

This is another division of the same company as the division identified as company FF.

The following is their "problem solving" procedure called the Open Door Policy.

If you have a problem or complaint, discuss it with your Supervisor immediately. An honest effort to resolve the problem at this level is highly desirable and should dispose of most problems and complaints.

If you and your Supervisor are unable to find a satisfactory solution or if you would prefer not to discuss your problem with your Supervisor, you should contact your Department Head.

You may then contact the Employee Relations Manager for disposition of your problem.

If you are still unable to find an equitable solution, you may contact the Plant Manager for a final decision.

Analysis of Company MM. As has been seen very frequently in this survey of grievance resolution procedures, the above procedure, described as an Open Door Policy, opens the doors of higher management only in a stipulated sequence. Also as previously seen, the role of the employee-relations manager is defined vaguely; although the employee approaches the employee-relations manager for "disposition of your problem" it is not stated whether a decision may be rendered or whether he or she may only coordinate a decision made by the supervisor or department head. Unlike some companies, employees of this division may not appeal over the plant manager to the corporate headquarters.

Company NN

This company has 350 employees. The first grievance step is to approach the supervisor and, if his decision is unsatisfactory, he may be asked to arrange an appeal with the superintendent. A further appeal is by asking the personnel manager to arrange a meeting with the president.

Analysis of Company NN. The only stipulated function of the personnel manager is to arrange meetings with company officials, but it is reasonable to assume that he or she will grasp the opportunity to analyze the employee's situation and offer the latter advice.

Company OO

There are written procedures for three plants of this company, which totals about 2,000 employees. In all three procedures the appeal steps are from the supervisor successively to the department head, the personnel manager, and the plant manager.

Although the appeal procedures are all identical, there are differences in the employee-relations manuals in the introductory statements regarding management's interest in dealing fairly with employees. However, the basic meaning expressed is the same in all cases. A second kind of difference is in the stipulating of an option for employees:

First plant. If, at any time you feel it necessary, you can ask to go directly to the department head or personnel manager.

Second plant. If, at any time, you feel it necessary, you can go directly to the department head or personnel manager. If you wish to go directly to the plant manager, the personnel manager will arrange that meeting.

Third plant. While employees are encouraged to use this complaint procedure, sensitive personal problems may be handled directly by the personnel manager or the plant manager by utilizing this plant's "open door policy."

Analysis of Company OO. In this company of 2,000 employees, divided into three plants, it is not advisable to draft individual written procedures for the plants, especially, as indicated above, when they differ only in minor details. In other words, the principle of decentralization does not appear, based on study of the three procedures, to offer any advantages. There is certainly no advantage in decentralizing the titles of the procedures, which are: Appeal-Complaint Procedure, Problem Resolution, and Employee Complaint Procedure.

Company PP

In this very small company of 200 employees, an appeal of an employee's grievance from the supervisor's decision may be taken to the employee-relations manager, who may decide to consult the supervisor, and a final appeal may be taken to the plant manager with the employee-relations manager, at the employee's request, "helping you to present your side of the question."

Analysis of Company PP. This simple procedure follows the practice of some companies of stipulating that the employee-relations department shall assist employees in presenting their grievances at certain levels of management.

Company QQ

In this 18,000-employee company, "it is the employee's privilege to take the problem directly to the Personnel Manager at any time. It is the Personnel Department's responsibility to ensure that the employee's problems will be given prompt attention and will be resolved in an equitable fashion." The "established procedure" is as follows:

The grievances may be appealed from the supervisor to the department manager, with the personnel manager present in the meeting, and if the decision is unsatisfactory to the employee, the personnel manager may be requested to arrange a meeting with the general manager.

Analysis of Company QQ. The duties of the personnel manager are not clearly delineated. In the case where an employee directly approaches him or her, it is logical to assume that, with the employee's permission, the personnel manager would contact the supervisor before seeking a solution from higher management. And in the case where the personnel manager's presence is required in a meeting of an employee with the department manager, his or her duties are left unstated. Those duties could be to assist the employee, or to advise the department manager regarding employee-relations policies, or both.

Company RR

The grievance resolution procedure of this company of 400 employees has been in effect for over 11 years.

"The 'Open Door Policy' means that any employee has the right to discuss any complaints or grievances with his Supervisor or Manager up to and including the President. This policy has seemed to work quite well. The appropriate approach is to register a complaint through the established procedure."

That "established procedure" is as follows. The "normal first step" is a meeting of the employee with the supervisor, and the decision may be appealed to the department manager. Further appeals may be made in sequence to the industrial relations manager, the vice president of industrial relations, the vice president of the employee's department, and the president. No more than a week should elapse at each step.

A subject of a "personal or confidential" nature may be taken to the industrial relations manager without the knowledge of the supervisor.

Analysis of Company RR. This company's open-door policy is defined—as is typical of most companies using the phrase—as all the doors of management at all levels being open to the employees. However, the limitation is that the "appropriate approach" is through the "established procedure" of a precise sequence of "steps" from the supervisor through middle management to the president, with the exception that an employee may take a matter which is "personal or confidential" directly to the industrial relations manager.

In the current copy of the written procedure, it is stated, obviously with substantial prior experience, that "this policy has seemed to work quite well," an indication that the employees have not objected to this company's very restrictive definition of the phrase "open door."

Company SS

This is a small consulting firm in the area of human resources management. Their procedure is as follows:

In order for this open door complaint policy to work, you must want it to work and use it. It's for your benefit. Our door is always open. If you follow these steps, no one will criticize you or penalize you in any way.

Step 1: Go talk to your immediate supervisor. Your supervisor knows more about you and your job than any other member of management, and is in the best position to handle your complaint.

Step 2: If you are not satisfied with the answer, your complaint or problem should then be placed in writing and given to the General Manager. You will have the opportunity to visit with him. A decision will be provided within seven (7) days.

Analysis of Company SS. It is noteworthy that no effort was made, as might be expected from a consulting firm specializing in human resources management, to design a grievance resolution procedure that could serve as a model for other companies. However, the inference may be drawn, from the fact that this firm saw fit to design a procedure satisfactory to itself, that the best procedure is one which is tailor-made for an individual company.

Another inference which may be drawn from this firm's procedure is that the firm subscribes to what this research is finding to be the dominant definition of an open-door policy, namely, that the doors of upper management are open to employees provided that a stipulated sequence of "steps" is followed from an employee's supervisor up to the highest level in the company, and often only in a plant or division. Pursuant to that definition, this consulting firm states that "Our door is always open" and then stipulates two required and restrictive "steps." This firm is too small to require a personnel manager, and no provision is made for any one to perform the employee-relations function relative to employees' grievances and other problems.

Company TT

The Dispute Resolution Policy; Problem Solving section of the employee-relations manual of this company of 2,500 employees was submitted to me under cover of this statement: "This is our first attempt at a formal grievance procedure and has just been approved. While we are optimistic that the policy will meet with success, I hesitated offering it for inclusion in Dr. McCabe's study as we have no solid track record on which to evaluate effectiveness."

It is the policy to provide an open and frank forum. No employee shall be penalized formally or informally for using the dispute resolution procedure. It is the employee's responsibility to give the procedure an opportunity to resolve the situation. It should not take more than three weeks. The employee may request a delay to gather additional information. The Human Resources Department will make an Employee Relations or EEO Specialist available to advise about how to use the procedure and to assist in preparing and presenting the employee's perception of the situation.

An employee should first discuss the issue privately with the supervisor, who should try to resolve the issue within three working days, with a delay explained to the employee. The supervisor shall make a decision based on the facts, company policy and a discussion with an Employee Relations Specialist if necessary, and, if the supervisor cannot resolve the issue, he or she should invite the employee to refer it to the next level of management.

That level shall investigate the facts, review company policy, and consult with the Employee Relations Manager if necessary, and render an opinion.

If that response is unsatisfactory to the employee, he or she may take the problem to the Division or Department head in writing on the form provided by the Human Resources Department, indicating the responses of lower management, the employee's 'reasons for disagreeing, and what he or she believes is the proper solution. The Division or Department head will review the employee's written statement with the supervisor or manager concerned to insure that the decision was correctly interpreted by the employee, and will obtain an interpretation of company policy from the Employee Relations Manager, and render a final decision.

Analysis of Company TT. It is interesting to examine this company's grievance resolution procedure from the viewpoint that, inasmuch as it is the first one in the company and just now established, it is reasonable to expect it to incorporate the best features gleaned from other companies' procedures. It is obvious that some attempt was made to do that.

Once again in this research a familiar concept is encountered: "an open and frank forum." And once again there is a rigid limitation on the openness by the stipulating of "steps" in the requirement of first approaching the immediate supervisor and then his or her manager before the doors of higher management will be "open."

Surprisingly, although higher levels of management are required to consult with the employee-relations department, the almost universal practice among companies of encouraging employees to consult informally at all times with that department is omitted in this company.

Another surprise is that, despite the company's "open and frank forum," no provision is made for an employee to appeal above "the Division or Department head" to the corporate officers, including the president, an appeal which is quite common among companies of this one's size.

There are good features in this company's procedure, which was scheduled to be established in the spring of 1987. However, despite its newness and therefore its opportunity to profit from other companies' procedures, it is not a model of grievance resolution worthy of verbatim copying by other companies.

Company UU

In this division of a laboratory-type company, employees are called "associates," with an Associate Problem Solving Policy which is described as one that "reflects good business practices and is a simple one. It is our intent that all supervisors maintain a positive associate relations climate in which integrity, trust and respect for each individual is evident. They should be dealt with recognizing their status and dignity as individuals regardless of race, color, religion, national origin, sex, age or handicap."

It is then stated:

It has always been the policy to maintain a free and open exchange of information and problems. Normally problems can be and are resolved between an associate and the immediate supervisor. It is intended that we respect the "chain of command" in this regard. That "chain of command" is stipulated as follows.

Step 1. All associates are encouraged to talk to their immediate supervisor.

Step 2. However, if that "chain of command" is perceived as an impediment to a healthy problem solving process, the associate or the supervisor may go to the next level of supervision or Personnel for assistance.

Step 3. If the problem persists, the matter should be reviewed with the next appropriate supervisor in that "chain of command" and Personnel for assistance.

Step 4. If the matter is still unresolved, the director of personnel should prepare a complete statement of the problem and apparent reasons that a satisfactory resolution of the problem could not be reached, which will be presented to the division president and the Vice President-Corporate Personnel for review and resolution.

Step 5. If necessary, the problem may even be reviewed with the Executive Vice President and the President.

Analysis of Company UU. It is becoming monotonous in this research to find company after company proclaiming an open-door policy in one breath, in this instance the words "a free and open exchange of information and problems," only to encounter in the next breath restrictions on the openness, in this instance the words "It is intended that we respect the chain of command in this regard."

In Step 2 the appeal is to higher supervision "or Personnel," and in Step 3 the phrase is changed to "and Personnel." A pertinent question is whether that change in terminology is intended or accidental and, if intentional, what is the reason? In Step 5 it is stated that the problem may "even" be reviewed by the top officers, although that quoted word has a tone of condescension toward employees, and could more properly be omitted. What this writer is here leading up to saying in his frequent annoyance, in studying and analyzing employee-relations manuals in this research, at encountering phraseology which is carelessly written and, for that or other reasons, subject to varying interpretation. Certainly a manual written for employees should be as meticulously and precisely prepared as are the blueprints used by them. A particularly glaring example is the almost universal claim that the doors of higher management are "open" to employees but, as this particular company requires, only in a "chain of command" sequence. This is condescending toward employees, offering them an "open door" but only on management's restrictive terms for management's benefit.

Company VV

This is another division in the same company as the division described as company MM, with an identical grievance resolution procedure.

Company WW

This company of 2,400 employees calls its grievance resolution procedure an Open Line Procedure designed "to provide a multi-step procedure to resolve any such problems and insure that employees have a way to express themselves to management."

A termination of employment may, within one week, be appealed directly to the president, who will respond within a week.

The grievance procedure is as follows: first a discussion with the supervisor or, if that "would not be comfortable or appropriate," with any member of management, including the human resources department. Higher appeal is then in sequence to the division manager, the executive vice president, and the president.

Analysis of Company WW. To continue a subject discussed regarding a previously examined company, this procedure is vaguely worded, due to its stipulating steps in the sequence of appeals but contrariwise providing that, if it is not "comfortable or appropriate" for the employee to approach his or her supervisor, "any member of management" may be consulted to obtain a decision regarding the grievance.

Company XX

"Whenever you have a problem or concern, you should discuss it with your supervisor. Normally, the majority of problems can be resolved in this manner." An appeal may be made to the superintendent, then to the plant manager, and "at the point, you may wish the assistance of the personnel department to assist you in presenting your case."

Analysis of Company XX. This is a small plant in a company totalling 4,000 employees. The three features which should be noted are that an appeal is not permitted above the plant level to the corporate officers; the assistance of the personnel department may not be requested by an employee until the case reaches the level of the plant manager; and a claim is not made that the company has an open-door policy.

Company YY

This large company with 15 plants has a policy called Open Door which is thus described: "While we believe an employee should refer problems to his or her immediate supervisor, and when necessary use the appeal procedure, an employee may, if desired, discuss the problem with any member of Management." Furthermore, it is stipulated, as a feature of the formal appeal procedure, that "An employee who prefers to talk to someone without direct supervision over him or her may discuss the problem with a member of the Personnel Department."

A decision of the supervisor may be appealed to the department manager, and then to the group president, the director of relations services, the president, or the chairman of the board.

Analysis of Company YY. Unlike some large companies, this one does not have grievance resolution procedures that are decentralized at the plant level.

In comparison with most companies, the open door of this one is exceptionally wide open to "any member of management," specifically to "discuss" a problem, and it is reasonable to expect that such a discussion will in some instances satisfy an employee so that he or she will not proceed with a formal grievance.

It is surprising that this company does not make provision in its formal appeal procedure for the assistance of the personnel department in presenting an employee's case at any levels of management.

Once again here is a vaguely phrased employee-relations manual. The appeal sequence in this company above the level of department manager is optionally to one of four corporate-level officials, a limitation that can be interpreted as conflicting with the open-door policy, which permits discussion "with any member of Management." Another possible interpretation is that, once an employee invokes the formal appeal procedure, that is equivalent to his or her waiving of the open-door privilege. It may be said that this is splitting hairs, but that is precisely what an attorney would do if an employee invokes the formal appeal procedure, selects the president as the highest official under that procedure, and then has his or her request denied to meet with the chairperson of the board pursuant to the open-door policy, whereupon the employee takes the grievance to court.

It should be noted that, in this survey of companies A through YY, none of them has a provision in the employee-relations manual that an employee's invoking of a formal appeal procedure is an automatic waiver of the employee's right to appeal from that procedure to a court of law. Neither is there an example of a prohibition of an employee's invoking a formal appeal procedure after having obtained a court decision in the matter. However, in the total of 78 employee-relations manuals which have been examined, there was one instance, outside of these A through YY companies, of a company prohibiting an employee to initially obtain a court decision and then, because it was deemed unsatisfactory, to seek a possibly more favorable decision by invoking the company's formal appeal procedure. The silence of companies regarding employees' grievances being taken to court could mean that the matter is not a problem for companies or they cannot do anything about it. Additionally, in the case in which an employee first goes to court and then invokes the company's formal appeal procedure in the hope of a more satisfactory decision, it is unlikely that a company would waive the decision made in its favor by the court. It is interesting that, in the one instance noted above of such an action by an employee being prohibited by a company, the formal appeal procedure in that company includes, as the very last step in the appeal sequence, a review of a grievance by an "internal tribunal," which is the subject matter of Chapter 4.

INTEGRATIVE ANALYSIS

What is here being reviewed is a simple question: "Do business firms have *formal* systems for the resolution of employees' grievances and, if so, what are the detailed provisions?"

What would be the logical expectation of someone who is unfamiliar with the subject? That expectation most likely should be (if consideration is given to the fact that grievances can have a devastating effect upon the morale not only of the employees immediately involved but also of their fellow employees in the departments affected, constituting in a very real sense "monkey wrenches in the gears of the company") that companies deem it an essential employee-relations function of management to provide a *formal* system for dealing with grievances, and even with what, as this research reveals, companies call "problems, concerns, and questions" which have not reached the status of grievances.

Such an expectation is emphatically validated by this research. Every one of the 78 companies (in some instances divisions or individual plants of decentralized companies) which were surveyed in this research had a *formal* procedure for handling employees' grievances, problems, and questions.

It is significant that the companies in this research vary in size from 30 employees to 60,000, and are therefore representative of many employee-relations situations, all of which appear to benefit by *formal* procedures. It is pertinent to repeat here the opening paragraph of the Introduction:

It is universally recognized by business executives that it is inevitable that the complexities of human relations in a company will generate employees' grievances. Consequently, good business practice requires suitable arrangements to systematize a company's handling of the grievances. It is axiomatic that the internal health of a company requires that its employees possess high morale, and this in turn requires that grievances, which are very destructive of morale, be dealt with as quickly as possible, and, of course, as satisfactorily as possible from employees' viewpoints. The very first requirement, therefore, is the maintenance by management of a company environment which encourages employees to reveal their grievances to management instead of keeping them hidden.

It should be noted that this research pertains to nonunion companies and to companies' nonunion divisions or plants, in which employees deal directly with management in the resolution of their grievances, including other problems and questions, without participation of union stewards pursuant to the provisions of union contracts concerning grievances. Consequently, this research reflects the thinking of management regarding what should be the detailed provision of *formal* grievance resolution procedures, without the modifications that a union might seek at the collective bargaining table.

There is a feature of management thinking which is expressly stated in a large percentage of the employee-relations manuals and unquestionably common to management in all companies: namely, that employees' grievances, together with various problems and questions, are inevitable; second, the employees' immediate supervisors are in the most favorable position to prevent and, if necessary, cure such difficulties; and, third, that therefore the employees should take their problems to their immediate supervisors before approaching other managerial personnel.

There are two corollaries of that thinking. The first is that if the number of employees' grievances, problems, and questions which employees appeal over a particular supervisor to higher management exceeds a desirable minimum, it is evidence that that supervisor is not performing his or her duties efficiently. And the second is that sometimes an employee will have what one company calls "a personal or confidential matter" which would make it embarrassing for some reason for the employee to deal with the immediate supervisor, thereby requiring, as many companies expressly provide in their employee-relations manuals, that the employee may bypass the supervisor and approach higher management or, as many companies favor, the employee-relations department.

When a company stipulates the formal steps to higher management that an employee should take in sequence to appeal a decision made at any level of management, it is often expressly stated in the manual that the employee is immune to unfavorable treatment of any kind as a result of his appeal. Furthermore, that protection of the employee's right to appeal is fortified in a few manuals in this survey by the additional provision that the discharging of an employee within a specified period of time after the appeal requires an investigation by higher management, and in one manual it is stipulated that a supervisor who discharges an employee in this context is also liable to being discharged.

Another provision which is often stipulated is that any member of management, most emphatically employees' immediate supervisors, from whom an employee appeals to higher management will properly assist the employee in going to higher management. It is obvious that that can be an embarrassing situation for a supervisor if he or she has reason to suspect that higher management will not support and uphold the decision which he or she made.

The concept of open-door policy was extensively reviewed in the introduction to this chapter, and what was there stated is confirmed by the above detailed examination of employee-relations manuals. It suffices here, consequently, to summarize the situation.

There appears to be an almost universal urge in management circles to be looked upon by employees as interested in their welfare as individuals. The justification for an observer's holding of such an impression is the attitude toward employees' grievances incorporated in employee-relations manuals. That attitude is symbolized by management's use of the term "open-door policy" to designate the procedure designed by management for the resolution of employees' grievances. The term has the connotation of a Welcome sign, indicating the readiness, and hopefully from employees' viewpoint the sincere desire, of management at all levels to assist employees in resolving their grievances against a particular supervisor or manager or against a management policy in general. This also includes as a secondary feature employees' problems and questions which are not in the status of grievances but are of substantial importance to the individual employees involved.

A cynic will reply that the situation is more complex than that. He or she will remind us that employee-relations manuals, including the sections pertaining to the resolution of employees' grievances, are written by the only office in a company, except for the infirmary, in which sympathy for an individual employee's problem is not compromised by the conflicting necessity of conforming with demanding budgets and schedules. That office is variously called Personnel, Employee Relations, Industrial Relations and, pursuant to the most recent management philosophy, Human Resources. The cynic will further suggest that, however sympathetic the motive of that office may be, when it submits its draft of the employee-relations manual to top management for approval, the motive of top management for approving the draft is most likely to be nothing more than cold-blooded self-interest. This would be a situation in which management considers the grievance resolution procedure to be a device not for the benefit of employees but merely for the benefit of management in disposing of a troublesome problem, to wit, a disgruntled employee whose low morale, whatever the cause, renders him or her a monkey wrench in the company's otherwise smoothly turning gears.

And how better, the cynic will conclude, can management encourage an employee to reveal a smoldering grievance to management and cooperate with management in resolving it than by advertising management's friendly open door? The term is a slogan. It has emotional appeal, and employees are very emotional people, just as emotional as management is.

But is the open door merely a slogan? That is what troubles the cynic, who reads in employee-relations manuals statements identified as open-door policy which are assertions that the doors of management at all levels are open at all times, but who then reads in the fine print that employees are *expected* to adhere to the stipulated *formal* appeal procedure with its steps, beginning with immediate supervisors and ending at some level of middle management, such as a plant or division manager, and in some companies proceeding a step higher to corporate officers. And even though employees deem it a sacred right for them to directly approach the personnel department informally and confidentially for advice and assistance at any time, a right cherished by soldiers with respect to Army chaplains, and even though practically all employee-relations manuals permit this on an *informal* basis, nevertheless, when the time comes for an employee to present his grievance *formally* to management in the appeal steps, in many companies the employee may not enlist the personnel department's assistance until higher steps have been reached.

Management's answer to the cynic's viewpoint is that employees' grievances, together with their various other problems and questions, must be subject, like all other phases of a business operation, to systemized control. Granted. And would not a *wide open* door flood the offices of middle management and top management with complaining employees whose personal problems would leave management little time to manage? That is the critical question, with the answer being no. To begin with, employees are adept at "sizing up" managers and would approach only the type which is temperamentally sympathetic to human troubles. Second, an employee's knowledge that the doors of management are open minimizes the frustration caused by a grievance, inducing the employee to think twice before approaching management and undoubtedly sometimes to decide that the grievance is not that important. And third, and most fundamentally, how many grievances per day per hundred employees does the average properly managed company have? Many employee-relations manuals state that grievances are inevitable, and that most of them can be resolved in discussions between employees and their immediate supervisor. On the other hand, a few employee-relations manuals state that, if too many grievances are generated in a supervisor's department, it is evidence that they are his or her fault, requiring appropriate corrective action by management.

More space has been given to the subject of open-door policy than is warranted, but management should be cautioned regarding the importance of being sincerely concerned about employees' personal problems *for the sake of the employees* rather than merely for the sake of the company, and the importance of employees understanding precisely what management means when it states in its employee-relations manual that its doors are "open."

It is obvious that management's proper motive for having its doors open is the maintenance of high morale among the employees. Only a couple of the surveyed employee-relations manuals stated the business axiom that the employees are the company's "most important asset." But, undoubtedly, most managers concede it, and a partial proof of that is the manuals that threaten supervisors with punishment if they retaliate against employees who appeal to higher management.

Considerable space in the introduction and here is accorded open-door policy because of its central status in the philosophy of management. It generates the proper attitude of management toward employees and of employees toward management. It is the keystone of sound employee relations.

CONCLUSION

The practical value of this research is that it saves the time and expense that a company would otherwise incur if it desires to study the experience of other companies before designing a Grievance Resolution Procedure for itself. This research not only presents the ideas of companies varying in size from 30 to 60,000 employees but also critically analyzes their good and bad features.

It was surprising to observe the popularity among companies of a *formal system* of appealing an immediate supervisor's decision regarding an employee's grievance, with precisely stipulated steps upward through successive management levels, including in many instances final decisions by corporate officers and even, in a couple of companies, by the chairperson of the board of directors. It was equally surprising to note the popularity among many companies of the inclusion of a complaining employee's "peer" employees as members jointly with management officials in internal tribunals, that is, jurylike committees which, at varying levels of appeal steps, are empowered to render decisions regarding grievances. Most but not all of the internal tribunals surveyed include peer employees as members.

All the companies surveyed have a *formal system*, described in detail in each company's employee-relations manual, for resolving employees' grievances. In all these companies the system includes a rather elaborate arrangement for an employee to appeal from his or her immediate supervisor's decision regarding a grievance to higher management in ascending steps, the extreme situation being the company in which it is possible for an employee to have a decision rendered six times, once by the immediate supervisor and five times in successive appeals upward through management's chain of command. That many appeals are ridiculous.

A major surprise is that 33 percent of the companies surveyed include an internal tribunal as described in Chapter 4 as one of the appeal steps. Inasmuch as many of the tribunals have one or more peer employees as members, one suspects that management's motive is to develop a "democratic" and participative environment as a factor in augmenting employees' morale. A similar motive appears to pertain to the popularity among the companies surveyed as to what they usually call their open-door policy, with considerable prominence given to it in employee-relations manuals' sections regarding resolving grievances. A certain degree of cynicism has developed regarding that "policy" because of the very high percentage of the companies which espouse it in a manual's introduction and then contradictorily and stringently limit it in a later part of the manual. That is, many companies assert that the doors at all levels of management are open to employees at all times for the discussion of grievances, including "problems and questions," but, as soon as an employee decides to appeal his or her immediate supervisor's decision regarding a grievance, all the so-called "open" doors automatically close except the next higher one in the employee's appeal "steps" upward through higher management levels.

The phrase "open door policy" is so highly popular among almost all companies that it would be instructive if each company came up with the following standardized definition of the phrase:

Open-Door Policy. We desire to maintain a democratic environment in which each employee who feels the need to discuss with management a personal or job-related problem or question will not hesitate to do so on an *informal*, confidential, and off-the-record basis. This would be preferably, of course, with the employee's immediate supervisor but with the employee encouraged to select whatever manager or corporate officer he or she deems most advisable in the situation. The only limitation would be that, if the employee decides afterward to present the problem to the company as a *formal grievance*, it will be done as stipulated in the following Grievance Resolution Procedure.

A peculiar situation noted is that many companies seem to be allergic to the word "grievance," with their employee-relations manuals speaking only of "problems and questions" and of a "problem solving procedure." There is nothing pejorative about the word "grievance." It is an honorable word, and, inasmuch as it has an important technical meaning in the area of employer-employee relations, it should be used when that meaning is intended. What is being advocated is a clear distinction between a company's open-door policy for the *informal* discussion of employees' "problems and questions" and the necessarily restrictive procedure when a *formal* grievance is submitted to an immediate supervisor, especially when the latter's decision is appealed to higher management.

For some reason the standard practice in employee-relations manuals is to present the formal appeal system under the heading of Open-Door Policy, which is an exaggeration if not a misnomer. Only one company provided an adequate definition of "grievance," stating that an employee's "problem" becomes a "grievance" as soon as it is submitted formally to the immediate supervisor for his decision.

Many surprises were encountered in this research, but not surprising is that only 6 of the 78 companies surveyed provide for an employee's final appeal of a grievance to an outside professional arbitrator. Executives are averse to submitting their destiny to influence by outsiders.

It is not practical in this conclusion to summarize the numerous and complex elements found in this survey of employee-relations manuals regarding the process of appealing an immediate supervisor's decision for a grievance to higher levels of management, and this information was made available above in the Integrative Analysis section.

A business axiom declares that a project will not be successful unless it is monitored and energized by the company's top executive. This is applicable to management's handling of employees' grievances, especially with regard to the "democratic," so-called open-door policy which is presently very popular, at least popular as an attractive slogan at the level of top management. Whether it is attractive at lower levels is a separate matter, partly because some supervisors and managerial personnel are temperamentally inclined to be more autocratic than participative—which is very likely one of the major reasons why employees' grievances are sufficiently numerous to necessitate companies having a formal grievance resolution procedure.

PART III
CONCLUSION AND
BIBLIOGRAPHY

Part III concludes the findings of this study. Chapter 6 outlines the executive summary of generalizable principles (that is, the human resources management lessons to be learned); delineates policy recommendations for human resource managers; and offers recommendations for future research.

Last, what is probably the most comprehensive bibliography on the subject of nonunion complaint/grievance procedures and systems has been compiled for use by both scholars and practitioners.

6
Conclusion

INTRODUCTION

Some general principles can be deduced from this study. Efforts to move from the specific to the general in any analysis should be attempted with caution, particularly in complex situations in which one or more factors may be exerting their weight in a direction different from that of other factors. In other words, to generalize about one factor will not be necessarily to arrive at the same conclusion as to generalize about another. Furthermore, to generalize about the composite of all the factors may involve a situation so unique that it will not again occur, rendering generalization of no value. It is important, therefore, to weigh the various factors, as the size and strength of varying waves and winds in a turbulent sea might be appraised in order to determine the probable direction of a ship that is at their mercy.

Also, the purpose of this chapter is to aid the reader who has carefully perused the entire study to gain a solid understanding of the procedural labyrinth and is not intended to be a substitute for a complete reading of the book. However, it is suggested that the busy practitioner and/or scholar who turns initially to this page, without an intention to read this entire study, also peruse the Integrative Analysis section of each chapter. In any event, it is hoped that this study will provide some guideposts for both employers and employees in future phases of the development of nonunion grievance procedures and systems.

EXECUTIVE SUMMARY OF GENERALIZABLE PRINCIPLES: HUMAN RESOURCES MANAGEMENT LESSONS TO BE LEARNED

It would be foolish to draft a procedure, and claim it to be "the ideal," for resolving employees' complaints and grievances. Like an organization chart, the procedure should be tailored to the situation of a particular company. On the other hand, it is practical, based upon the research, to propose a summary of general principles which should be considered when preparing a manual's Grievance section. Hopefully the following items will assist a company in drafting what is for it, in its particular situation, a grievance resolution procedure which approaches an ideal.

1. Have the above surveyed procedures, which reflect the thinking and experience of a number of companies, been examined by you in search of ideas which may be beneficial for your company?
2. Do you consider it advisable, as a few companies do, to state, either in the introduction of your employee-relations manual or in its section on Grievances, your company's philosophy that "Our employees are our most important asset," together with some explanation for it?
3. What title do you think will be best for the manual's section regarding grievances, such as How to Handle a Grievance?
4. Consider the advisability, as some companies do, of providing a specific definition of "grievance" as your management desires employees to understand the word. Some companies define a grievance as a complaint by an employee against treatment by management which violates the terms of employment described in the employee-relations manual. Some companies state that a grievance may be initiated against supervisors' and managers' "application or interpretation" of a company policy published in the manual, but not against the policy itself. All such companies surveyed ignore in their manuals the possibility that a policy may be defective and that it can be in the best interest of a company to provide employees with an orderly procedure for complaining about it.
5. Consider the advisability, as some companies do, of including in the grievance resolution procedure not only formal grievances as your company defines them but also such annoyances to employees as miscellaneous "problems and questions."
6. If you are a "participative management" company, that is, one in which fresh ideas are generated in management committees in which employees are also members, such a committee should contribute its thinking to the grievance procedures project.
7. If you are a decentralized company, with substantially autonomous divisions or plants, each will probably have its own locally prepared grievance resolution procedure. In this instance, a key question will be whether the highest level of management to which an employee may appeal a grievance is a local official or an official at the corporate headquarters, and the decision should be made by that headquarters based on its human resources management policy.
8. Before any detailed provisions of the grievance resolution procedure are written, a decision should be made regarding the scope of participation of human resources management personnel, including those at the corporate headquarters of a decentralized company. This matter should be considered jointly with item 9, which pertains to open-door policy.

a. In a few companies, human resources management personnel perform the ombudsman function, that is, they are paid by management to represent the interests of employees when any of the latter are in a conflict situation with management.

b. In most companies, if not all, employees are urged to approach human resources management personnel informally and confidentially for advice at any time.

c. In some companies, an employee may formally present a grievance initially to human resources management personnel instead of initially to the immediate supervisor if for some reason the latter action would be embarrassing or distasteful to the employee. In an extremely few companies an employee must initially present a formal grievance to the immediate supervisor even though the employee may approach human resources management personnel later when using the steps of a procedure of appeal to higher management.

d. There is considerable variation among companies as to the level of management in the steps of appealing a grievance, at which a human resources management official is designated as the next member of management to be approached by the employee.

   (1) A major deficiency noted in many employee-relations manuals surveyed is failure to stipulate clearly the authority of a human resources management official designated as a step of appeal of a grievance to higher management. In some instances it is stipulated that he or she will render a decision regarding the grievance, even though it may overrule (modify or cancel) a decision of the immediate supervisor and/or of the latter's manager. The advisability of a human resources management official having authority to overrule a decision of line management, especially in the few instances surveyed in which that official is the final step of appeal, is questionable. My recommendation is that the function of human resources officials be limited to assisting employees in processing their grievances and in coordinating and advising line managers in rendering decisions regarding grievances which conform with the company's human resources policies.

   (2) It should be noted that many employee-relations manuals state the opinion of management that most employees' grievances are resolved in meetings of the employees with their immediate supervisor, and this should be stated in a manual as encouragement to employees to approach their supervisors optimistically. In a mood of exceptional frankness, one manual surveyed stated bluntly that the occurrence of too many grievances in a supervisor's department is probably evidence that he or she is incompetent.

9. You will probably desire, as most companies do, to announce in the employee-relations manual that your company has an open-door policy. Its primary advantage is undoubtedly psychological, that is, giving employees a sense of intimate relationship with management as contrasted with a sense of isolation from management.

a. The danger is that "open-door policy" may be little more than a nice-sounding slogan, with little practical significance. To avoid that danger, top management must force itself and lower management to "mean what they say" in declaring that their doors are "open" to employees.

b. A second danger is inconsistency, which is evident in those companies that announce that management's doors are "open" and then provide restrictions, an example being the company that states contradictorily that its management doors are "open" and that employees are "expected" to adhere strictly to the formal appeal procedure steps, including first approaching the immediate supervisor.

c. The ideal open door is undoubtedly one which is wide open, at all levels of management at all times on a very informal basis, including the door of the chairperson of the board of directors. This ideal is best exemplified by the owner-president of a small company who strolls frequently among the employees chatting with them on a first-name basis. If too many employees take advantage of the "open door" with unjustified grievances, which is unlikely, the company's auditor should balance that fact against the column in his books which indicates the high level of employees' morale generated by the open-door policy.

10. A decision should be made regarding the policy, which was found in only a few of the surveyed companies, of "confidentially" of a grievance, whereas some companies favor publishing the decision regarding it, but with most companies remaining silent on this subject. If there is a conflict in a particular case between the employee's best interest and the company's best interest, the former should prevail.

a. It should be noted that some companies stipulate that any written record of the processing of a grievance shall include a copy in the files of the human resources management department but excluding the placing of a copy in the employee's personnel file.

(1) A written record of the processing of a grievance should be restricted to the minimum required by a manager to whom a grievance is appealed from a decision of a lower level of management. No known company uses written records for statistical purposes and the best argument against such a practice is the generally acknowledged fact that most grievances are resolved, usually informally, by immediate supervisors as a normal function of their day-to-day duties. The basic question is whether statistical analysis of written records serves a meaningful purpose with respect to appealed grievances. Statistical analysis should be introduced only if—and when—a specific need for it is determined.

11. Serious consideration should be given to the practice of many companies of stipulating in their employee-relations manuals that employees may feel secure from retribution against them by a supervisor or manager because of the initiation and/or appeal of a grievance. A few of the surveyed companies require an investigation of the circumstances of the discharge within a stipulated time of an employee who processed a grievance, and the manual of one company threatens supervisors with being themselves discharged if they penalize an employee for having processed a grievance.

12. The following questions are the most fundamental ones which must be answered when drafting the grievance section of an employee-relations manual:

a. Should the company have an open-door policy?

b. Should the company have formal appeal steps to higher levels of management for the processing of an employee's grievance?

c. Should the company have as one of the appeal steps the submission of a grievance at the option of the employee to an internal tribunal, defined as a jury the members of which are some management personnel and some of the employee's peers, that is, fellow employees with about the same status as he or she in the company?

   (1) There are numerous differences among companies in the method of appointment of the members of an internal tribunal. The management members may be appointed by management; or the employee may exercise a veto over an appointed manager; or the employee may select at least one of the management members. The members who are peer employees may be appointed by the management members, in this instance customarily chosen at random from a roster of suitable employees who in some cases have received training for the purpose, usually with the employee having a veto privilege, or, these members may be selected from among all of the company's employees by the employee who has the grievance, with or without a veto by management. Finally, to cite a specific example from a company surveyed by this writer, management may appoint two of its members to serve on the internal tribunal, the complaining employee will then select two of his peer employees, and then those four appointees will unanimously select a third peer, providing the desirable odd number of members for voting purposes and, it should be noted, giving the complaining employee's peers majority control of the internal tribunal.

   (2) Sometimes an internal tribunal has a mandated member selected from the human resources management department, who then is customarily designated as the tribunal's chairperson. The advantage here is that this person is officially neutral between management and the complaining employee and, in addition, can advise the tribunal on the company's human resources policies. Sometimes he or she has a vote in the tribunal only when necessary to break a tie.

   (3) In most companies having an internal tribunal render its decision comes at the highest level of appeal steps and is final, although in a few companies its decision may be overruled by top management. Companies have many names for it, a frequent one being Board of Review, but Grievance Appeal Board is recommended as being most descriptive of its function.

d. Should the company have a provision authorizing an employee and/or manager to invoke arbitration by an outside professional arbitrator as the final step in appealing a grievance to higher management?

   (1) The advantage of arbitration is its professional neutrality, and the disadvantage from a management viewpoint is that the company surrenders its control of a grievance to an outsider.

13. There should be no difficulty in designing the appeal steps for an employee's grievance, because, if an employee dislikes the decision of his immediate superior, the steps are progressively through higher levels of management strictly in conformity with the chain of command.

   a. It is exceptional for an employee to skip at his or her option one or more of the stipulated levels of management, for companies only rarely permit it.

b. Special provision must be made in the step sequence when one of the steps is a designated member of the human resources department, which is not in the chain of command. Such a step is usually at or somewhat above the mid-point of the steps and rarely at the last step, the obvious reason being that top management desires to have the last word in disposing of an appealed grievance. An advantage of placing this person near the mid-point of the steps is that, as an officially neutral person between employees and management, he or she is able before rendering a decision regarding a grievance to consult informally and off the record with managers below and above the mid-point location, thereby being able to inform the complaining employee that his or her decision is the best which that employee probably should expect.

c. It is at this point that a decentralized division or plant must determine whether the appeal steps shall include one or more members of top management at the corporate headquarters.

14. Many companies prescribe a maximum number of working days within which a person at any level of management must provide a decision regarding an employee's grievance, and some companies permit the employee to proceed to the next appeal level if no decision is provided within the time limit. Inasmuch as "Justice delayed is justice denied," care must be taken that the total elapsed time of all permitted appeal steps is not unreasonable from an employee's viewpoint.

15. Discharges are given special treatment in some companies, undoubtedly because of the urgency of processing the employee's appeal, with the employee permitted to begin an appeal at a high level of management, such as a plant manager.

16. It is surprising that, with one exception, the companies surveyed appear to ignore the question of whether there is at least a theoretical maximum justifiable number of appeal steps. In one company, an employee is permitted to obtain six decisions regarding a grievance, namely, the decision of his or her supervisor and the decisions at five appeal steps above that manager. The mentioned exception is a centralized company having a different number of management levels in its various facilities, with the final appeal being to a member of the corporate executive committee, and with a maximum of four decisions permitted, including that of the immediate supervisor. The question each company must answer for itself is: How many appeals over the decision of an immediate supervisor are "fair and reasonable" for both the complaining employee and management?

a. The best answer is that after an immediate supervisor has rendered a decision, the first appeal should be to that supervisor's manager and the next and final appeal to a permanent Grievance Appeal Board consisting of a member of middle management, a member of top management, and a high level member of the human resources department as a voting chairperson. The obvious advantage of such a committee is continuity of experience in judging the merits of grievances, uniformity of decisions, and the accumulation of data for the recommending of corrective action when too many grievances of a given type, or too many grievances from a particular department, reach the committee.

b. A related question is the advisability of including provision for an employee's peers to participate in the above-recommended permanent Grievance Appeal

Board. That is, of course, the participative management thing to do. Personally, I would prefer to appeal a grievance to a permanent committee of the company, with the expertise that permanence generates, than to an internal tribunal which is merely ad hoc—that is, assembled as a temporary committee to hear a particular grievance, and including one or more peer employees picked, as is frequently done, more or less at random and having no previous experience in resolving a grievance.

17. Only a few of the companies surveyed use a specially designed paper form as a record of the processing of a grievance, and usually only if the decision of the immediate supervisor is to be appealed. Some other companies require an employee to initiate an appeal in the form of a letter, especially when the appeal is to a member of top management. It is customary to stipulate that an employee may ask for the assistance of a member of the human resources management department in the preparation of any required document.

18. Ambiguity in the phraseology of an employee-relations manual should be no more tolerated than it is in an engineer's blueprint. One of the manuals surveyed states that, if a complaining employee is dissatisfied with the superintendent's decision regarding a grievance, "you may request either a private meeting with the Personnel Manager or a joint meeting with the Superintendent, Personnel Manager and Manager of Manufacturing." The inference in that statement, as it is worded, is that, if the employee selects the "private meeting with the Personnel Manager" as his "either-or" option, the Personnel Manager has authority to overrule the Superintendent's decision, with the additional inference that, if the employee selects "a joint meeting with the Superintendent, Personnel Manager and Manager of Manufacturing," the final decision will be made by the Manager of Manufacturing after consultation with the Superintendent and Personnel Manager. Another ambiguity is in whatever distinction this company's manual intends to make between a meeting with the Personnel Manager and a "private meeting" with him or her, and, indeed, what precisely is the meaning of "private" in this context? Does it mean secretive?

    a. Another example of ambiguity is the manual of a company that authorized appeal steps to higher management but states: "As long as your supervisor is aware that you intend to talk to one of his supervisors about your problem, your job status will not be affected." How would it be affected? Who would make the change, the supervisor on his or her own authority or with the manager's approval? Could an employee's grievance against such a change in his or her job status be considered legitimate? Was it intentional on the part of management to phrase its statement as a threat?

       A third example of ambiguity is the manual which states that, if an employee is dissatisfied after appealing a grievance to the department head, "You may then contact the Employee Relations Manager for disposition of your problem," after which a final appeal may be made to the plant manager, the ambiguity being uncertainty regarding the authority of the Employee Relations Manager in this situation, inasmuch as he or she is a member of the organization's "staff" and not an official in the "chain of command."

19. What ideas do you have which should be considered for inclusion in your company's Grievance/Complaint Resolution Procedure but which are not included in this survey?

POLICY RECOMMENDATIONS FOR EXECUTIVES AND HUMAN RESOURCE MANAGERS

A characteristic of the development of nonunion grievance procedures has been the unpredictability of their suitability. In this section, with the past as a lesson learned, a look will be taken into the future, not as a prediction but in the form of policy recommendations.

The following actions should be taken where appropriate by human resource managers, general managers, neutrals, agencies, or employers, or in combination as required based upon the research of this entire study.

1. Human resource managers and executives should utilize the good offices of such organizations and groups as the American Arbitration Association (AAA) for proffering and listing experienced arbitrators for the nonunion grievance procedure process. The AAA, in particular, exists for such a purpose and it can aid employers, executives, managers, and employees with pedagogical seminars for comprehending the benefits of such a process. The AAA enthusiastically recommends the arbitration process as an alternative form of dispute resolution (ADR) in nonunion employer-employee relationships. It is up to human resource managers, general managers, and employers to realize that nonunion arbitration of employee complaints and grievances can function just as well as the traditional forms of labor-management arbitration in resolving conflict in the workplace. This expeditious functioning was discussed in Chapter 3.

2. Much more experimentation and use of nonunion grievance arbitration systems and procedures should be tried in universities and colleges. For example, impartial and neutral third-party arbitration can be utilized as the last step in nonunion faculty grievance procedures in certain nonunion institutions. Also, private sector hospitals, eleemosynary institutions, and other service organizations may find such systems useful and expeditious in settling human conflict in the workplace. Therefore, managers in nonprofit institutions should study Chapter 3 for potential procedural transferability.

3. Greater reliance should be placed by human resource managers on the Expedited Employment Arbitration Rules and the Alternative Dispute Resolution Program of Resolving Business Disputes of the American Arbitration Association in relation to nonunion grievance arbitration systems. These rules should be studied carefully and this program of the AAA should be given careful consideration by managers.

4. Management in nonunion companies should encourage arbitration procedures, internal tribunals and peer review systems, and legitimate open-door policies designed to resolve employment-related disputes in order to foster industrial justice and jurisprudence and an enlightened and passionate sense of due process for dissatisfied employees. This is sound corporate social responsibility.

5. In nonunion grievance arbitration systems, both executives and employees should try to select, whenever possible, less experienced arbitrators. The reason for this policy recommendation is that very often the most experienced arbitrators are seldom available and thus justice delayed is justice denied (a major principle in this study).

6. Where nonunion grievance and complaint arbitration is used, it should be severely limited to review of contested applications of company policy and not of the policy itself, as was seen in Chapter 3.

7. When adopting an internal tribunal or peer review system for handling employee complaints, it is important to stipulate in the employee-relations manual that the tribunals and peer review panels are not allowed to set policy, as was discussed in Chapter 4.

8. To foster a climate of true and legitimate peer review, the composition of an internal tribunal should ideally be that of three of the complainant's peers and two management representatives, as was discussed in Chapter 4.

9. A peer review tribunal requires the wholehearted support of employers and top management. Furthermore, the process per se must also be seen as enduring. Finally, there must be a concomitant and corresponding commitment at all management levels in the hierarchy and scalar chain of command to employee due process and equitable treatment as was discussed in Chapter 4. Without top management's total support, any peer review system will inevitably fail.

10. Employers and executives must realize that definitive, lucid, equitable, and just human resources management policies that are effectively communicated are the foundational cornerstone of sound employer-employee relations (especially in the nonunion environment) and good business ethics.

11. Managers should adopt a contingency theory of nonunion complaint procedures. That is, they should realize that there is no one single and best system for all companies or organizations and that no two firms should have identical or similar systems merely for the sake of uniformity. Each procedure or system should be specifically tailored to fit the unique size, complexity, and endemic operating conditions and idiosyncrasies of the organization. This policy recommendation can be based upon the unique experiences of the firms studied in Chapters 3, 4, and 5.

12. The National Academy of Arbitrators and the Federal Mediation and Conciliation Service (FMCS) can also be used by human resource managers as a source of neutral and impartial arbitrators to serve in the final step in nonunion grievance arbitration procedures, or to serve as individual members of an internal corporate tribunal or peer review process where such systems call for a neutral and dispassionate outsider as part of their membership composition. Potential examples of where such proferred arbitrators could be used might be seen in Chapter 3 and 4.

13. Companies that adopt peer review and internal tribunal systems must establish a sound and very rigorous training program for potential panelists. A critical and fundamental element of this intensive training should be a simulated grievance or complaint hearing. Having a reliable simulation is an integral part of a valid and reliable panelist training program. As was seen in Chapter 4, some companies have superb panelist training programs.

14. Human resource managers, if they have not already acknowledged it in their employee-relations literature, need to recognize intrinsically the due process or fair process rights of their employees and workers to seek restitution of complaints and grievances. Furthermore, employers and executives must provide for the

exercise of these procedural and substantive rights through the institutionalization of formal policies, procedures, and systems. These two principles are the raison d'être of this study.

15. Based upon this study's research, human resource managers would well serve their organizations by advocating either peer review or arbitration as the terminal step of the nonunion grievance/complaint procedure rather than a mere informal open-door process. Based upon this study of 78 firms, it appears that either system would provide the requisite credibility to foster maximum worker confidence in an organization's system of due process and just treatment.

16. A nonunion complaint resolution system is valuable only if employees and workers are not oblivious to it—that is, they must be totally aware of it and knowledgeable about how it works in terms of its procedural nuances. Therefore, human resource managers must do an excellent and thorough job in publicizing this aspect of the nonunion employment relationship through the proper organizational and employee communication channels. Employees must also observe that absolutely no retribution from management ever takes place against those workers using the procedure. A sound, valid, and reliable system forbids any form of reprisals against any employee filing complaints. It was seen in this study that many companies will terminate supervisors who retaliate against employees for filing complaints.

17. The human resources management department in nonunion companies must play an even greater strategic and tactical role in the nonunion complaint and grievance process. The department of human resources should take the aggressive lead in developing fair and just organizational due process mechanisms and forcefully selling these systems especially to finance, accounting, and marketing executives.

18. Executives with institutionalized and operational nonunion grievance procedures must be totally consistent and uniform when utilizing them. They must comply fully with organizational procedures and policies delineated in employee-relations manuals and other human resources management literature as well as company past practice. Procedures should never be short-circuited for the sake of expediency.

19. Some companies should help to expedite the settlement of employee complaints and grievances by establishing an ombudsman office headed by respected and neutral individuals who report directly and only to the CEO or president. Firms that have already adapted ombudsmen should be meticulously studied and analyzed by organizations seeking to institutionalize this relatively new human resources management tool. Thus, the use of ombudsmen in nonunion companies in which specific circumstances might indicate that he or she can contribute meaningfully to improving employer-employee relations is recommended. This policy recommendation was illustrated in Chapter 2.

20. The real key to the ultimate success of any nonunion complaint procedure is total employee participation in its planning, development, and implementation. Executives must be unequivocally committed to the process of allowing employees to help in the formulation and execution of the procedure or system.

RECOMMENDATIONS FOR FUTURE RESEARCH

This study began with the observation that the question of nonunion grievance procedures in private industry (and in organizations in general) has received little academic attention. General understanding of the subject is still remarkably meager. The research in this study, confined as it has been to companies under the umbrella of the National Association of Manufacturers, is merely a first step in updating the body of knowledge in this area for both scholars and practitioners. Nonunion grievance procedures, undoubtedly because they sometimes engender intense feelings, are not an easy subject for an outsider to investigate. Several companies declined to open their files to this writer. The purpose of this final section is to outline some of the gaps which remain in the public knowledge of the topic which, if other organizational files are opened, offer additional research opportunities. Those opportunities are indicated by the following very succinct descriptions of development in all types of organizations.

Nonunion Grievance Mechanisms in Academic Institutions

Interest in mediation and other alternative ways of solving employee complaints—what some term "alternative dispute resolution"—is receiving greater attention in universities. A few universities are studying the idea to see if it can viably work to settle faculty and staff complaints and grievances. Can academic institutions utilize some form of mediation to supplement existing nonunion grievance procedures? The idea here is to get employees to sit down in a very nonconfrontational and nonlitigious atmosphere and merely talk, the essence of mediation, unlike decision-making arbitration, being the effort by a neutral third party to assist disputants in resolving their conflict. This technique might go a long way in solving employees' complaints and problems.[1]

But is nonunion grievance mediation appropriate for every type of academic problem? Grievances involving promotion, tenure, and reappointment at many universities are heard by university committees.[2]

Various colleges and universities, in their role as employers, have nonunion grievance systems which include the feature of mediation, an appropriate area for additional research.[3]

Measuring the Effectiveness of the Nonunion Grievance Process

According to Lewin and Peterson, some additional research is needed before it is possible to draw any definitive and generalizable conclusions about the grievance process per se. First of all, there is a need to construct a conceptual and theoretical framework "to identify the key factors affecting grievance activity and to derive hypotheses concerning the unique relationships among independent, intervening and dependent variables in the grievance process." Furthermore, "where there is theoretical support for a specific relationship, this needs to be clearly identified. Such identification would help us to gain a better appreciation of the multivariate nature of the grievance procedure."[4]

Second, Lewin and Peterson believe that we should rechannel our research energies toward attempting to measure grievance effectiveness "as an outcome of the grievance process." What constitutes a satisfactory measure of effectiveness needs to be answered by marching into the organizations and questioning the parties themselves. What may be judged an effective grievance system by the employer may be viewed quite differently by the employees. The expectations and definitions of an effective procedure may vary among employees and within the membership even of a single division of a company.[5]

Finally, it should be noted that many factors may influence grievance resolution effectiveness in any given individual employer-employee relationship. In this matter, future research might well include longitudinal methodological designs to capture the effects of changes in the idiosyncrasies of employee relations and management leadership in a particular firm.[6]

Mediation of Employee Rights Disputes in Corporations

Solomon notes that mediation can be a very appropriate part of the grievance process in nonunionized corporations. Mediation can be used in settling disputes concerning ethical issues of working life and can provide alternative means for institutionalizing the protection of employee rights in the corporation.[7] Should mediation occur at the first stage or at the final stage of the procedure? Can we develop a generalized model for handling grievances with mediation, which then can be tailor-made according to the employee-relations philosophy, size, and other normative characteristics of an organization? Can a proposed procedure include due process, administrative simplicity, and attention to financial costs?[8]

Solomon suggests a grievance mediation model in which, if a grievance is not resolved in a meeting, preferably as informal as possible, between the complaining employee and his or her supervisor, then the grievance is subjected to mediation as the next step, based on the employee's written statement of the nature of the grievance, the employee's argument, and the outcome sought. The key element in Solomon's model is the presence in the company of a formal mediation office, or such an office in each department of the company which is large enough to justify a local office. Circumstances will determine whether the office will have a single mediator provided from the ranks of management or a mediation panel with, normally, one management representative and one employee as members. Solomon points out that an even number is not disadvantageous inasmuch as mediation does not involve a decision made by the mediator or mediators, and he adds that two mediators may be better than one in offering the disputants "alternative solutions."

Solomon's mediation model includes provision for a decision arrived at by the mediated parties to be reviewed by management, which should break the agreement only if company policy or a legal requirement has been violated.

The final step in Solomon's model, if mediation fails, is arbitration.[9]

The question here proposed for future research is whether the mediation model proposed by Solomon is adequate to protect the rights of both management and complaining employees.[10] In this research, the only actual use of mediation among the companies surveyed is whatever informal mediation a representative of the human resources department may provide. It should also be noted that in this research, the key feature in the grievance resolution surveyed is progressive appeal by an employee up through successively higher levels of management in the hope of ultimately securing the decision which the employee desires. Solomon's model does not provide for any management decision making in the grievance process above the level of the employer's immediate supervisor.

Equal Employment Opportunity and Nonunion Grievance Systems

What role can nonunion grievance and complaint procedures play in resolving equal employment opportunity grievances? Will internal due process systems benefit minority employees, ensure individual justice, and present organizational discrimination against individuals?

One study by two human resources management scholars noted that nonunion grievance systems can offset racial discrimination against individuals. According to Salipante and Aram, the most direct means by which appeal procedures have these positive effects is through the opportunity a minority has to challenge and appeal a particular decision in a timely fashion.[11]

Those authors emphasize the fact that the mere existence of a company's employees' right of appeal to higher management "places constraints on the immediate supervisors," discouraging them from violating the company's antidiscrimination policy. Furthermore, management's analysis of actual appeals against instances of discrimination can enable corrective action to be taken before the development of pressure from sources outside the company.[12]

The research of those two authors differentiated between "informal" and "more formal" systems of appeal of discrimination grievances upward through higher levels of management, with the following determination:

Our exploratory research indicates that the appeal procedures currently available in many organizations—chiefly, informal appeal to one's superior and on up the chain of command—are inadequate to produce the above effects. Minority employees reported that this informal procedure was not likely to lead to redress of complaints, and that grievants were likely to be labeled as trouble-makers, ruining their career opportunities in the organization. In organizations with more formal grievance procedures, grieving employees were more likely to find assistance, usually from the organization's employee-relations or equal employment opportunity unit, and protection from later recrimination.

The general conclusion, then, is that formal systems of employee appeal offer promise for preventing discriminatory treatment and for changing organizational practices which permit discrimination in promotion, pay, and disciplinary decision.[13]

Therefore, a major future research question emanating out of this study is what definitive nonunion grievance systems will be perceived by the employees of a firm to give a just and equitable hearing and a fair resolution in the special case of equal employment opportunity, thereby earning their full participation in the process.[14]

Fact-finding in Employee Complaint Resolution

Can conflict in areas of the employer-employee relationship outside of the collective bargaining agreement be subject to an orderly avenue of redress? That is, is it viable for employers to consider formal, structured mechanisms for the resolution of their employees noncontractual complaints?[15]

One human resources management scholar has described such a procedure:

Step (1): the complainant is required to discuss the nature of the conflict with the immediate supervisor. This gives the supervisor an opportunity to resolve the matter informally.
Step (2): if the dispute is not resolved between employee and supervisor, the employee may file a formal complaint with the personnel office.
Step (3): a representative of the Personnel Department attempts to mediate between the complainant and supervisor. If mediation produces an agreement, it is reduced to writing and signed by both parties.
Step (4): unsuccessful mediation results in a "first level formal review" by the complainant's department head. The department head prepares a written statement of relevant facts and provides reasons for granting, compromising, or denying the requested remedy.
Step (5): if not satisfied with the results of Step (4) the complainant may request a "second level review" by a higher level of management. In addition, the complainant can invoke fact-finding by an independent third party appointed by the policy development office.
Step (6): employees may appeal second level decisions to the highest management official.[16]

What are the advantages and disadvantages of such a structured procedure for examining employee noncontractual grievances? Is a review procedure such as that described above useful and appropriate for all employer-employee relationships, particularly where employees' noncontractual grievances are remaining unresolved?[17]

Nonunion Grievance Procedures in Nonprofit Organizations

Chruden and Sherman determined that persons working for nonprofit organizations "do not necessarily have fewer grievances than those in profit-making organizations; in fact, they may have more because wages and other conditions of employment frequently are less satisfactory than those provided by profit-making firms."[18] Thus, these authors note, "it is becoming increasingly common to have formal grievance procedures established in charitable foundations, community service organizations, hospitals, and colleges. Even churches have grievance procedures for resolving disputes and differences of opinion occurring within their organizations."[19]

Future research can determine what demand there is for more democratic procedures in solving human resources management problems in these types of organizations.[20]

Nonunion Grievance Procedures in Governmental Agencies

In most governmental jurisdictions, according to Chruden and Sherman, civil service systems "provide procedures by which employees may appeal management decisions affecting them. Those procedures established by the governing body are referred to as statutory procedures. Employee input in determining the procedures usually is limited to what political influence they can bring to bear upon the governing body. Employee appeals terminate with an adjudication decision by an appeals body such as a civil service commission or by an adjudicator appointed by it."[21]

Additional research is suggested regarding a comparison between various types of civil service appeals procedures and corporate nonunion grievance systems.[22]

Unionism and Nonunion Grievance Procedures

Professor William Scott of De Paul University, in his treatise on appeal systems in organizations, stated the following:

While unions would never directly encourage and support a unilateral management plan for appeal settlement, a case for indirect influence on the establishment of these programs can be made. This influence is positive and negative.

Negatively, a business firm may institute an appeal system as a counter-measure to the union's promise to employees of a negotiated grievance procedure. In this respect, the unilateral system is employed as an anti-union device.

Positively, a union's initiative in negotiating grievance procedures for members of the bargaining unit may prompt management to institute appeal programs for all employees, especially those not covered by a contract. While I am not denying anti-union overtones here, I am also suggesting a "halo" effect which is analogous to the positive influence that unionization has on wages for nonunion employees in the same firm.

There is no denying that the influence of unionization has motivated, either positively or negatively, the management of some companies to install appeal systems. But his explanation does not rate unqualified acceptance. It does not, for instance, account for appeal systems in non-business organizations which are relatively free from union pressures. . . . Unionism, while plausible in certain isolated business cases, must be rejected as a general explanation of the appeal phenomenon.[23]

An interesting Ph.D. dissertation in human resources management might be one utilizing empirical methodologies to test for the existence and nature of this "halo" effect, and one that would be able to differentiate between both indirect and direct influences. Also, does "developing a union-avoidance strategy for its own sake usually result in a dysfunctional adversarial relationship between management and the workers?"[24] It has been noted that "despite the apparent popularity of nonunion grievance procedures in management literature, empirical data on such measures are sparse."[25]

Nonunion Conflict Resolution in High Technology Firms

Professor David Lewin of Columbia University's Graduate School of Business Administration has raised a number of research questions in relation to nonunion conflict resolution which need further answering. A number of these questions are particularly important when studying the topic in nonunion high technology firms. For example, how often are those nonunion grievance systems actually used? Which employees use these appeal systems and which ones do not?[26] "How (if at all) does appeal activity affect employee and supervisor job performance, turnover, work attendance, and promotion? Do appeal filers and those against whom appeals are filed suffer in terms of subsequent performance and organizational rewards, compared to employees and supervisors/managers who are not officially in appeal activity?"[27] "Do nonunion appeal systems in high technology firms in effect serve as a substitute for employee unionization?"[28]

The Impact of Strategic Human Resource Policies on Union Organizing

"There seems to be a consensus in the speculative and case study literature to the effect that the growth of union substitution policies (for example, high compensation, employee participation, grievance procedures) has reduced certification rates and union success more generally."[29] However, "does it matter whether a nonunion grievance procedure includes the possibility of a final decision by an impartial umpire? Are some elements of union substitution strategies more effective than others? Are some counterproductive?"[30] Additional research will be needed to answer these questions.

International Human Resource Management Comparisons

There is a research need to examine foreign experience in the area of nonunion complaint procedures and systems. The following statement by Steiber and Blackburn is pertinent: "Many people are absolutely convinced that nothing is adaptable in the sense of taking the actual device and transmitting it to foreign soil and expecting it to grow. But an examination of foreign experience is extremely important primarily because it teaches us to look at American problems from a somewhat different perspective. Foreign experience may suggest new or different approaches that merit our attention."[31]

CONCLUSION

The development of sound and just nonunion complaint and grievance procedures within companies and organizations has made significant progress in recent years. Evolutionary and yeoman changes in the procedures themselves, and the adoption of the written procedures into the overall strategic and tactical corporate human resources management system of firms have enhanced the opportunities for the growth of this very important management developmental process.

Some problems remain unsettled. But the continued development of nonunion grievance and complaint procedures which are equitable for both employees and employers will continue to mature. We may disagree as to whether the pace is fast enough but the direction is clear and encouraging. Simply put, this is an exciting new area in human resources management which will warrant further observance and research.

In closing, the purpose of this study was not just to provide an analysis of the procedures and processes, but, more importantly, to establish a springboard hopefully pointed in the proper direction for the ultimate smooth resolution of remaining problems and issues.

NOTES

1. Liz McMillen, "Colleges Are Trying New Ways to Settle Campus Grievances," *The Chronicle of Higher Education*, 6 May 1987, 14.

2. Ibid.

3. Ibid., 17.

4. David Lewin and Richard B. Peterson, "A Model for Measuring Effectiveness of the Grievance Process," *Monthly Labor Review* 105 (April 1982): 48; see also Richard B. Peterson and David Lewin, "A Model for Research and Analysis of the Grievance Process," in *Industrial Relations Research Association Series, Proceedings of the Thirty-Fourth Annual Meeting, December 28–30, Washington*, ed. Barbara D. Dennis (Madison, WI: Industrial Relations Research Association, 1982), 303–12.

5. Ibid.

6. Ibid.

7. Janet Stern Solomon, "Mediation of Employee Rights Disputes," in *Proceedings of 1986 Annual National Conference, The Council on Employee Responsibilities and Rights, October 16–17, 1986, Virginia Beach, Virginia*, ed. Dietrich Schaupp and Randall Elkin (Virginia Beach, VA: The Council on Employee Responsibilities and Rights, 1986), 35.

8. Ibid., 35–36.

9. Ibid., 36–38.

10. Ibid., 38.

11. Paul F. Salipante, Jr., and John D. Aram, "A System for Individual Equity in Equal Employment Opportunity," *Monthly Labor Review* 102 (April 1979): 46–47; and Paul F. Salipante, Jr., and John D. Aram, "The Role of Special Grievance Systems in Furthering Equal Employment Opportunity," in *Industrial Relations Research Association Series, Proceedings of the Thirty-First Annual Meeting, August 29–31, 1978, Chicago*, ed. Barbara D. Dennis (Madison, WI: Industrial Relations Research Associations, 1979), 299–307.

12. Ibid.

13. Salipante and Aram, "A System for Individual Equity in Equal Employment Opportunity," 16–17.

14. Salipante and Aram, "The Role of Special Grievance Systems in Furthering Equal Employment Opportunity," 307.

15. Steven Briggs, "Beyond the Grievance Procedure: Factfinding in Employee Complaint Resolution," *Labor Law Journal* 33 (August 1982): 454–55.

16. Ibid., 456–57.

17. Ibid., 458–59.

18. Herbert J. Chruden and Arthur W. Sherman, Jr., "Procedures in Nonprofit Organizations," in *Personnel Management*, 5th ed. (Cincinnati: South-Western, 1976), 420.

19. Ibid.

20. Ibid.

21. Herbert J. Chruden and Arthur W. Sherman, Jr., "Grievance Procedures in Government Organizations," in *Managing Human Resources*, 7th ed. (Cincinnati: South-Western, 1984), 394.

22. Ibid.

23. William G. Scott, *The Management of Conflict: Appeal Systems in Organizations* (Homewood, IL: Richard D. Irwin, and The Dorsey Press, 1965), 94–95.

24. Fabius P. O'Brien and Donald A. Drost, "Non-Union Grievance Procedures: Not Just an Anti-Union Strategy," *Personnel* 61 (September-October 1984): 69.

25. James K. McCollum and Dwight R. Norris, "Nonunion Grievance Machinery in Southern Industry," *Personnel Administrator* 29 (November 1984): 107.

26. David Lewin, "Conflict Resolution in the Nonunion High Technology Firm," in *Human Resource Management in High Technology Firms*, ed. Archie Kleingartner and Carolyn S. Anderson (Lexington, MA: D.C. Heath, 1987), 137–39.

27. Ibid., 148.

28. Ibid., 150.

29. Jack Fiorito, Christopher Lowman, and Forrest D. Nelson, "The Impact of Human Resources Policies on Union Organizing," *Industrial Relations* 26 (Spring 1987): 114.

30. Ibid., 124.

31. Jack Steiber and John Blackburn, eds., *Protecting Unorganized Employees Against Unjust Dismissal: Proceedings of a Conference Held at Michigan State University* (East Lansing, MI: School of Labor and Industrial Relations, College of Social Science, Michigan State University, 1983), 46.

Bibliography

BOOKS

Scott, William G. *The Management of Conflict: Appeal Systems in Organizations.* Homewood, IL: Richard D. Irwin, and The Dorsey Press, 1965.

SECTIONS OF BOOKS

Armstrong, Michael, and John F. Lorentzen. "Industrial Relations Procedures for Nonunionized Companies or Employees;" "Grievance Procedure." In *Handbook of Personnel Management Practice: Procedures, Guidelines, Checklists, and Model Forms.* Englewood Cliffs, NJ: Prentice-Hall, 1977.

Barry, Vincent. "Just Cause" and "Due Process." in *Moral Issues in Business.* Belmont, CA: Wadsworth Publishing Co., 1979.

Beach, Dale S. "Grievance Settlement for Nonunion Employees." In *Personnel: The Management of People at Work.* 4th ed. New York: Macmillan Publishing Co., 1980.

————. "Grievance Settlement for Nonunion Employees." In *The Management of People at Work.* 5th ed. New York: Macmillan Publishing Co., 1980.

————. "Where Ombudsmen Work Out." In *Managing People at Work: Readings in Personnel.* 3d ed. New York: Macmillan Publishing Co., 1980.

Beavers, Wiley I. "Employee Relations Without a Union." In *ASPA Handbook of Personnel and Industrial Relations, Volume III, Employee and Labor Relations,* edited by Dale Yoder and Herbert C. Heneman, Jr. Washington, D.C.: The Bureau of National Affairs, 1979.

————. "Employee Relations Without a Union." In *ASPA Handbook of Personnel and Industrial Relations, Volume III, Employee and Labor Relations,* edited by Dale Yoder and Herbert C. Heneman, Jr. Washington, D.C.: The Bureau of National Affairs, 1976.

Beer, Michael, Bert Spector, Paul R. Lawrence, D. Quinn Mills, and Richard E. Walton. *Human Resource Management: A General Manager's Perspective—Text and Cases.* New York: The Free Press, 1985.

———. *Managing Human Assets.* New York: The Free Press, 1984.

Boone, Louis E., and David L. Kurtz. "Labor-Management Relations in Nonunionized Organizations." In *Contemporary Business.* 5th ed. Hinsdale, IL: The Drydren Press, 1987.

Burack, Elmer H., and Robert D. Smith. "Maintaining Nonunion Status." In *Personnel Management: A Human Resource System Approach.* New York: John Wiley & Sons, 1982.

Byars, Lloyd L., and Leslie W. Rue. "Discipline in Nonunionized Organizations." In *Human Resource and Personnel Management.* Homewood, IL: Richard D. Irwin, 1984.

Carrell, Michael R., and Frank E. Kuzmits. "Grievance Handling in Nonunion Organizations." In *Personnel: Human Resource Management.* 2d ed. Columbus, OH: Merrill Publishing Co., 1986.

———. "Nonunion Organizations." In *Personnel: Management of Human Resources.* Columbus, OH: Charles E. Merrill Publishing Co., 1982.

Carroll, Steven J., and Randall S. Schuler, eds. "Labor Relations in Nonunion Companies." In *Human Resource Management in the 1980s.* Washington, D.C.: The Bureau of National Affairs, 1983.

Catt, Stephen E., and Donald S. Miller. "Handling Grievances in Nonunion Organizations." In *Supervisory Management and Communication.* Homewood, IL: Richard D. Irwin, 1985.

Cherrington, David J. "Grievance Procedures in Nonunion Organizations." In *Personnel Management: The Management of Human Resources.* 2d ed. Dubuque, IA: Wm. C. Brown Co., 1987.

———. "Grievance Procedures in Nonunion Organizations." In *Personnel Management: The Management of Human Resources.* Dubuque, IA: Wm. C. Brown Co., 1982.

Chruden, Herbert J. "Procedures in Nonprofit Organizations." In *Personnel Management.* 5th ed. Cincinnati: South-Western Publishing Co., 1976.

Chruden, Herbert J., and Arthur W. Sherman, Jr. "Disciplinary Actions and Appeal Procedures." In *Managing Human Resources.* 7th ed. Cincinnati: South-Western Publishing Co., 1984.

———. "Formal Grievance Procedure." In *Personnel Management: Cincinnati: South-Western Publishing Co., 1959.*

Comstock, Thomas W. *"Dealing With Complaints and Grievances." In Modern Supervision.* Albany, NY: Delmar Publishers, 1987.

Crane, Donald P. "Grievance Procedures." In *Personnel: The Management of Human Resources.* 3d ed. Boston: Kent Publishing Co., 1982.

Davis, Keith. "Grievance Systems." In *Human Relations In Business.* New York: McGraw-Hill, 1957.

Davis, Keith, and Robert L. Blomstrom. "Corporate Constitutionalism." In *Business and Society: Environment and Responsibility.* 3d ed. New York: McGraw-Hill, 1975.

De George, Richard T. "Employment-at-Will: Rights in Hiring, Promotion, and Firing." In *Business Ethics.* 2d ed. New York: Macmillan, 1986.

Dressler, Gary. "Grievance Handling in Nonunion Organizations." In *Personnel Management: Modern Concepts and Techniques*. Reston, VA: Reston Publishing Co., 1978.

————. *Management Fundamentals: Modern Principles & Practices*. 4th ed. Reston, VA: Reston Publishing Co., 1985.

Douglas, John, Stuart Klein, and David Hunt. "Discipline and Discharge." In *The Strategic Managing of Human Resources*. New York: John Wiley & Sons, 1985.

Ewing, David W. "Due Process and Freedom of Inquiry." In *Do It My Way or You're Fired!": Employee Rights and the Changing Role of Management Prerogatives*. New York: John Wiley & Sons, 1983.

————. "Making Due Process a Reality." In *Freedom Inside the Organization: Bringing Civil Liberties to the Workplace*. New York: E. P. Dutton, 1977.

Flippo, Edwin B. "Human and Organizational Conflicts." In *Personnel Management*. 5th ed. New York: McGraw Hill, 1980.

————. "Human and Organizational Conflicts." In *Principles of Personnel Management*. 4th ed. New York: McGraw-Hill, 1976.

————. "The Management of Conflict." In *Personnel Management*. 6th ed. New York: McGraw-Hill, 1984.

Fossum, John A. "Employee Relations in Nonunion Organizations." In *Labor Relations: Development, Structure, Process*. 3d ed. Plano, TX: Business Publications, 1985.

Foulkes, Fred K. "Grievance Procedures." In *Personnel Policies in Large Nonunion Companies*. Englewood Cliffs, NJ: Prentice-Hall, 1980.

————. "Large Nonunionized Employers." In *U.S. Industrial Relations, 1950–1980: A Critical Assessment*. Industrial Relations Research Association Series, ed. Jack Stieber, Robert B. McKersie, and D. Quinn Mills. Madison, WI: Industrial Relations Research Association, 1981.

————, ed. "How Top Nonunion Companies Manage Employees." In *Strategic Human Resource Management: A Guide for Effective Practice*. Englewood Cliffs, NJ: Prentice Hall, 1986.

French, Wendell L. "Organizational Justice." In *The Personnel Management Process: Human Resources Administration and Development*. 6th ed. Boston: Houghton Mifflin Company, 1987.

————. "Organizational Justice." In *The Personnel Management Process: Human Resources Administration and Development*. 5th ed. Boston: Houghton Mifflin Company, 1982.

————. "Organizational Justice." In *The Personnel Management Process: Human Resources Administration and Development*. 4th ed. Boston: Houghton Mifflin Company, 1978.

Garrett, Thomas M., and Richard J. Klonoski. "Due Process." In *Business Ethics*. 2d ed. Englewood Cliffs, NJ: Prentice-Hall, 1986.

George, Claude S., Jr. "What Are the Grievance Procedures in Nonunionized Companies?" In *Supervision in Action: The Art of Managing Others*. 4th ed. Reston, VA: Reston Publishing Co., 1985.

————. "What Are the Grievance Procedures in Nonunionized Companies?" In *Supervision in Action: The Art of Managing Others*. 3d ed. Reston, VA: Reston Publishing Co., 1982.

————. "What Are the Grievance Procedures in Nonunionized Companies?" In *Supervision in Action: The Art of Managing Others*. Reston, VA: Reston Publishing Co., 1979.

Glueck, William F. "Hierarchial Discipline Systems;" "Other Discipline and Appeal Systems." In *Foundations of Personnel*. Dallas: Business Publications, 1979.

————. "Hierarchial Discipline Systems;" "Other Discipline and Appeal Systems." In *Personnel: A Diagnostic Approach*. Rev. ed. Dallas: Business Publications, 1978.

————. "Hierarchial Discipline Systems;" "Other Discipline and Appeal Systems." In *Personnel: A Diagnostic Approach*. Dallas: Business Publications, 1974.

Glueck, William F. Revised by George T. Milkovich. *Personnel: A Diagnostic Approach*. 3d ed. Plano, TX: Business Publications, 1982.

Gordon, Judith R. "Approaches to Resolving Grievances in Nonunion Organizations." In *Human Resource Management: A Practical Approach*. Boston: Allyn and Bacon, 1986.

Greenlaw, Paul S., and John P. Kohl. "Employee-Management Relations: The Managerial Decision Process." In *Personnel Management: Managing Human Resources*. New York: Harper & Row, 1986.

Griffin, Ricky W. "Grievance Procedures." In *Management*. 2d ed. Boston: Houghton Mifflin Co., 1987.

Haimann, Theo, and Raymond L. Hilgert. "Adjudicating Grievances." In *Supervision: Concepts and Practices of Management*. 2d ed. Cincinnati: South-Western Publishing Co., 1977.

————. "Handling Employee Complaints and Grievances." In *Supervision: Concepts and Practices of Management*. 3d ed. Cincinnati: South-Western Publishing Co., 1982.

Hampton, David R., Charles E. Summer, and Ross A. Webber. "Adjusting Conflict through Hierarchial Appeal." In *Organizational Behavior and the Practice of Management*. 5th ed. Glenview, IL: Scott, Foresman and Co., 1987.

Heneman, Herbert G., III, Donald P. Schwab, John A. Fossum, and Lee D. Dyer. "Labor-Management Relations in the Nonunion Organization." In *Personnel/Human Resource Management*. 3d ed. Homewood, IL: Richard D. Irwin, 1986.

————. "Labor-Management Relations in the Nonunion Organization." In *Personnel/Human Resource Management*. Rev. ed. Homewood, IL: Richard D. Irwin, 1983.

————. "Labor-Management Relations in the Nonunion Organization." In *Personnel/Human Resource Management*. Homewood, IL: Richard D. Irwin, 1980.

Holley, William H., and Kenneth M. Jennings. "Characteristics and Policies of the Nonunion Employer." In *Personnel/Human Resource Management: Contributions and Activities*. 2d ed. Hinsdale, IL: Dryden Press, 1987.

————. "Characteristics and Policies of the Nonunion Employer." In *Personnel Management: Functions and Issues*. Chicago: The Dryden Press, 1983.

Holloway, William J., and Michael J. Leech. "Remedies Within the Employer Organization." In *Employment Termination: Rights and Remedies*. Washington, D.C.: The Bureau of National Affairs, 1985.

Ivancevich, John M., and William F. Glueck. "Grievances;" "The Rights of Employees in Nonunionized Situations." In *Foundations of Personnel/Human Resource Management*. Plano, TX: Business Publications, 1983.

Jackson, John H., and Timothy J. Keaveny. "The Grievance Procedure in Nonunion Organizations." In *Successful Supervision*. Englewood Cliffs, NJ: Prentice-Hall, 1980.

Keegan, Elizabeth A. "Grievances." In *Index to AMA Resources: 1977–1981*. New York: American Management Associations, 1982.

Klatt, Lawrence A., Robert G. Murdick, and Frederick E. Schuster. *Human Resource Management*. Columbus, OH: Charles E. Merrill Publishing Co., 1985.

Kochan, Thomas A., and Thomas A. Barocci. "Due Process Procedures for Nonunion Employees." In *Human Resource Management and Industrial Relations: Text, Readings, and Cases*. Boston: Little, Brown, 1985.

Kochan, Thomas A. "Management Strategies for Avoiding Unions." In *Collective Bargaining and Industrial Relations: From Theory to Policy and Practice*. Homewood, IL: Richard D. Irwin, 1980.

Lewin, David. "Conflict Resolution in the Nonunion High Technology Firm." In *Human Resource Management in High Technology Firms*. Edited by Archie Kleingartner and Carolyn S. Anderson. Lexington, MA: Lexington Books, 1987.

Lewis, Philip V. "Handling Grievances." In *Managing Human Relations*. Boston: Kent Publishing Co., 1983.

Lopez, Felix M., Jr. "The Grievance Interview." In *Personnel Interviewing: Theory and Practice*. New York: McGraw-Hill, 1965.

Luthans, Fred, Richard M. Hodgetts, and Kenneth R. Thompson. "Dispute Resolution and Procedures for Employee Justice." In *Social Issues in Business*. 3d ed. New York: Macmillan, 1980.

———. "Employee Justice Systems." In *Social Issues in Business: Strategic and Public Policy Perspectives*. 5th ed. New York: Macmillan, 1987.

Mathis, Robert L., and John H. Jackson. "Nonunion Grievance Procedures." In *Personnel: Human Resource Management*. 4th ed. St. Paul, MN: West Publishing Co., 1985.

———. "Non-union Grievance Procedures." In *Personnel: Contemporary Perspectives and Applications*. 3d ed. St. Paul, MN: West Publishing Co., 1982.

Megginson, Leon C. "Handling Complaints in Nonunion Organizations." In *Personnel Management: A Human Resources Approach*. 5th ed. Homewood, IL: Richard D. Irwin, 1985.

———. "Handling Complaints in Nonunion Organizations." In *Personnel and Human Resources Administration*. 3d ed. Homewood, IL: Richard D. Irwin, 1977.

Mills, Daniel Quinn. "Methods of Handling Communication and Grievances." In *Labor-Management Relations*. 2d ed. New York: McGraw-Hill, 1982.

———. "Nonunion and Union." In *Labor-Management Relations*. 3d ed. New York: McGraw-Hill, 1986.

———. "Nonunion versus Union Grievance Handling." In *Labor-Management Relations*. New York: McGraw-Hill, 1978.

Miner, Mary Green, and John B. Miner. "Employee Conduct and Discipline." In *Policy Issues in Contemporary Personnel and Industrial Relations*. New York: Macmillan, 1977.

———. "Grievance Procedures." In *Personnel and Industrial Relations: A Managerial Approach*. 4th ed. New York: Macmillan, 1985.

Miner, John P. "Appeal Procedures and Organizational Due Process." In *The Man-*

agement Process: Theory, Research, and Practice. 2d ed. New York: Macmillan, 1978.

Mondy, R. Wayne, Robert M. Noe III, Harry N. Mills, Jr., and Arthur Sharplin. "Grievance Handling for Nonunion Employees." In *Personnel: The Management of Human Resources.* 2d ed. Boston: Allyn and Bacon, 1984.

———. "Grievance Handling for Nonunion Employees." In *Personnel: The Management of Human Resources.* Boston: Allyn and Bacon, 1981.

Mondy, R. Wayne, and Robert M. Noe. "Union Free Organizations." In *Personnel: The Management of Human Resources.* 3d ed. Newton, MA: Allyn and Bacon, 1987.

Myers, Donald W. "Employee Relations and Communications." In *Human Resources Management: Principles and Practice.* Chicago, IL: Commerce Clearing House, 1986.

Newman, William H., E. Kirby Warren, and Andrew R. McGill. "Prompt Settlement of Grievances." In *The Process of Management: Strategy, Action, Results.* 6th ed. Englewood Cliffs, NJ: Prentice-Hall, 1987.

Pigors, Paul, and Charles A. Myers. "Complaints and Grievances." In *Personnel Administration: A Point of View and a Method.* 9th ed. New York: McGraw-Hill, 1981.

———. "Complaints and Grievances." In *Personnel Administration: A Point of View and a Method.* New York: McGraw-Hill, 1977.

———. "Complaints and Grievances." In *Personnel Administration: A Point of View and a Method.* New York: McGraw-Hill, 1956.

Pingpank, Jeffrey C., and Thomas B. Mooney. "Wrongful Discharge: A New Danger for Employers." In *Readings in Managing Human Resources.* 6th ed. Edited by Herbert J. Chruden and Arthur W. Sherman, Jr. Cincinnati: South-Western Publishing Co., 1984.

Saltonstall, Robert. "Hidden Meaning of Grievances and Complaints." In *Human Relations in Administration: Text and Cases.* New York: McGraw-Hill, 1959.

Sandver, Marcus Hart. "Change in Employer Policies of Human Resource Management." In *Labor Relations: Process and Outcomes.* Boston: Little, Brown, 1987.

Schneier, Craig Eric, Richard W. Beatty, and Glenn M. McEvoy, "Erosion of the Employment-at-Will Doctrine." In *Personnel/Human Resource Management Today: Readings and Commentary.* 2d ed. Reading, MA: Addison-Wesley Publishing Co., 1986.

Schoen, Sterling H., and Douglas E. Durand. "Effective Grievance Procedures." In *Supervision: The Management of Organizational Resources.* Englewood Cliffs, NJ: Prentice-Hall, 1979.

Schuler, Randall S. "Employer Strategies for Employee Job Security Rights." In *Personnel and Human Resource Management.* 3d ed. St. Paul, MN: West Publishing Co., 1987.

———. "Nonunion Employee Relations." In *Personnel and Human Resource Management.* St. Paul, MN: West Publishing Co., 1981.

Seybold, Geneva. "Labor Relations and Grievances." In *Employee Communication: Policy and Tools.* Personnel Policy Study No. 200. New York: National Industrial Conference Board, 1966.

Sikula, Andrew F. "Nonunion Grievances." In *Personnel Administration and Human Resources Management*. Santa Barbara, CA: John Wiley & Sons, 1976.

Silver, Isidore. "The Corporate Ombudsman." In *Personnel Management Series, Reprints from Harvard Business Review*. No. 21145. Boston: Harvard Business Review, 1968.

Sloane, Arthur A. " 'Just Cause' Statutory Job Protection." In *Personnel: Managing Human Resources*. Englewood Cliffs, NJ: Prentice-Hall, 1983.

Sovereign, Kenneth L. "Employee Complaint Procedures: A Defense for Concerted Activity." In *Personnel Law*. Reston, VA: Reston Publishing Co., 1984.

Steiner, George A., and John F. Steiner. "The Rights Movement in Corporations." In *Business, Government, and Society*. 4th ed. New York: Random House, 1985.

Sturdivant, Frederick D. "Employee Rights." In *Business and Society: A Managerial Approach*. 3d ed. Homewood, IL: Richard D. Irwin, 1985.

Sturdivant, Frederick D. "Openness of the System: Corporate Governance." In *Business and Society: A Managerial Approach*. Rev. ed. Homewood, IL: Richard D. Irwin, 1981.

Thrash, Artie Adams, Annette N. Shelby, and Jerry L. Tarver. "Grievance Interviews." In *Speaking Up Successfully: Communication in Business and the Professions*. New York: Holt, Rinehart and Winston, 1984.

Tosi, Henry L., John R. Rizzo, and Stephan J. Carroll. "Ombudsmen." In *Managing Organizational Behavior*. Marshfield, MA: Pitman, 1986.

Trotta, Maurice S. "Handling Employee Complaints in a Nonunion Company." In *Handling Grievances: A Guide for Management and Labor*. Washington, D.C.: The Bureau of National Affairs, 1976.

Velasquez, Manuel G. "The Right to Due Process." In *Business Ethics: Concepts and Cases*. Englewood Cliffs, NJ: Prentice-Hall, 1982.

Webber, Ross A. "Appeal Procedures." In *Management: Basic Elements of Managing Organizations*. Homewood, IL: Richard D. Irwin, 1975.

Webber, Ross A., Marilyn A. Morgan, and Paul C. Browne. "Open-Door Appeal;" "Appeal to Arbitration;" and "The Ombudsman." In *Management: Basic Elements of Managing Organizations*. 3d ed. Homewood, IL: Richard D. Irwin, 1985.

Werhane, Patricia H. "The Right to Due Process" and "Policies for the Institution of Due Process in the Workplace." In *Persons, Rights, and Corporations*. Englewood Cliffs, NJ: Prentice-Hall, 1985.

Westin, Alan F., ed. "New Management Policies and Procedures: The Inside Mechanisms." In *Whistle Blowing: Loyalty and Dissent in the Corporation*. New York: McGraw-Hill, 1981.

Yoder, Dale, and Paul D. Staudohar. "Grievance Settlement." In *Personnel Management and Industrial Relations*. 7th ed. Englewood Cliffs, NJ: Prentice-Hall, 1982.

MONOGRAPHS

Bales, Robert E. *Appeal System—A Different Approach to Resolving Employee Problems*. Washington, D.C.: CUE—An Organization for Positive and Progressive

Employee Relations, National Association of Manufacturers, Number Nine—Studies in Employee Relations, 1981.

Bambrick, James J., Jr., and John J. Speed. *Grievance Procedures in Non-unionized Companies*. Conference Board Reports. Studies in Personnel Policy, No. 109. New York: National Industrial Conference Board, 1950.

Berenbeim, Ronald. *Nonunion Complaint System: A Corporate Appraisal*. A Research Report from The Conference Board, Conference Board Report No. 770. New York: The Conference Board, 1980.

Caras, Harvey S. *Peer Grievance Review—A Proven Approach to Employee-Problem Resolution*. Washington, D.C.: CUE—An Organization for Positive Employee Relations, National Association of Manufacturers, Number 41—Studies in Employee Relations, 1986.

Gill, Brian W., and Daniel B. Loftus. *Union-Free Complaint Procedures—25 Samples*. Washington, D.C.: CUE—An Organization for Positive Employee Relations, National Association of Manufacturers, 1984.

Industrial Relations Department, National Association of Manufacturers. *Settling Complaints in the Union-Free Operation*. Washington, D.C.: National Association of Manufacturers, June 1982.

Master Printers of America. *Due Process for Nonunion Companies: Complaint Procedures*. Arlington, VA: Master Printers of America, 1984.

Miner, Mary Green. *Policies for Unorganized Employees*. Personnel Policies Forum. PPF Survey No. 125. Washington, D.C.: The Bureau of National Affairs, April 1979.

Thomson, A. W. J., "The Structure of Procedures in Non-Unionized Companies." In *The Grievance Procedure in the Private Sector*. Ithaca, NY: Publications Division, New York State School of Industrial and Labor Relations, 1974, 11–12.

JOURNAL ARTICLES

Abbasi, Sami M., Kenneth W. Hollman, and Joe H. Murrey, Jr. "Employment at Will: An Eroding Concept in Employment Relationships." *Labor Law Journal* 38 (January 1987): 21–32.

Aram, John D., and Paul F. Salipante, Jr. "An Evaluation of Organizational Due Process in the Resolution of Employee/Employer Conflict." *Academy of Management Review* 6 (April 1981): 197–204.

Balfour, Alan. "Five Types of Non-Union Grievance Systems." *Personnel* 61 (March-April 1984): 67–76.

Blades, Lawrence E. "Employment at Will vs. Individual Freedom: On Limiting the Abusive Exercise of Employer Power." *Columbia Law Review* 6 (December 1967): 1,404–35.

Bohlander, George. "Employee Protected Concerted Activity: The Nonunion Setting." *Labor Law Journal* 33 (June 1982): 344–51.

Bonner, Walter V. "Handling Grievances of Nonunionized Employees." *Personnel* 39 (March-April 1962): 56–62.

Boyce, Michael T. "Protected Activities of Nonunion Employees." *Employee Relations Law Journal* 9 (Autumn 1983): 292–307.

Bradshaw, David A., and Linda Van Winkle Deacon. "Wrongful Discharge: The Tip of the Iceberg?" *Personnel Administrator* 30 (November 1985): 74–76.

Briggs, Stephen. "Beyond the Grievance Procedure: Factfinding in Employee Complaint Resolution." *Labor Law Journal* 33 (August 1982): 454–59.

Clark, Kim E. "Improve Employee Relations with a Corporate Ombudsman." *Personnel Journal* 64 (September 1985): 12–13.

Clausen, A. W. "Listening and Responding to Employees' Concerns." *Harvard Business Review* 58 (January-February 1980): 101–14.

Clutterbuck, David. "Norton Delegates Personnel Affairs to the Workers." *International Management* 30 (June 1975): 48–52.

Condon, Thomas J. "Use Union Methods in Handling Grievances." *Personnel Journal* 64 (January 1985): 72–75.

Condon, Thomas J., and Richard H. Wolff. "Procedures that Safeguard Your Right to Fire." *Harvard Business Review* 63 (November-December 1985): 16–18.

Coombe, John D. "Peer Review: The Emerging Successful Application." *Employee Relations Law Journal* 9 (Spring 1984): 659–71.

Cooper, M. R., B. S. Morgan, P. M. Foley, and L. B. Kaplan. "Changing Employee Values: Deepening Discontent?" *Harvard Business Review* 57 (January-February 1979): 117–25.

Coulson, Robert. "An Informal Way to Settle Disputes." *Modern Office Procedures* (June 1980): 182, 184–85.

Drost, Donald A., and Fabius P. O'Brien. "Are There Grievances Against Your Non-Union Grievance Procedure?" *Personnel Administrator* 28 (January 1983): 36–40, 42.

Epstein, Richard L. "The Grievance Procedure in the Non-Union Setting: Caveat Employer." *Employee Relations Law Journal* 1 (Summer 1975): 120–27.

Evan, William M. "Due Process of Law in Military and Industrial Organizations." *Administrative Science Quarterly* 7 (September 1962): 187–207.

———. "Organization Man and Due Process of Law." *American Sociological Review* 26 (August 1961): 540–47.

Ewing, David W. "Due Process: Will Business Default?" *Harvard Business Review* 60 (November-December 1982): 114–22.

———. "How to Negotiate With Employee Objectors." *Harvard Business Review* 61 (January-February 1983): 103–10.

———. "What Business Thinks About Employee Rights?" *Harvard Business Review* 55 (September-October 1977): 81–94.

———. "Who Wants Corporate Democracy?" *Harvard Business Review* 49 (September-October 1971): 12–14, 16, 18–21, 24–28, 146–49.

———. "Who Wants Employee Rights?" *Harvard Business Review* 49 (November-December 1971): 22–24, 26, 28, 30–32, 34–35, 155–58, 160.

———. "Winning Freedom on the Job: From Assembly Line to Executive Suite." *The Civil Liberties Review* 4 (July/August 1977): 8–22.

Fiorito, Jack, Christopher Lowman, and Forrest D. Nelson. "The Impact of Human Resource Policies on Union Organizing." *Industrial Relations* 26 (Spring 1987): 113–26.

Florey, Peter. "A Growing Fringe Benefit: Arbitration of Nonunion Employee Grievances." *Personnel Administrator* 30 (July 1985): 14, 16, 18.

Foegen, J. H. "An Ombudsman as Complement to the Grievance Procedure." *Labor Law Journal* 23 (May 1972): 289–94.

Foulkes, Fred K. "How Top Nonunion Companies Manage Employees." *Harvard Business Review* 59 (September-October 1982): 90–96.

Gorlin, Harriet. "An Overview of Corporate Personnel Practices." *Personnel Journal* 61 (February 1982): 125–30.

Hayford, Stephen L., and Richard Pegnetter. "Grievance Adjudication for Public Employees: A Comparison of Rights Arbitration and Civil Service Appeals Procedures." *The Arbitration Journal* 35 (September 1980): 22–29.

Heshizer, Brian P., and Harry Graham. "Discipline in the Nonunion Company: Protecting Employer and Employee Rights." *Personnel* 59 (March-April 1982): 71–78.

Heshizer, Brian. "The New Common Law of Employment: Changes in the Concept of Employment at Will." *Labor Law Journal* 36 (February 1985): 95–107.

Hiley, David R. "Employee Rights and the Doctrine of At Will Employment." *Business & Professional Ethics Journal* 4 (Fall): 1–10.

Hundley, John R., III. "Listening Posts." *Personnel* 53 (July-August 1976): 39–43.

Joiner, Emily A. "Erosion of the Employment-at-Will Doctrine." *Personnel* 61 (September-October 1984): 12–18.

Klein, Stuart M., and Kenneth W. Rose. "Formal Policies and Procedures Can Forestall Unionization." *Personnel Journal* 61 (April 1982): 275–81.

Lewin, David, and Richard B. Peterson. "A Model for Measuring Effectiveness of the Grievance Process." *Monthly Labor Review* 105 (April 1982): 47–49.

Lewin, David. "Dispute Resolution in the Nonunion Firm: A Theoretical and Empirical Analysis." *Journal of Conflict Resolution* 31 (September 1987): 465–502.

Lo Bosco, Maryellen. "Nonunion Grievance Procedures." *Personnel* 62 (January 1985): 61–64.

McCollum, James K., and Dwight R. Norris. "Nonunion Grievance Machinery in Southern Industry." *Personnel Administrator* 29 (November 1984): 106–9, 131.

McCulloch, Kenneth. "Alternative Dispute Resolution Techniques: Pros and Cons." *Employment Relations Today* 11 (Autumn 1984): 311–19.

Michael, Stephen R. "Due Process in Nonunion Grievance Systems." *Employee Relations Law Journal* 3 (Spring 1978): 516–27.

Miller, Ronald L. "Grievance Procedures for Nonunion Employees." *Public Personnel Management* 7 (September-October 1978): 302–11.

O'Brien, Fabius P., and Donald A. Drost. "Non-Union Grievance Procedures: Not Just an Anti-Union Strategy." *Personnel* 61 (September-October 1984): 61–69.

Olsen, Theodore A. "Wrongful Discharge Claims Raised By At Will Employees: A New Legal Concern for Employers." *Labor Law Journal* 32 (May 1981): 265–97.

Olson, Fred C. "How Peer Review Works at Control Data." *Harvard Business Review* 62 (November-December 1984): 58–59, 62, 64.

Rendero, Thomasine. "Grievance Procedures for Nonunionized Employees." *Personnel* 57 (January-February 1980): 4–10.

Robbins, Lee P., and William B. Deane. "The Corporate Ombuds: A New Approach to Conflict Management." *Negotiation Journal* 2 (April 1986): 195–205.

Rowe, Mary P., and Michael Baker. "Are You Hearing Enough Employee Concerns?" *Harvard Business Review* 62 (May-June 1984): 127–35.

Salipante, Paul F., and John D. Aram. "A System for Individual Equity in Equal Employment Opportunity." *Monthly Labor Review* 102 (April 1979): 46–47.

Scott, William G. "An Issue in Administrative Justice: Managerial Appeal Systems." *Management International* 1 (1966): 37–53.

Shaw, Reid L. "A Grievance Procedure for Non-Unionized Employees." *Personnel* 36 (July-August 1959): 66–70.

Sirota, David, and Alan D. Wolfson. "Pragmatic Approach to People Problems." *Harvard Business Review* 51 (January-February 1973): 120–28.

Stieber, Jack. "Most U.S. Workers Still May Be Fired Under the Employment-at-Will Doctrine." *Monthly Labor Review* 107 (May 1984): 34–38.

Summers, Clyde W. "Protecting *All* Employees Against Unjust Dismissal." *Harvard Business Review* 58 (January-February 1980): 132–39.

Swann, James P., Jr. "Formal Grievance Procedures in Non-Union Plants." *Personnel Administrator* 26 (August 1981): 66–68, 70.

Trisler, Stewart. "Grievance Procedures: Refining the Open-Door Policy." *Employment Relations Today* 11 (Autumn 1984): 323–27.

Trotta, Maurice S., and Harry R. Gudenberg. "Resolving Personnel Problems in Nonunion Plants." *Personnel* 53 (May-June 1976): 54–63.

Trueman, Allen K. "You Can Resolve Employee Grievances." *Administrative Management* 25 (March 1964): 56–58.

Vogel, Alfred. "Your Clerical Workers are Ripe for Unionization." *Harvard Business Review* 49 (March-April 1971): 48–54.

Walters, Kenneth D. "Your Employees' Right to Blow the Whistle." *Harvard Business Review* 53 (July-August 1975): 26–28, 30, 32, 34, 161–62.

Warren, William H. "Ombudsman Plus Arbitration: A Proposal for Effective Grievance Administration without Public Employee Unions." *Labor Law Journal* 29 (September 1978): 562–69.

Wohlking, Wallace. "Effective Discipline in Employee Relations." *Personnel Journal* 54 (September 1975): 489–93, 500.

Yenney, Sharon L. "In Defense of the Grievance Procedure in a Non-Union Setting." *Employee Relations Law Journal* 2 (Spring 1977): 434–43.

Youngblood, Stuart A., and Gary L. Tidwell. "Termination at Will: Some Changes in the Wind." *Personnel* 58 (May-June 1981): 22–33.

PROCEEDINGS

Coulson, Robert. "Justice in the Workplace: Organized or Unorganized Employees." In *Proceedings of 1986 Annual National Conference, the Council on Employee Responsibilities and Rights, October 16–17, 1986, Virginia Beach, Virginia.* Edited by Dietrich Schaupp and Randyl Elkin. Virginia Beach, VA: The Council on Employee Responsibilities and Rights, 1986, 99–101.

Epstein, Henry B. "Comment." In *Arbitration Issues for the 1980s: Proceedings of the Thirty-Fourth Annual Meeting, National Academy of Arbitrators, Maui, Hawaii, May 4–8, 1981.* Edited by James L. Stern and Barbara D. Dennis. Washington, D.C.: The Bureau of National Affairs, 1982, 62–67.

Howlett, Robert G. "Due Process for Nonunionized Employees: A Practical Proposal."

In *Industrial Relations Research Association Series, Proceedings of the Thirty-Second Annual Meeting, December 28–30, 1979, Atlanta*. Edited by Barbara D. Dennis. Madison, WI: Industrial Relations Research Association, 1980, 164–70.

Kolb, Deborah M. "Corporate Ombudsmen." In *Bringing the Dispute Resolution Community Together, 1985 Proceedings, Thirteenth International Conference, October 27–30, 1985, Boston, Massachusetts, Society of Professionals in Dispute Resolution*. Edited by Cheryl Cutrona. Washington, D.C.: Society of Professionals in Dispute Resolution, 1986, 401–2.

Littrell, Lawrence R. "Grievance Procedure and Arbitration in a Nonunion Environment: The Northrup Experience." In *Arbitration Issues for the 1980s, Proceedings of the Thirty-Fourth Annual Meeting, National Academy of Arbitrators, Maui, Hawaii, May 4–8, 1981*. Edited by James L. Stern and Barbara D. Dennis. Washington, D.C.: The Bureau of National Affairs, 1982, 35–42.

Olson, Fred. "The Counseling Approach to Work-Problem Resolution." In *Bringing the Dispute Resolution Community Together, 1985 Proceedings, Thirteenth International Conference, October 27–30, 1985, Boston, Massachusetts, Society of Professionals in Dispute Resolution*. Edited by Cheryl Cutrona. Washington, D.C.: Society of Professionals in Dispute Resolution, 1986, 366–79.

Peterson, Richard B., and David Lewin. "A Model for Research and Analysis of the Grievance Process." In *Industrial Relations Research Association Series, Proceedings of the Thirty-Fourth Annual Meeting, December 28–30, 1981, Washington*. Edited by Barbara D. Dennis. Madison, WI: Industrial Relations Research Association, 1982, 303–12.

Reckford, Jonathan. "Ombudsman Workshop: An Exploration of Professional Development, Research Agendas, and Legislative Initiatives." In *Ethical Issues in Dispute Resolution, 1983 Proceedings, Eleventh Annual Conference, October 5–7, 1983, Philadelphia, Pennsylvania, Society of Professionals in Dispute Resolution*. Edited by Charlotte Gold. Washington, D.C.: Society of Professionals in Dispute Resolution, 1984, 86–90.

Rowe, Mary P. "Ombudsman Sector Workshop." In *Bringing the Dispute Resolution Community Together, 1985 Proceedings, Thirteenth International Conference, October 27–30, 1985, Boston, Massachusetts, Society of Professionals in Dispute Resolution*. Edited by Cheryl Cutrona. Washington, D.C.: Society of Professionals in Dispute Resolution, 1986, 363–65.

Salipante, Paul F., Jr., and John D. Aram. "The Role of Special Grievance Systems in Furthering Equal Employment Opportunities." In *Industrial Relations Research Association Series, Proceedings of the Thirty-First Annual Meeting, August 29–31, 1978, Chicago*. Edited by Barbara D. Dennis. Madison, WI: Industrial Relations Research Association, 1979, 299–307.

Schauer, John S. "Discussion." In *Industrial Relations Research Association Series, Proceedings of the Thirty-Second Annual Meeting, December 28–30, 1979, Atlanta*. Edited by Barbara D. Dennis. Madison, WI: Industrial Relations Research Association, 1980, 183–86.

Solomon, Janet Stern. "Mediation of Employee Rights Disputes." In *Proceedings of 1986 Annual National Conference, The Council on Employee Responsibilities and Rights, October 16–17, 1986, Virginia Beach, Virginia*. Edited by Dietrich

Schaupp and Randyl Elkin. Virginia Beach, VA: The Council on Employee Responsibilities and Rights, 1986, 35–38.

St. Antoine, Theodore J. "Protection Against Unjust Discipline: An Idea Whose Time Has Long Since Come." In *Arbitration Issues for the 1980s: Proceedings of the Thirty-Fourth Annual Meeting, National Academy of Arbitrators, Maui, Hawaii, May 4–8, 1981.* Edited by James L. Stern and Barbara D. Dennis. Washington, D.C.: The Bureau of National Affairs, 1982, 43–62.

Stieber, Jack. "The Case for Protection of Unorganized Employees Against Unjust Discharge." In *Industrial Relations Research Association Series, Proceedings of the Thirty-Second Annual Meeting, December 28–30, 1979, Atlanta.* Edited by Barbara D. Dennis. Madison, WI: Industrial Relations Research Association, 1980, 155–63.

Stieber, Jack. "Employment-at-Will: An Issue for the 1980s." In *Industrial Relations Research Association Series, Proceedings of the Thirty-Sixth Annual Meeting, December 28–30, 1983, San Francisco.* Edited by Barbara D. Dennis. Madison, WI: Industrial Relations Research Association, 1984, 1–13.

Stieber, Jack, and John Blackburn, eds. *Protecting Unorganized Employees Against Unjust Dismissal: Proceedings of a Conference Held at Michigan State University.* East Lansing, MI: School of Labor and Industrial Relations, College of Social Science, Michigan State University, 1983.

Wachter, Michael L. "Comment." In *Arbitration 1986: Current and Expanding Roles, Proceedings of the Thirty-Ninth Annual Meeting, National Academy of Arbitrators, Philadelphia, Pennsylvania, June 2–6, 1986.* Edited by Walter J. Gershenfeld. Washington, D.C.: The Bureau of National Affairs, 1987, 67.

Waxman, Merle. "Employee Responsibilities and Rights: Reactive and Proactive Strategies Using the Ombudsman Concept." In *Proceedings of 1986 Annual National Conference, The Council on Employee Responsibilities and Rights, October 16–17, 1986, Virginia Beach, Virginia.* Edited by Dietrich Schaupp and Randyl Elkin. Virginia Beach, VA: The Council on Employee Responsibilities and Rights, 1986, 107–11.

Wolf, Mary Jean. "Trans World Airlines' Noncontract Grievance Procedure." In *Arbitration 1986: Current and Expanding Roles, Proceedings of the Thirty-Ninth Annual Meeting, National Academy of Arbitrators, Philadelphia, Pennsylvania, June 2–6, 1986.* Edited by Walter J. Gershenfeld. Washington, D.C.: The Bureau of National Affairs, 1987, 27–33.

PERIODICALS

Brody, Michael. "Listen to Your Whistleblower." *Fortune*, 24 November 1986, 77–78.

Caffrey, Charles A. "Before the Union Calls . . . " *Industry Week*, 11 June 1973, 65–66.

Caulkins, Charles S. "Rating Employee Relations Programs." *Profit*, January/February 1986, 16–17.

Engel, Paul G. "Preserving the Right to Fire." *Industry Week*, 18 March 1985, vol. 224, no. 3, 39, 40.

Glaberson, William B. "Rolling Back the Boss's Right to Fire At Will." *Business Week*, 8 July 1985, 74–75.

Hoerr, John, William G. Glaberson, Daniel B. Moskowitz, Vicky Cahan, Michael A. Pollock, and Jonathan Tasini. "Beyond Unions: A Revolution in Employee Rights Is In The Making." *Business Week*, 8 July 1985, 72–77.

Rowe, Mary P. "The Growing Phenomenon of the Ombuds." *Alternatives to the High Cost of Litigation*, October 1986, 3–5, 16.

Suters, Everett T. "Hazards of an Open-Door Policy." *Inc.: The Magazine for Growing Companies*, January 1987, 99–100, 102.

Tasini, Jonathan, and Patrick Houston. "Letting Workers Help Handle Workers' Gripes." *Business Week*, 15 September 1986, 82–86.

"A Fight Over the Freedom to Fire." *Business Week*, 20 September 1982, 116.

"How the Xerox Ombudsman Helps Xerox." *Business Week*, 12 May 1973, 188–90.

"The Antiunion Grievance Ploy." *Business Week*, 12 February 1979, 117, 120.

"The Growing Costs of Firing Nonunion Workers." *Business Week*, 6 April 1981, 95, 98.

"Where Ombudsmen Work Out." *Business Week*, 3 May 1976, 114, 116.

NEWSPAPER ARTICLES

Kramer, Andrew M. "The Hazards of Firing at Will." *The Wall Street Journal*, 9 March 1987, Sec. 1, 20.

McMillen, Liz. "Colleges Are Trying New Ways to Settle Campus Grievances." *The Chronicle of Higher Education*, 6 May 1987, 14–15, 17.

Reibstein, Larry. "More Firms Use Peer Review Panel to Resolve Employees' Grievances." *The Wall Street Journal*, 3 December 1986, Sec. 2, 29.

Rout, Lawrence. " 'Hyatt Hotels' Gripe Sessions Help Chief Maintain Communications with Workers." *The Wall Street Journal*, 16 July 1981, Sec. 2, 27, 33.

"Complaint Systems Help Some Firms Stave Off Unions." *The Wall Street Journal*, 29 February 1980, Sec. 1, 1.

OTHER SOURCES

American Arbitration Association. *Expedited Employment Arbitration Rules*. As amended and in effect, July 1, 1986. New York: American Arbitration Association, 1986.

American Arbitration Association. *Resolving Business Disputes: The Alternate Dispute Resolution Program of the American Arbitration Association*. New York: American Arbitration Association, 1986.

Baderschneider, Earl, ed. "Hold Put on Inapplicability of Nonunion Weingarten Rights." *Study Time*, A Quarterly Letter of News and Comment for the AAA Labor Arbitrator, no. 3, 1986, American Arbitration Association, 1–2.

Brown, Alverta. "Non-Union Grievance Procedures." *Newspaper Personnel Relations Association Newsletter*, May 1982, 3–4.

Brown, Laura Ferris. *Grievance Procedures for Unionized and Non-Unionized Employees*. New York: American Arbitration Association, 1986, 4–5.

"A Formal Grievance System." *Small Business Report*, September 1982, pp. 23–27.

Levin, Edward R. "Do Internal Grievance Procedures Preclude Outside Litigation?" *CUE Legal Alert* 7 (May 15, 1986).

UNPUBLISHED WORKS

Caras, Harvey S. "Peer Grievance Review: The Proven Approach to Employee Problem Solving." A Presentation to CUE, November 19, 1985. Dallas: Performance Systems Corporation, 1985.

Hellwig, Susan A., and Catherine A. Sullivan. "An Examination of Current Grievance Interviewing Practices in Major American Corporations." San Diego: Department of Speech Communication, San Diego State University, 1982.

Rowe, Mary P. "The Corporate Ombudsman." Draft Copy. Cambridge: Massachusetts Institute of Technology, 1986, 1–16.

Index

About the Author

DOUGLAS M. MCCABE is Associate Professor of Human Resources Management at Georgetown University's School of Business Administration, Washington, D.C. He is the author of over 100 articles, proceedings, speeches, and papers presented at professional and scholarly meetings in the field of employee relations. He is also an active consultant in the human resources area.

Considered by the media to be an expert in his field, Dr. McCabe has appeared over 60 times on international, national, statewide, and local television and radio as the networks have sought his views on critical issues in employee relations.

His television credits include ABC's "World News Tonight;" Cable News Network's "NewsWatch," "DayWatch," and "Take Two;" NBC's "Overnight;" the Canadian Broadcasting Corporation; Independent Network News; WRC's (NBC) "Cover Story," Washington, D.C.; Washington, D.C., television station channel 5 (Metromedia); and Washington, D.C., television station channel 9 (CBS).

His radio credits include ABC News Radio, KVON-AM (NBC), San Francisco Bay Area; WISN News-Talk Radio, Milwaukee, Wisconsin; WXYT News-Talk Radio, Detroit, Michigan; RKO Radio, New York; the Mutual Broadcast System; WIOD (ABC), Miami, Florida; KMPC Radio, Los Angeles, WRC's (NBC) News-Talk Radio, Washington, D.C.; and Washington, D.C. Radio Station WASH FM.

Additionally, he has been quoted in *Business Week, U.S. News & World Report, USA TODAY*, the *Los Angeles Times*, and *The Washington Post.* Dr. McCabe has also conducted over 50 management development programs in the area of employer-employee relations.

Dr. McCabe was also a member of the Advisory Committee, Task Force on Law and Business Schools, American Arbitration Association, New York City, New York, and was Chair of its Subcommittee on Incorporation, Alternate Dispute Resolution (ADR). Furthermore, he was a member of the Board of Governors, Washington, D.C. Chapter, Industrial Relations Research Association and was a member of the Board of Directors, Washington, D.C. Chapter, Society of Professionals in Dispute Resolution.

His professional and scholarly organizational affiliations include the Academy of Management, the International Personnel Management Association, Industrial Relations Research Association, the International Industrial Relations Association, and the Society of Professionals in Dispute Resolution.

Finally, Dr. McCabe holds a Ph.D. in human resources management and industrial relations from Cornell University and is a member of Phi Beta Kappa.